AF664438

Globalization, Growth and Employment

Globalization, Growth and Employment

Challenges and Opportunities

Edited by

Lancy Lobo

Jayesh Shah

RAWAT PUBLICATIONS

Jaipur • New Delhi • Bangalore • Hyderabad • Guwahati

ISBN 978-81-316-0510-3

© Contributors, 2012

No part of this book may be reproduced or transmitted in any form or by any means, electronic or mechanical, including photocopying, recording or by any information storage and retrieval system, without permission in writing from the publishers.

Published by
Prem Rawat for **Rawat Publications**
Satyam Apts, Sector 3, Jawahar Nagar, Jaipur 302 004 (India)
Phone: 0141 265 1748 / 7006 Fax: 0141 265 1748
E-mail: info@rawatbooks.com
Website: www.rawatbooks.com

New Delhi Office
4858/24, Ansari Road, Daryaganj, New Delhi 110 002
Phone: 011 2326 3290

Also at *Bangalore, Hyderabad* and *Guwahati*

Typeset by Rawat Computers, Jaipur
Printed at Chaman Enterprises, New Delhi

Contents

Acknowledgements

This volume is the outcome of two seminars. The first was held on 16th and 17th July 2010 at the Centre for Culture and Development, Vadodara, on "Changing Scenario of Employment in Gujarat: 1960-2010" sponsored by ICSSR Western Region, Mumbai. The second was held on 4th and 5th March 2011 at the Department of Business Economics, The M.S. University of Baroda, on "Employment Scenario in India in the Post-Reform Period" sponsored by UGC. We are thankful to Dr Dinkar Nayak for permitting us to incorporate the selected papers presented in the first part of this volume. Finally, we thank Mr Pranit Rawat for speedy publication of this volume.

List of Tables

Chapter 4

Chapter 5

Chapter 6

Chapter 7

Chapter 8

Chapter 9

Chapter 10

Chapter 11

Chapter 12

Chapter 13

List of Figures

Chapter 5

Chapter 12

List of Abbreviations

GATS	General Agreement on Trade in Services
GDP	Gross Domestic Product
IT	Information Technology
ITES	Information Technology-Enabled Services
NAS	National Accounts Statistics
NDP	Net Domestic Product
NSS	National Sample Survey
OFDI	Outward Foreign Direct Investment
RBI	Reserve Bank of India
WTO	World Trade Organization

List of Contributors

Akash Kumra, Lecturer, Department of Business Economics, The M.S. University of Baroda, Vadodara.

Amita Shah, Director, Gujarat Institute of Development Research, Ahmedabad.

Arpita Mukherjee, Senior Fellow and Professor, Indian Council for Research on International Economic Relations, New Delhi.

Aswini Trivedi, Lecturer, Department of Business Economics, The M.S. University of Baroda, Vadodara.

Dinkar Nayak, Associate Professor, Department of Business Economics, The M.S. University of Baroda, Vadodara.

Guy Standing, Professor of Economic Security at the University of Bath, UK.

Jayesh Shah, Research Associate, Centre for Culture and Development, Vadodara.

Jeemol Unni, Director, Institute of Rural Management, Anand.

Kiran Desai, Associate Professor, Centre for Social Studies, Surat.

Lancy Lobo, Director, Centre for Culture and Development, Vadodara.

Manjira Dasgupta, Research Scholar, Department of Business Economics, The M. S. University of Baroda, Vadodara.

Niti Mehta, Associate Professor, Sardar Patel Institute of Economic & Social Research, Ahmedabad.

Paramita Saha, Associate Professor, Department of Applied Economics, Tripura University, Tripura.

R.C. Popat, Director, Sandipani Institute of Economic Research, Rajkot.

Ravikiran Naik is Research Associate at the Institute of Rural Management, Anand.

Renana Jhabvala, Chair, Self-Employed Women's Association Bharat, the National Federation of SEWA Organizations, Delhi.

Sangeeta Jha, Lecturer, Department of Geography, Faculty of Science, The M.S. University of Baroda, Vadodara.

Shankar Jha, Lecturer, Department of Business Economics, The M.S. University of Baroda, Vadodara.

Tanu M. Goyal, Research Associate, Indian Council for Research on International Economic Relations, New Delhi.

Trupti Shah, Lecturer, Department of Business Economics, The M.S. University of Baroda, Vadodara.

Uma Rani, Senior Development Economist at the International Institute of Labour Studies, ILO, Geneva.

1

Introduction

Lancy Lobo and Jayesh Shah

The world economy is undergoing a lot of changes due to liberalization. This change is affecting all national economies irrespective of whether it is a transitional, controlled, socialist, or market economy. The result of this change is a paradigm shift in the employment structure of most of the countries. What is required at this point of time is to align it strategically so that maximum advantage is taken from its competencies and the existing weaknesses is removed or nullified.

Liberalization refers to the removal of government restrictions from trade between nations. Rapidly increasing flows of goods and services across national borders have been the most visible aspect of the increasing integration of the global economy in recent decades. There is a vast body of literature which shows that trade is good for economic growth which in turn is also good for poverty reduction. It suggests that liberalization may raise labour productivity in the developing economies but it also has differential impact on their wages and employment. Higher trade has mostly been associated with higher employment but lower wages. In this context, the impact of liberalization on employment is of particular significance. The present edited volume has examined the changes in the employment scenario of India following the pursuance of the liberalization strategy and the possible effects of further liberalization.

The economic boom that is being experienced in India is largely attributed to the globalization and liberalization of the Indian economy. The era prior to the 1990s was quite averse to the concept of an open market policy. The Indian markets were predominantly closed in nature. The Government of India, however, ruled and regulated Indian markets but with the globalization and liberalization of the Indian economy, the whole market scenario changed in no time. The reforms progressed further in the areas of opening up to foreign investment, reforming capital markets, deregulating domestic business, and reforming the trade regime. Liberalization has done away with the License Raj (investment, industrial, and import licensing) and ended many public monopolies, allowing automatic approval of foreign direct investment in many sectors. Government's goals were reducing the fiscal deficit, privatizing the public sector, and increasing investment in infrastructure. Trade reforms and changes in the regulation of foreign direct investment were introduced to open India to foreign trade while stabilizing external loans.

Critics of liberalization have blamed it for a host of ills such as rising unemployment and wage inequality in the advanced countries, increased exploitation of workers in developing countries, and a 'race to the bottom' with respect to employment conditions and labour standards, the de-industrialization and marginalization of low-income countries, increasing poverty, global inequality, and degradation of the environment. These views have spread in spite of the fact that the benefits of free trade, in terms of improved allocation of resources and consequent gains in productive efficiency and economic growth, are basic tenets of mainstream economic analysis.

India's labour force is growing at a rate of 2.5 per cent annually, but employment is growing at only 2.3 per cent. Thus, the country is faced with the challenge of not only absorbing new entrants to the job market (estimated at seven million people every year), but also clearing the backlog. Sixty per cent of India's workforce is self-employed, many of whom remain very poor. Nearly 30 per cent are casual workers (that is they work only when they are able to get jobs and remain unpaid for the rest of the days they have no job). Only about 10 per cent are regular employees, of which two-fifths are employed by the public sector. More than 90 per cent of the labour force is employed in the 'unorganized sector', that is sectors which do not provide social security and other benefits of employment as in the 'organized sector'. In the rural areas, agricultural workers form the bulk of the unorganized sector. In urban India, contract and sub-contract as well as migratory agricultural labourers make up most of the unorganized labour force.

This volume makes an attempt to evaluate the employment scenario in different sectors of Indian economy since the inception of liberalized policies. A common trend observed worldwide is that employment is moving away from traditional agriculture to industry and more to services. This is the result of, first, static wages and efficiencies of agricultural sector which need much lesser number of people, and second, rapidly increasing demand for services and associated higher wages. Appropriate technology to suit the indigenous needs, removal of rural urban disparities in service sector, replacement of production-oriented plan with employment-oriented plan, changing educational system, population control, etc., are suggested to solve the sectoral disparities in India.

It is observed that the performance of the primary sector is pessimistic, moderate in manufacturing sector and satisfactory in service sector. It is disappointing to note that the employment of the primary sector is found negative. In the manufacturing sector, the results have not indicated any significant impact up to the expectations of the policy makers.

In India, this trend is visible more in the developed states of Gujarat, Maharashtra, Karnataka, Tamil Nadu, and Andhra Pradesh where a significant proportion of employment has shifted to services. This phenomenon is throwing up a lot of challenges as well as opportunities for the states, which is forcing each of them to take stock of its capabilities and weaknesses. As the state of Gujarat is celebrating golden jubilee, we have selected some of the papers on Gujarat in second part.

If we look at the overall employment situation in Gujarat, it has improved after globalization, but the share of regular employment has declined and the share of casual labourers has increased. The unemployment rate in Gujarat, however, is lower than that of the rest of the country. It was 4.63 per cent in 2000 compared to 7.29 per cent for the country. Gujarat ranked 10th among the major states of India with respect to unemployment rate. Gujarat thus appears to be in a relatively better position with regard to overall employment. However, there are several developments, such as the increased share of marginal workers, the declining workforce participation rate with respect to main workers, the declining share of the organized sector, and the declining rate of growth of employment, all of which need careful attention of policy makers in the Golden Jubilee year of the state of Gujarat.

Despite the high growth performance of the economy of Gujarat in the last one decade, the continuing high incidence of poverty and of other forms of deprivation, resulting in despair, has prompted the planners and policy makers for the state of Gujarat to advocate 'inclusive growth'. Despite the rhetoric of inclusive growth, however, the overbearing emphasis is on attaining higher growth rate and not on improving human development. Absence of any commitment to provide social security and related protection for a semblance of decent work conditions for those in the unorganized sector, are hardly the initiatives that would help promote inclusion.

In addition, there is no well-articulated strategy for harnessing the untapped potential of the tribal communities and of artisans to generate productive employment. Policies and programmes for reducing wide gaps between the various districts in a whole range of economic and social indicators are also conspicuous by their absence. The policy makers should also provide an alternative paradigm for inclusive development and growth with particular reference to the issue of employment in which the state has to play a leading role.

Human capital which is responsible for generating employment in Gujarat, most ostensibly in the form of education, would be an inescapable input for ensuring competitive levels of productivity in various sectors, and for accelerating the overall pace of economic growth and human development in the state. The quality of workforce poses a frightening scenario in agriculture, mining, quarrying, and construction. The rural–urban and male–female contrasts are no less frightening, as globalization has raised apprehensions and expectations, more often the former than the latter, in respect of its impact on the workforce. Dislocation and reduced social protection are feared to be the short-term fallouts, while the widening and diversification of employment opportunities, the rising real earnings, and the improvements in conditions of work are expected to be the benefits that labour can realize from globalization in the medium and in the long run.

The Gujarat experience so far has produced the negative more often than the positive impact on labour. Where employment has increased, it is mostly in the informal sector and in its more 'flexible', i.e., casual, contract and temporary, forms. As a result, the 'decent work' deficit has increased and the coverage of social protection to workers has declined. Assuming that the expectation of faster expansion of employment opportunities is realized through market-based faster economic growth and through greater flexibility in the use of labour, lack of social protection is likely to emerge as a major problem, which can be tackled only by the state and social activism. The policy makers can introduce a few interventions, for example, improving the quality of would-be workers in the coming decades, training and retraining of the existing workforce to make them competitive in the current international scenario, and enhancing focus on manufacturing.

Though the unemployment rate in Gujarat is lower than that in the rest of the country, the number of unemployed educated youth is a worrying problem for any growing state. The policy makers should explore both the macro and the micro dimensions of the educated youth unemployment issue at the district as well as the gender level during the two decades. The youths constituting more than half of the total Gujarat population represent its greatest asset for the present and the future. Nearly 50 per cent of the total educated youth are facing serious vulnerability problems all over the state due to some or other reasons. Tracking the unemployment rate for the educated youth and setting a target for its reduction; and identifying policy interventions, assumed importance, and urgency for the state of Gujarat at the time of celebration of its golden jubilee. Migration history of unemployed youth does not support the hypothesis that higher youth unemployment in urban areas reflects the transmission of open unemployment in the rural areas.

The recent policy discourse in Gujarat is marked by unequivocal emphasis on revival of growth in the agriculture sector. This is mainly due to the significant poverty-reducing impact of the sector. The next round of agricultural growth offers a huge potential for welfare enhancement, provided that the policies are robust enough to bring in a paradigm shift in the manner in which the expected growth in productivity is achieved. The conventional sources of productivity enhancement, especially since the Green Revolution and the White Revolution, has centred on water as well as input intensive practices.

The challenge now is to shift towards water-efficient and employment-intensive systems of agricultural production. Achieving them would require a more nuanced approach, incorporating differential agro-ecological features on the one hand, and employment and livelihood needs on the other. The policy makers should be able to cover a number of goals simultaneously: imperatives for workforce diversification; employment in agriculture; linkages between farm and non-farm employment, crop-specific labour use, importance of irrigation, changing the locus of growth to the lagging districts of Gujarat, growth and variation among different districts of Gujarat; expanding opportunities by reviving farming systems approach, watershed development in dry land areas, and diversified and high-valued agriculture.

Let us now shift from agriculture to the qualitative aspects of population. The latter has great importance from the viewpoint of development of a state and the welfare of its people. Healthy, educated, well-trained, well-fed, and enthusiastic people contribute a great deal to development. Education, in particular, is a potentially important determinant of employment. It improves an individual's prospects for jobs as well as increases his or her ability to allocate time to work efficiently among income producing activities.

In early phases of development many rural activities require only low levels of schooling. But the state of Gujarat is now passing through the intensive phase of developmental activities. During this phase, a positive relationship between modern occupations (such as mechanical repair of tractors, modern textiles, and wooden furniture making) and the level of education is expected, but a negative relationship between the level of education and traditional occupations (such as basket makers, carpet makers, barbers, tailors, potters, and carpenters) is also not desirable.

The planners should examine the relationship between education and skills and rural employment in different districts of Gujarat, including tribal areas. Why the quality of the educated rural labour force is not of the employable kind in the current intensive development phase needs to be examined in detail. How the human capital base of the rural workforce should be improved and strengthened requires deliberation.

One more area which is hardly studied systematically is the trends of growth and the productivity of trading units in the unorganized sectors in Gujarat. In view of the arrivals of mega 'malls', the unorganized trading sector needs to be investigated, as these trading units provide good amount of employment all over Gujarat. The managers of mega malls purchase the products directly from the producers and avoid the intermediary traders in their business. Trading means the activities of intermediaries, who do not actually purchase or sell the goods but arrange their purchase and sale, and thereby earn profit by way of brokerage or commission. Distributive agencies, which undertake trading activity on commercial basis, are also included in the trading sector. In addition, the activities of collection and sale of honey and other minor forest products, collection of fish for sale, and collection of waste paper for sale are also treated as trading activities. Trading enterprises account for a very large proportion of total enterprises in Gujarat, as the Gujarati people are known for their trading capabilities since centuries. The share of trading activities has gone up in the last two decades. But after the entry of mega mall culture, the small trading communities are adversely affected. The trends in employment and productivity levels in the unorganized trading sector should be analysed in different districts.

It is now a well-known fact that the structure of employment in Gujarat has moved away from both the primary sector, i.e., from agriculture, and the secondary sector, i.e., the manufacturing sector, to the tertiary or the services sector. Can we call this process 'de-industrialization'? This is definitely not the stylized growth path, viz., 'agriculture to industry to service' attained by the developed economies. Would it be correct to say that Gujarati people prefer services to manufacturing goods or to agricultural production? Does emphasizing the demand side help explain the structural transformation in Gujarat? If not, what does? Is the growth supply induced? Are we the odd ones to have skipped industry and leapfrogged from agriculture to services? What lessons do the sectoral shifts in workforce in Gujarat suggest?

In order to answer these questions, the scholars and planners need to examine how wages, corrected for inflation, changed in both the formal and informal sectors of Gujarat economy in the last 20 years. If informal and casual sector employment increases simultaneously with a rise in the real wages of these workers, the outcome could not be said to be as devastating as is made out to be. We may also analyse how women fared in the liberalized economy's labour market. Is the workforce market more feminized in the post-reform period than in the pre-reform period? Are women discriminated against as workers? If so, what kind of discrimination do they face? Does the extent of discrimination increase with liberalization? More importantly, does gender inequality in incomes decrease or increase during the liberal regime?

II

This volume contains two parts: the first few chapters are on India and the remaining on Gujarat. Dinkar Nayak and Akash Kumra have argued that India has initiated the liberalization process since 1991. The reforms in the 1990s mainly dealt with industry and trade policy. The chief objective of initiating the reform was to make the country more competitive, and thereby enhance economic growth. It was held that rapid growth will lead to generation of new employment opportunities. Thus, it has been asserted that economic reforms will have a positive impact on employment. The question here is whether the economic growth has actually created more employment opportunities or not. This is attempted in the present study. The whole study is sub-divided into two sub-periods, i.e., adjustment period and post-adjustment period.

Jeemol Unni and Ravikiran Naik discuss that the most dynamic sector in the last decade globally has been the service sector. India has outpaced many countries as a result of its growth in the services sector, powered by software programming and business process outsourcing (BPO) services. A large proportion of India's export growth has also been fuelled by the growth in the services sector. This paper examines whether any of this high-productivity, high-income growth in the service sector is occurring in rural India, and if so, to what extent. This paper addresses three questions: (a) While India has experienced high economic growth led by the services sector in the last decade, to what extent has rural structural transformation taken place? (b) India has seen a spurt in the export of services. How does the Indian services sector perform in the context of the General Agreement on Trade in Services (GATS)? How is this reflected in rural India? (c) The information technology (IT) and BPO revolution is considered the engine of the recent growth in the services sector. To what extent has the rural workforce gained from this revolution? Communications, banking and insurance, and business services were identified as the most dynamic segments of the service sector. Expansion in terms of both income and employment in these new sectors was restricted to urban areas. The benefits of rapid economic growth in the more productive and high-income-earning sectors were not obtained in rural areas.

Trupti Shah and Aswini Trivedi argue that the consistent high-growth rate in the Indian economy since last few years and fast paced recovery in the face of world financial crises is not reflected in the employment data for the economy. It challenges the underlying assumption of the Indian planning that investment will automatically generate employment. In spite of the growth story of India as an 'emerging economy' of the world, more than 90 per cent of the working population is forced to rely on the unorganized sector for the livelihood, thanks to the non-existence of effective employment policy. This paper analyses recent data from 64th round of NSSO 2007–08 and compares it with the data from the various rounds of NSSO in pre- and post-reform surveys for the social groups such as male, female, SC, ST, and OBC and analyses the draft employment policy which was formulated in 2008 but not yet passed by the Parliament of India. It argues that the steps to protect and promote employment, livelihood and improvement in the condition of working poor are the precondition for the 'inclusive growth'.

Paramita Saha and Manjira Dasgupta take up the issue of social security, an indispensable aspect of employment concerns in a developing country context. Security considerations/employment benefits form an important aspect of conditions of employment, and in the absence of secured employment social security issues become all the more important. This is particularly relevant in the dynamic employment scenario of post-reform and post-global crisis India, where an increasing proportion of the labour force lies outside the purview of formal employment opportunities and therefore beyond the scope of policies targeted at the organized sector. This paper follows the conceptual framework of Kannan et al. (2007) to survey in detail the state of basic and contingent social security in India in the context of economic reforms and the recent global financial crisis. The various schemes in force and their working and coverage are examined. The ongoing efforts at social security reforms are discussed in some detail.

Reviewing the state of affairs, the paper concludes that while considerable and undeniable progress has been made, India still has a host of problems to address and a long way to go towards reforming its social security scene – an imperative that is all the more challenging in the aftermath of the financial crisis of 2008.

III

These are some of the issues and the trends in the last 50 years in the employment sector for the state of Gujarat. The following papers in this volume throw light on the major trends of the changing scenario of employment in Gujarat.

R.C. Popat, in his paper, 'Changing Scenario of Agriculture and Rural Employment in Gujarat: Challenges and Opportunities' shows that the scenario of agricultural labour has undergone considerable change in respect of both the demand and supply side. With the technological improvements in agriculture and the increase in gross cultivated area, there has been remarkable increase in the demand for the workers, both regular and casual in agriculture in Gujarat. The qualitative demand for agricultural workers has also undergone a lot of changes in the last decade. Popat tries to prove his argument that the supply of agricultural labour is found declining year by year during the post-reform period of Gujarat. He emphatically argues that NREGA has highly affected the supply of migrant labour in agriculture.

Niti Mehta in her paper 'Quality and Employability: Aspects of Rural Labour Force in Gujarat' highlights the employability aspect of the rural workforce, mainly in three contexts: the extent to which the rural labour force has the capability for full-time employment, the extent to which the rural workers are fully employed in the non-primary sectors, and the extent to which the workers have shifted and/or have the ability to engage in urban jobs. Between 1991 and 2001, the rural workers fell by 6 per cent (from 70% to 64%). The marginal workers in the rural population rose from 9 per cent to 12.2 per cent. Absolute numbers of marginal workers fell; evidence suggests a definitive shift of these workers towards urban jobs along with declining marginalization of rural workers. Regions having progressive and diversified agriculture and those with larger degree of urbanization are witnessing decrease in the extent of marginalization of workforce in their rural locations. Evidence since 2000 suggests that gradual decline in share of agriculture in rural areas continued and the slow pace of rural workforce diversification is equally shared by the secondary and tertiary sectors. Employment diversification is occurring in varying degrees, but is possibly distress driven. Jobs in non-primary sectors are not always remunerative and of good quality, as is indicated by increasing marginalization of workers in urban areas. Gradual shift towards urban locations, particularly in tertiary activities, is a reflection of being pushed out from the over-burdened agriculture and has distress connotations. Backward regions require special interventions for improving access to education, skills, creation of better infrastructure, and efforts to improve the productivity of primary sector activities.

Shankar and Sangeeta Jha's paper 'Globalization and Employment: A Case Study of Changing Structure of Employment in Gujarat' shows that there is a sectoral change in the employment patterns for the state of Gujarat in the last 50 years. There are more employment opportunities available in secondary and tertiary sectors. Jha provides district-wise data for the average annual growth in employment for the state of Gujarat, which reflect the industry-wise changing structure of employment for the state of Gujarat in the last 50 years. A majority of workers continue to work in the unorganized sector outside the statutory cover and earn wages below the subsistence level, and their share of self-employment increased at a rapid rate in the last 10 years.

Kiran Desai in his paper 'Options of Survival for Marginalized Labour in Deteriorating Employment Situation: Floating in Informal-Fringe Sector' narrates the labour market scenario at the bottom rung of the urban economy with reference to a few pockets of Gujarat state in the present context of globalization regime. He has observed the condition of workers seeking livelihood in industrial and other activities of informal sector, mainly in the urban settings of two prominent industrial centres of south Gujarat region, namely, Surat and Vapi. He attempts to arrive at a generalized statement pertaining to employment situation at the lowest level of the labour market in the urban setting. He informs that many scholars have critically and clinically analysed the impact of new economic regime on labour as such and have candidly established nature and magnitude of detrimental effects on labouring poor. He emphatically presents that at present, cities, large or small, offer much in terms of employment opportunities in the informal sector only. Those seeking livelihood are getting information regarding this changing scenario from their friends, relatives and acquaintances working at different places. They prefer to move to the places where a group of persons from their own caste or village has already been working and has established strong links, through which they can get work as well as other support system required at a new place. The workers eking out their livelihoods from various informal sector activities, industrial as well as non-industrial, are exposed to extremely adverse conditions. Their powerlessness and debility have been exploited by the owners and the affluent section to gain maximum advantage. They are denied their legal rights. They are made to work in oppressive conditions and the wages they received cannot be called attractive and substantial. He raises some questions for marginalized workers.

Amita Shah in her paper 'Implementing NREGS in Gujarat: Evidence from the Initial phase' observes that the implementation of the NREGA throws up significant challenges, given the multiple objectives on the one hand, and breaking through the micro level dynamics – political as well as administrative – on the other hand. The most important initial hurdles seem to emanate from demand-driven nature of the scheme. This, among other things, essentially calls for revitalizing local communities and institutions of decentralized governance such as Gram Sabha and Panchayats at village level. She also highlights the difficulties in planning for creating productive assets and generation of awareness in the community. She notes that the administrative delays in starting the work, continuity, seasonality, and transparency in payment, remain the major issues during the initial phase of implementation of a demand driven NREGA.

Jeemol Unni et al., in their paper 'Social Income: Community, State and Private Support Mechanisms for Inclusive Growth in Gujarat' explores whether the poorer sections of the society experienced the benefits of the rapid growth in the state of Gujarat. They also examine the concept of social income. She argues that besides the money income earned by individual members, the households also gain from support by other institutions such as the community, the state and the private initiatives or investments. They had searched the extent to which these support mechanisms help households to improve their economic situation. They suggest that the platform of 'inclusive growth', a worthy slogan and a benchmark by which to judge all income-related policies, should include a strategy to make incomes less unequal. A progressive redistribution of money income, complemented by a reduction in the inequality of community, state and private benefit income, is desirable.

Arpita Mukherjee and Tanu Goel in their paper 'Fuelling the Retail Boom: Need for the Right Employment Policy for Gujarat' present that retail is the second largest employer after agriculture, and retail employment is divided into direct and indirect employment. The retail sector is growing, and employment in the retail sector is rising, but there is difference in the skill sets of modern and traditional sector employees in the retail sector. The traditional retail outlets are owned largely by families, and recruit family members as a source to get work done in their traditional retail outlets, while modern retail outlets are owned by leading corporate houses and provide organized employment with better pay and working conditions. Gujarat is traditionally known for its trader communities. Retail is a priority sector having around 12 per cent share in SGDP. Organized retail accounts for 12 per cent of retail in the state of Gujarat which is much higher than the national average. But Gujarat has not been able to attract foreign retailers or mega foreign stores such as Wal-Mart. Modern retailers are facing skill shortage in Gujarat. Urban planning problems had affected the growth of modern retail outlets. Hence, by identifying skill shortage and designing the curriculum as per retailer's requirement and initiating policy with public–private partnership may solve the problem. Gujarat should link developments in retail with other labour-intensive sector such as tourism and should organize shopping festivals, etc., as it is organized in Dubai and Malaysia.

The last chapter by Lancy Lobo and Jayesh Shah explores the character of special economic zones (SEZs) and special investment regions (SIRs). The state is in various stages of the implementation of SEZs and SIRs and these will have singular thrusts in the domain of employment and consequences such as immigration and their effects on Gujarat society and culture.

Part I
Growth and Employment Scenario in India

2

The Employment Intensity of Economic Growth in India during the Reforms Period

Dinkar Nayak and Akash Kumra

India has initiated the liberalization process since 1991. The reforms in the 1990s mainly dealt with industry and trade policy. The chief objective of initiating the reform was to make the country more competitive, and thereby enhance economic growth. It was asserted that reforms bring about change through promotion of economic growth. This is in terms of increase in real per capita income, the increase in share of services sector in gross domestic product (GDP) and the increase in share of services in employment.[1]

Thus, it is held that rapid growth will lead to generation of new employment opportunities. Several studies have been conducted to examine the relationship between economic growth and employment growth. These studies have analysed the link through estimation of employment elasticity.

In one such study, Boltho and Glyn (1995) found elasticities of employment with respect to output growth in the order of 0.5–0.6 for a set of OECD countries. Thus, as per this study, a 1 per cent economic growth leads to about 0.6 per cent growth in employment. According to another study by the International Labour Organization (ILO, 1996), it was concluded that the responsiveness of employment growth to GDP growth has not declined in industrialized countries as a whole.

However, a country-by-country analysis revealed mixed results with little relationship found in Germany, Italy, and the UK in the 1990s, thus implying a jobless recovery. Pianta et al. (1996) discovered evidence suggesting that restructuring of major economic sectors reduces the relationship between economic growth and employment. Among the G7 countries studied (Canada was excluded), a positive and significant relationship between growth in value added and employment was found only in Germany and the United States.

Padalino and Vivarelli (1997) found significant differences in employment elasticities between different countries, with an elasticity of approximately 0.5 for the United States and Canada, while elasticities for Japan, France, Germany, Italy, and the United Kingdom were close to zero. But Pini (1997) estimated that the employment elasticities in Germany and Japan rose between the period 1979–95 compared with 1960–79, while it declined in France and Sweden and showed little change in Italy, United Kingdom, and United States. He also detected negative employment elasticities in Italy and Sweden for the period 1990–95.

Walterskirchen (1999) found employment elasticities of 0.65 when employing a cross-country analysis of EU countries from 1988 to 1998. Using data from 1970 to 1998 for seven countries plus the EU as a whole, employment elasticities ranged from 0.24 for Austria to 0.76 for Spain (the elasticity for the United States was 0.53).

Kapsos (2005) looked at the growth rate of GDP and employment in many countries and estimated employment elasticity. He found that the elasticity has indeed decreased in some countries, whereas Seyfried (2006) estimated that employment elasticity is in the range of 0.31–0.61 in specific states with an estimate of 0.47 for the United States as a whole.

Most of the above studies pertain to the developed world. Further, it was mostly conducted prior to the global slowdown. Very few studies have been undertaken with India as the backdrop. It is in this context that a study pertaining to the relationship between employment and economic growth is particularly necessary, when global slowdown has brought the economic growth from 9.00 per cent rate during the years 2006–07 and 2007–08 to the level of 6.7 per cent in 2008–09.[2] This paper, thus, makes an attempt to find the relationship between economic growth and employment growth in India in the post-reforms period. The rest of the paper is divided into four sections. In the following section, data source and methodology is discussed. Findings are presented in the third section and finally in the fourth section our conclusions are drawn.

Data Sources and Methodology

(a) *Data:* Time series data for the period from 1990–91 to 2007–08 on real GDP and its components at constant prices and employment in public sector and organized private sector by industry have been obtained from the various issues of the "Handbook of Statistics on Indian Economy" published by Reserve Bank of India and as well as different issues of "Economic Surveys" published by Ministry of Finance, Government of India. The data have been collected by dividing the whole post-reform period into the following sub-periods.[3]

Sub-period	*Year*
Adjustment period	1990–91 to 1994–95
Post-adjustment period	1995–96 to 2007–08
Overall period	1990–91 to 2007–08

(b) *Methodology:* To investigate the issue whether there is an acceleration of growth rate of economy and employment in the post-reform period, the following model is designed:

$$\text{Log } Y_t = b_0 + b_1 t + b_2 D + b_3 D.t + u_t \qquad \text{...(1)}$$

where Y_t is the time series under study or the determinant, t is the time variable and D is the intercept dummy which assumes the value 1 for the post-adjustment period and zero for the adjustment period, $D.t$ is the slope dummy which is nothing but the time variable during the post-adjustment period and zero otherwise. The coefficient b_1 will be the growth rate of variables in the adjustment period and $(b_1 + b_3)$ will give the growth rate of variable in the post-adjustment period. The slope coefficients b_1 and $(b_1 + b_3)$ give the instantaneous (at a point in time) rate of growth. The compound growth can be computed by taking the anti-log of b_1 and $(b_1 + b_3)$, subtract 1 from it and multiply the difference by 100. If the coefficient of, say, slope dummy, b_3, is statistically significant and positive, it can be concluded that the regression equation for the post-adjustment period is different from that of the adjustment period and that the rate of growth in the series is higher during the post-adjustment period (as $b_3 > b_1$).

Furthermore, to study the relationship between economic growth and employment growth, this study makes use of graph and regression techniques. Comparable to Boltho and Glyn (1995) and Padalino and Vivarelli (1997) studies, the employment intensity of economic growth is estimated using the following model:

$$\text{Empgrowth} = \beta_0 + \beta_1 \text{ economic growth} + \varepsilon \qquad \ldots(2)$$

where empgrowth is the annual per cent change in employment for the respective industry; economic growth is the annual growth rate of real GDP and β_1 is the estimated elasticity. The estimated elasticity provides a measure of the employment intensity of economic growth, i.e., the growth in employment resulting from growth.

The above models estimated the simple relationship between employment growth and economic growth. However, one should consider the possibility of persistence in employment growth. That is, years with positive growth in employment are likely to be followed by further increases in employment and vice versa. Thus, Equation (2) is augmented by the inclusion of lagged employment growth, resulting in the following equation:

$$\text{Empgrowth} = \beta_0 + \beta_1 \text{ economic growth} + \beta_2 \text{ lagged empgrowth} + \varepsilon \qquad \ldots(3)$$

Lagged employment growth provides further insight into the relationship between employment growth and economic growth. In the augmented models, β_1 represents the partial elasticity of employment, while β_2 is an estimate of the degree of persistence of employment growth. By persistence, we mean the correlation between past and current employment growth; in other words, does employment growth have momentum such that periods of positive growth which are followed by further growth which eventually declines and tends to be followed by further declines? By ignoring the potential effect of lagged employment growth, the previous studies may have obtained misleading results.

Findings

The analysis is done in two parts; in the first part, growth rate of economy and employment is presented. The second part deals with the relationship between economic growth and employment growth.

Growth Analysis

Economic Growth

Table 1 shows the growth rate of real GDP and its components at constant prices. During the study period, the economy has grown at a significant rate of 6.60 per cent. A higher and significant growth is recorded by THR (9.50%) and TSC (8.32%). During the post-adjustment period also, economy grew at the rate of 6.28 per cent. This is mainly due to the higher growth recorded by the sector such as THR (10.05%), CONST (9.90%) and FIRB (8.53%).

Table 1

Growth Rate of GDP and Its Components at Constant Prices Base Year: 1999–2000

Sectors/components	*1990–91 to 1994–95*	*1995–96 to 2007–08*	*1990–90 to 2007–08*
In A&A	3.57*	2.63	2.87*
In Agriculture	3.56*	2.50	2.80*
In Industry	8.60*	6.06**	6.30*
In M&Q	4.50*	4.95	4.73*

Cont'd...

...Cont'd

In MANU	9.46*	6.4**	6.67*
In EGW	7.81*	4.84*	5.48*
In TSC	6.68*	8.83**	8.32*
In CONST	3.65**	9.90*	8.09*
In THR	8.76*	10.05	9.50*
In FIRB	7.18*	8.53	8.14*
In CSPS	4.67*	6.54**	6.67*
In GDPfc	6.15*	6.88	6.60*

*Significant at 1 per cent level of significance.

**Significant at 5 per cent level of significance.

Note: The growth rates are estimated based on the model given in Data Sources and Methodology section. A&A = Agriculture and Allied, M&Q = Mining and Quarrying, MANU = Manufacturing, EGW= Electricity, Gas and Water Supply, CONST = Construction, THR=Trade, Hotels and Restaurants, TSC= Transport, Storage and Communication, FIRB = Financing, Insurance, Real Estate and Business Services, CSPS= Community, Social and Personal Services.

The overall analysis shows a significant improvement in the economic growth during the post-reforms period. This indicates that the reforms are in the right direction as far as acceleration of growth was concerned.

Employment Growth

Tables 2 and 3 represent the growth rate of employment in the private as well as public sector by industry. During the study period, total employment registered a negative growth. If we compare the adjustment period with the post-adjustment period, then it shows that the employment growth has declined significantly from 0.70 per cent to –0.57 per cent. The employment in the private sector has registered a significant growth of 0.51 per cent during the study period. This is mainly due to the higher employment growth in sectors such as FIRB (4.91%), TSC (3.23%), and THR (2.86%).

However, towards the latter part of the reforms, the growth rate of employment in the private sector has declined from a significant 1.08 per cent in adjustment to –0.19 per cent in post-adjustment period. This is mainly due to the decline in employment in industries such as M&Q, MANU, EGW, THR, and CSPS.

Table 2
Growth Rate of Employment in the Private Sector by Industry (lakh person)

Sectors/industry	*1990–91 to 1994–95*	*1995–96 to 2007–08*	*1990–91 to 2007–08*
ln A&A	–0.26	0.67	0.42**
ln M&Q	0.01	–2.07	–2.28*
ln MANU	1.13	–1.36*	–0.12
ln EGW	5.76	2.10	1.16**
ln CONST	–10.10**	–2.11**	–2.16*
ln THR	47.42	3.45	2.86*
ln TSC	2.19**	3.00	3.23*
ln FIRB	3.50	5.37	4.91*
ln CSPS	1.92*	0.95**	1.21*
ln Pvt	1.08**	–0.19**	0.51*
ln Emp	0.70**	–0.57*	–0.16

*Significant at 1 per cent level of significance.

**Significant at 5 per cent level of significance.

Note: The growth rates are estimated based on the model given in Data Sources and Methodology section.

Table 3
Growth Rate of Employment in the Public Sector by Industry (lakh person)

Sectors/Industry	*1990–91 to 1994–95*	*1995–96 to 2007–08*	*1990–91 to 2007–08*
ln A&A	–1.12	–0.92	–1.01*
ln M&Q	0.62	0.73	–0.01
ln MANU	–1.42	–3.85	–3.38*
ln EGW	0.89	–1.00*	–0.45*
ln CONST	0.40	–2.27*	–1.71*
ln THR	1.74	1.19	1.12*
ln TSC	0.59	–1.17**	v0.70*
ln FIRB	1.93**	0.85	0.81*
ln CSPS	0.80	–0.36**	0.03
ln Pub	0.55	–0.79**	–0.47*
ln Emp	0.70**	–0.57*	–0.16

*Significant at 1 per cent level of significance.

**Significant at 5 per cent level of significance.

Note: The growth rates are estimated based on the model given in Data Sources and Methodology section.

Employment in the public sector fails even to register a positive growth during entire period as well as during post-adjustment period (see Table 3). Within the public sector, the increase in the employment growth is indicated by the industry THR (1.12%) and FIRB (0.81%) during the study period.

During the post-adjustment period, the positive employment growth is attained by the THR (1.19%) and FIRB (0.85%), rest all recorded the negative employment growth. The overall employment growth analysis shows a grim picture and casts doubt on the perception that economic reforms have generated more employment.

This requires an analysis to link economic growth with employment growth. This is attempted next.

Relationship between Economic Growth and Employment Growth

Figure 1 shows the trend in economic and employment growth during the entire study period.[4] From the figure, it is evident that there is more or less no relationship between these two.

Figure 1

Economic Growth and Employment Growth

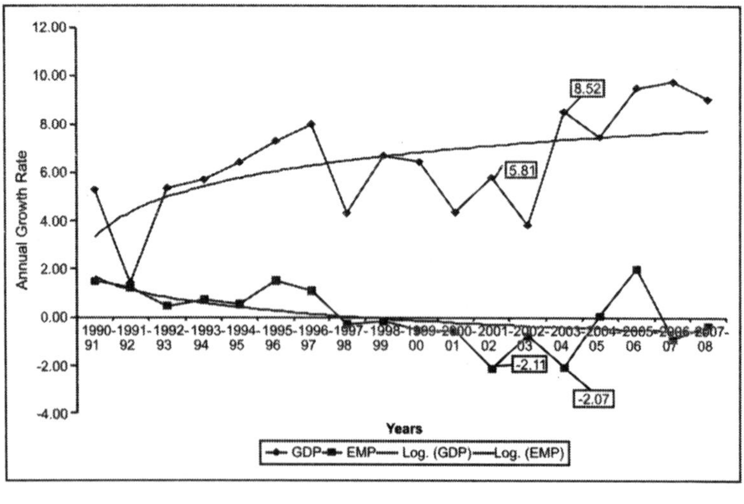

Economic growth, for instance, grew during 2000–01 from 4.35 per cent to 5.81 per cent in 2001–02. However, during the same period, employment growth declined from -0.61 per cent to -2.11 per cent. A similar pattern has been witnessed during 2003–04 and 2006–07.

Figure 2

Economic Growth and Public and Private Employment

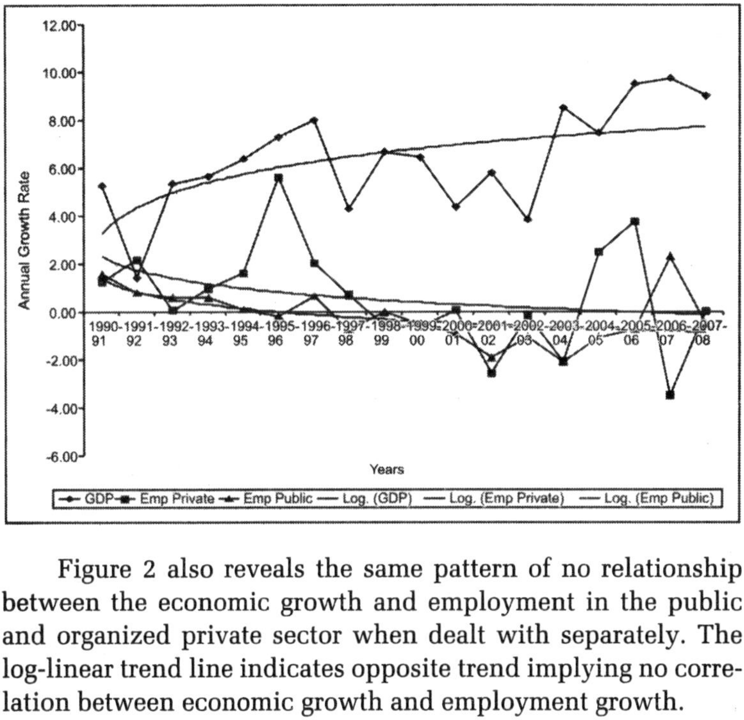

Figure 2 also reveals the same pattern of no relationship between the economic growth and employment in the public and organized private sector when dealt with separately. The log-linear trend line indicates opposite trend implying no correlation between economic growth and employment growth.

Further, employment elasticity with respect to the economic growth indicates a declining trend from 1991–92 onwards. Elasticity declined from 0.84 in 1991–92 to 0.08 in 1992–93, thereafter it continuously declined and reached at -0.37 in 2000–01. It has shown some improvement during 2005–06 (0.21).

But the overall analysis shows that employment elasticity was less elastic. This indicates a poor effect of the economic growth on the employment. Not only does this indicate that with the onset of reforms, the economic growth failed to generate employment, suggesting little correlation between economic growth and employment growth (a jobless recovery).

Figure 3

Employment Elasticity with Respect to Economic Growth

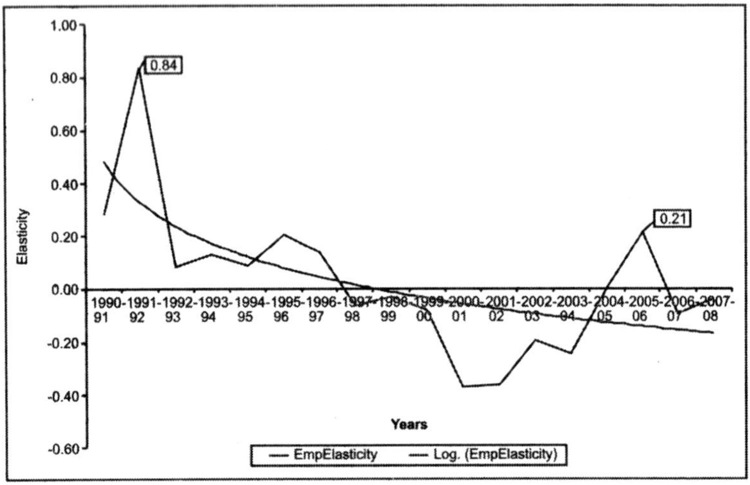

Further, the relationship can also be verified with the help of Equation (2). The estimated elasticity provides a measure of the employment intensity of economic growth, i.e., the growth in employment resulting from growth in output.

The results are presented in Table 4. It is evident from the table that none of the results are statistically significant indicating no significant impact of economic growth on the total employment as well as on the employment of industry. Although the employment in the industry such as M&Q, MANU, CONST, and THR were positively related to the growth rate of the real GDP, but it is not significant.

Tables 5 and 6 indicate the regression results of economic growth and employment growth in public and private sector separately. Here also none of the result was found to be statistically significant. This further shows that individually also economic growth failed to generate any significant impact on the employment of public as well as on the employment of the private sector.

Table 4

Relationship between Employment Growth and Economic Growth

Empgr Y	*Constant* β_0	*Ecogr* β_1	R^2	AdR^2	*F*
Empgr	0.0563	–0.0062	0.0001	–0.0624	0.0019
t	0.0593	–0.0439			
A&A	2.0036	–0.2955	0.0440	–0.0157	0.7369
t	0.8645	–0.8584			
M&Q	–4.0146	0.6791	0.0415	–0.0184	0.6923
t	–0.7307	0.8321			
MANU	–1.5881	0.1709	0.0216	–0.0396	0.3524
t	–0.8196	0.5936			
EGW	0.7363	–0.1223	0.0163	–0.0452	0.2648
t	0.4603	–0.5146			
TSC	–0.2295	–0.0161	0.0003	–0.0622	0.0047
t	–0.1461	–0.0688			
CONST	–2.8310	0.2665	0.0490	–0.0105	0.8240
t	–1.4322	0.9077			
THR	–1.4733	0.6876	0.0094	–0.0526	0.1511
t	–0.1237	0.3887			
FIRB	5.0430	–0.5059	0.0778	0.0201	1.3490
t	1.7199	–1.1615			
CSPS	1.1856	–0.1237	0.0318	–0.0287	0.5256
t	1.0319	v0.7250			
PUB	–0.0563	–0.0136	0.0007	–0.0618	0.0112
t	–0.0650	–0.1058			
PVT	1.1415	–0.0783	0.0059	–0.0562	0.0950
t	0.6679	–0.3082			

t: denotes '*t*' value.

Table 5

Relationship between Economic Growth and Employment in Organized Private Sector by Industry

Empgr Y	*Constant* β_0	*Ecogr* β_1	R^2	AdR^2	*F*
A&A	2.0606	–0.2442	0.0151	–0.0505	0.2303
t	0.5949	–0.4799			
M&Q	–0.3784	–0.0997	0.0004	–0.0662	0.0059
t	–0.0429	–0.0770			
MANU	–0.5539	0.1116	0.0074	–0.0588	0.1113
t	–0.2432	0.3337			
EGW	16.9337	–2.0086	0.0301	–0.0345	0.4661
t	0.8455	–0.6827			
TSC	5.6050	–0.4473	0.1087	0.0493	1.8290
t	2.4895**	–1.3524***			
CONST	–0.5709	–0.1073	0.0003	–0.0664	0.0038
t	–0.0483	–0.0618			
THR	–4.3042	1.4099	0.0190	–0.0464	0.2908
t	–0.2419	0.5393			
FIRB	7.1215	–0.3858	0.0082	–0.0579	0.1241
t	0.9552	–0.3523			
CSPS	2.8985	–0.2657	0.1115	0.0522	1.8819
t	2.1986**	–1.3718***			
PVT	1.1415	–0.0783	0.00590	–0.0562	0.0950
t	0.6679	–0.3082			

[*Significant at 1 per cent level of significance.

**Significant at 5 per cent level of significance.

provided the significance of '**' and '***'.]

Table 6

Relationship between Economic Growth and Employment in Public Sector by Industry

Empgr Y	*Constant* β_0	*Ecogr* β_1	R^2	AdR^2	*F*
A&A	1.23261	–0.29805	0.05682	–0.00606	0.90366
t	0.57750	–0.95061			
M&Q	–5.12992	0.83755	0.05998	–0.00269	0.95704
t	–0.88020	0.97828			
MANU	–5.40879	0.43934	0.06210	–0.00043	0.99310
t	–1.80224**	0.99655			
EGW	0.00479	–0.02788	0.00111	–0.06548	0.01673
t	0.00326	–0.12935			
TSC	–0.43728	0.00194	0.00000	–0.06666	0.00006
t	–0.25058	0.00758			
CONST	–3.39228	0.33427	0.07608	0.01448	1.23513
t	-1.65679***	1.11137			
THR	6.67295	–0.84478	0.14780	0.09099	2.60151
t	1.87154**	–1.61292***			
FIRB	4.04774	–0.48061	0.10255	0.04272	1.71410
t	1.61975***	–1.30924			
CSPS	0.58313	–0.06903	0.00642	–0.05982	0.09686
t	0.38618	–0.31122			
PUB	–0.0563	–0.0136	0.0007	–0.0618	0.0112
t	–0.0650	–0.1058			

*Significant at 1 per cent level of significance.

**Significant at 5 per cent level of significance.

***Significant at 10 per cent level of significance.

t: denotes '*t*' value.

The above regression analysis (models) estimated the simple relationship between employment growth and economic growth. However, one should consider the possibility of persistence in employment growth. That is, years with positive growth in employment are likely to be followed by further increases in employment and vice versa. Thus, Equation (2) was augmented by the inclusion of lagged employment growth, resulting in Equations (3).[5]

Table 7

Relationship between Employment Growth, Economic Growth and Lagged Employment Growth

Y	*Constant* β_0	*Ecogr* β_1	*Lagempgr* β_2	R^2	AdR^2	*F*
A&A	1.4486	–0.2181	–0.2039	0.0791	–0.0525	0.6013
t	0.5768	–0.5895	–0.7791			
M&Q	–5.0031	0.8086	–0.2847	0.1290	0.0045	1.0364
t	–0.8788	0.9660	–1.1408			
MANU	–0.9607	0.1028	0.5226	0.2918	0.1906	2.8842
t	–0.5270	0.3870	2.2998**			
EGW	0.6382	–0.1141	–0.0867	0.0209	-0.1190	0.1493
t	0.3688	–0.4487	–0.3284			
TSC	–0.3054	–0.0064	0.0391	0.0016	–0.1410	0.0113
t	–0.1786	–0.0252	0.1452			
CONST	–3.0632	0.3229	0.2880	0.1601	0.0401	1.3345
t	–1.5615***	1.1259	1.2169			
THR	0.3432	0.6200	–0.3650	0.1418	0.0192	1.1564
t	0.0285	0.3512	–1.4817***			
FIRB	4.9414	–0.4608	–0.1596	0.0966	–0.0324	0.7487
t	1.5729***	–0.9985	–0.6321			
CSPS	–1.3444	0.3130	0.3183	0.1538	0.0329	1.2719
t	–0.8959	1.4545***	1.0264	0.0329		
PUB	–0.5151	0.0480	0.3270	0.1196	–0.0061	0.9514
t	–0.6210	0.3907	1.3759***			
PVT	1.1264	–0.0964	0.1502	0.0267	–0.1124	0.1917
t	0.6113	–0.3517	0.5615			
EMP	–0.1948	0.0168	0.4469	0.2189	0.1073	1.9615
t	–0.2229	0.1309	1.9770**			

*Significant at 1 per cent level of significance.

**Significant at 5 per cent level of significance.

***Significant at 10 per cent level of significance.

t: denotes '*t*' value.

Results of lagged regression model are presented in Table 7. The lagged employment growth provides further insight into the relationship between employment growth and economic growth. It shows that although economic growth does not have a significant impact on the employment growth, but it exhibits significant degree of persistence. Similarly, employment in the MANU industry has indicated a significant degree of persistence. But, the overall analysis shows that neither economic growth nor lagged employment growth has significant effect on the employment growth in the majority of the sectors or industry.

Conclusion

In this study, we examined the nature of the relationship between employment and economic growth in the nine sectors both in the public and private sector.

The results help provide insight to the nature of the relationship between employment and economic growth. The difference between the original model and the one incorporating lagged employment growth suggest that though economic growth does not provide an impetus to employment, employment growth may take on a momentum of its own such that periods of poor employment growth are followed by further periods of poor employment growth.

The above analysis shows that liberalization has not benefited or increased employment opportunities in the organized sector. Recent experience, however, suggests that most of the new employment opportunities are likely to be generated in the unorganized sector and will be characterized by poor conditions of work, and lack of employment and social security. If this trend continues, then in the coming years a majority of workers will continue to have no social protection against the risks of work-related hazards, unemployment, sickness and old age. Even within the organized sector, an increasing number of workers are being employed in a 'flexible' manner on casual or contract basis, without the social security benefits available to regular workers. Thus, reforms have not brought about inclusive growth in the sense that it has not enhanced employment opportunities.

Notes

1. Eschenbach, F., and Hoekman, B. (2006).
2. Report on Effect of Economic Slowdown on Employment in India (Jan–March 2010), Government of India.
3. Here it is to be noted that reform process is long-term process and it takes some time to adjust. We cannot expect quick and immediate

results. It is for this reason that the post-reforms period is subdivided into adjustment and post-adjustment period.
4. Trend is estimated through the log-linear trend line.
5. See Data Sources and Methodology section.

References

Boltho, Andrea, and Andrew Glyn. (1995) 'Can macroeconomic policies raise employment?', *International Labour Review* 134, 451–470.

Eschenbach, F, Hoekman, B (2006), Services Policy Reform and Economic Growth in. Transition Economies *Review of World Economics*, 142 (4), pp. 746–764.

International Labour Office/Organization (ILO). 1996. World Employment 1996197: National policies in a global context (Geneva).

Kapsos, Stepen. (2005) *The Employment Intensity of Growth: Trends and Macroeconomic Determinants*. ILO.

Padalino, Samanta, and Marco Vivarelli (1997) 'The employment intensity of economic growth in the G-7 countries', *International Labour Review* 136:191–213.

Pianta, Mário, Rinaldo Evangelista and Giulio Perani (1996) 'The dynamics of innovation and employment: An international comparison', *Science Technology Industry Review* 18: 67–93.

Pini, Paolo. (1997) 'Occupazione, Tecnologia e Crescita: Modelli Interpretativi ed Eevidenze Empiriche a Livello Macroeconomico'. Paper presented at the Conference of the Accademia Nazionale dei Lincei on 'Sviluppo tecnologico e disoccupazione: trasformazione della societa', Rome, 16–18 January.

Seyfried, William. (2006) 'Examining the relationship between employment and economic growth in the ten largest states', *Southern Economic Journal* 13–23.

Walterskirchen, Ewald. (1999) 'The relationship between growth, employment and unemployment in the EU', European Economist for an Alternative Economic Policy Workshop, Barcelona, Spain.

3

Rural Structural Transformation

The Case of the Service Sector in India[1]

Jeemol Unni and Ravikiran Naik

The most dynamic sector in the last decade globally has been the service sector. India is said to have outpaced a number of countries with its growth in the service sector, powered by software and business process outsourcing (BPO) services. A large share of the export growth in the country is also fuelled by the growth of the service sector. Even in the 1990s, it was seen that the share of the service sector was increasing. There was, however, a debate as to whether this was growth-led or low-productivity residual employment crowding into the sector due to poor agricultural growth and the slowing down of the manufacturing sector. However, in the decade beginning 2000, India has seen an economic boom and the service sector is clearly surging ahead. What concerns us in this paper is whether much, or any, of this high-productivity, high-income growth in the service sector is occurring in rural India. This paper addresses three questions in the following sections: While India experienced high economic growth led by the service sector in the recent decade, to what extent has structural transformation in rural areas taken place? India has seen a spurt in the export of services. How does the Indian service sector perform in the context of General Agreement on Trade in Services (GATS)? How is this reflected in the rural scenario? The information technology (IT) and BPO revolution is considered the engine of the recent growth in the service sector. To what extent has the rural workforce gained from this revolution?

Structural Transformation

Growth and Share of GDP and Employment in India

According to the Planning Commission's (2008) 'Report of the High Level Group on Services Sector', the service sector has been the key driver of the fast growth of the Indian economy in recent years. The Indian economy grew at a rapidly increasing rate from nearly 6 per cent in 2001 to 9.7 per cent per annum in 2006–2007; the service sector outstripped this growth rate in most years. According to National Accounts Statistics (NAS), since 2005, service sector growth has been closer to 11 per cent per annum. The service sector is now seen as the new engine of growth, replacing manufacturing (Dasgupta and Singh, 2005). India's performance is also contrasted with that of China where industry, with an emphasis on mass production, has led to the country's rapid growth in recent decades (Li et al., 2003).

Traditional structural change was also not visible in India. Even in 2000, the service sector contributed nearly half of India's gross domestic product (GDP). The share of services grew to nearly 60 per cent of India's GDP in 2008–2009. The share of agriculture (a primary sector) fell sharply from 25 per cent of GDP in 1999–2000 to 17 per cent in 2008–2009, while industry maintained its position with about 25 per cent.

While the share of GDP in agriculture fell rapidly from 25 per cent in 1999–2000 to 20 per cent in 2004–2005 and to 17 per cent in 2008–2009, the share of employment fell from 60 per cent to 57 per cent only during 1999–2005. In rural areas, nearly three-fourths of the workforce is still dependent on the agricultural sector as the main source of livelihood, with industry and services each constituting 13 per cent of the share of employment.[2] Industry and services have grown in the rural sector as well. Indeed, while the agricultural sector has a large share of employment with a low share of income, it is the service sector that has more than a 50 per cent share of GDP while employing only a quarter of the workforce in India. The service sector has been dynamic and productive, and has helped sustain India's high growth rates in the last decade.

India's Export in Services in the Context of GATS

The Indian service sector has experienced rapid integration with the world economy. India's export in services increased dramatically in the last decade, from US$ 16 billion in 2000 to nearly US$ 73 billion in 2006 (RBI, 2006). It grew by an average annual rate of 12 per cent during the same period. The growing foreign direct investment (FDI) flows to the service sector also facilitated India's integration into the world economy (Chanda, 2007). India has shown global competitiveness in the supply of services, primarily in computer and IT-related services and BPO. However, its share in world trade in services is minuscule, rising from 1 per cent in 2000 to 2.7 per cent in 2006. With the rapid growth in services in the past few years, India's export in services outdid her import in services since 2004, obtaining a trade surplus in the sector (RBI, 2006).

India's Export of Services in Different Modes

With the advent of this new technology, an interesting shift has occurred in the composition of India's export of services, a move away from traditional sectors such as transport and travel to new sectors such as software and business services. The rise in IT-related software and non-software services began around 1997 and picked up sharply in 2000 (Figure 1). Among these new services, software accounted for the largest share, nearly 45 per cent of all exports in 2008. Among the non-software miscellaneous services, business services had the largest share, nearly 20 per cent of all exports in 2006–2007, which declined slightly in 2008–2009. The other components were financial services and communication, which rose to 4.2 per cent and 3.2 per cent respectively in 2006–2007 (Figure 2).

Trade via Mode 3 implies commercial presence through the movement of capital. In recent years, India's outward FDI (OFDI) is steadily increasing and dominated by exports of the services particularly by non-financial services such as communication, software, and business services. Service sector's share increased from 18.1 per cent in 2000–2001 to 30.2 per cent in 2005–2006. Some Indian companies are setting up subsidiaries in segments such as software and health.

Figure 1

Composition of India's Export in Services, 1990–2009

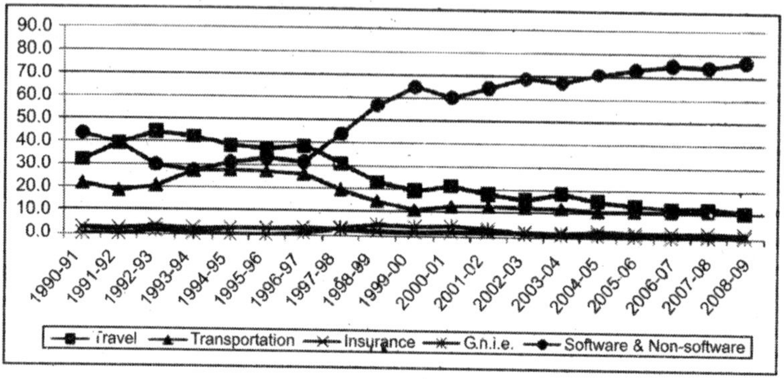

Source: Reserve Bank of India Bulletin, November 2006.

Figure 2

Detailed Composition of India's Export in Services, 2000–2009

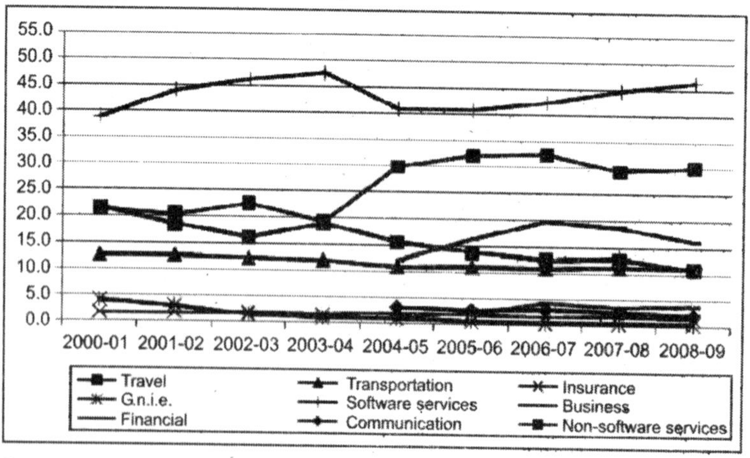

Source: Reserve Bank of India Bulletin, November 2006.

Growth of the Service Sector and Its Composition

The Planning Commission (2008) noted that while the growth of the service sector was broad based, certain services such as communication, of which telecommunication was the principal component, and insurance and banking grew more rapidly. We found that while the overall growth in GDP in services was closer to 11 per cent, that of communication was nearly 26 per cent, and that of banking and insurance was 15 per cent in 2007–2008 (NAS, various years).

Further, the overall share of the service sector in GDP grew from 49 per cent to 57 per cent. The share of the traditional sectors such as trade, hotels and restaurants, and transport remained stagnant, while that of communication and banking and insurance sectors grew. These latter segments are the new dynamic services.

The nature and delivery of communication has seen major changes under the new policy measures regarding IT industry. Finance, insurance, and business services have benefited from new technologies.

Rural Transformation in Sectoral Incomes and Employment

Economic diversification has been occurring in the various sectors in India, which is clear evidence of dynamic structural change. To what extent is this reflected in rural areas? Or is the dynamism, particularly in the modern service sector, restricted to urban areas? A rise in the share of the service sector is often followed by a subsequent rise in total employment. But in the Indian case, service-sector-led growth has failed to create a significant number of jobs in the economy (Banga, 2006). While we had noted a faster rate of growth of services in GDP in India, we find that the growth of employment was higher in industry than in services (Table 1). This could imply that, on the whole, the service sector is more productive than the industry sector. Overall, employment growth was much higher in urban areas (3.2%) compared to rural areas (1.6%) in the period 1993–1994 to 2004–2005 (Table 1). A rural–urban comparison showed that the growth of employment was higher in industry in rural areas, while employment grew faster in urban areas in the service sector.

Table 1

Growth Rate (%) of Employment in Rural and Urban Areas, 1993–2005

Sector	*Rural*			*Urban*		
	1993–1994 to 1999–2000	*1999–2000 to 2004–2005*	*1993–1994 to 2004–2005*	*1993–1994 to 1999–2000*	*1999–2000 to 2004–2005*	*1993–1994 to 2004–2005*
Agriculture, etc.	0.18	1.70	0.87	–3.36	4.43	0.18
Industry	2.48	6.35	4.24	2.28	5.57	3.77
Mining and quarrying	–2.41	2.67	–0.10	–4.53	4.43	–0.46
Manufacturing	1.56	4.48	2.88	1.58	6.03	3.60
Electricity, gas and water supply	0.63	2.67	1.56	–3.72	4.43	–0.02
Construction	5.94	10.58	8.05	6.21	4.43	5.40
Services	2.03	4.52	3.16	3.30	3.74	3.50
Trade, hotels and restaurant	3.47	6.25	4.74	7.67	2.64	5.38
Trade	3.45	6.32	4.75	7.97	2.13	5.32
Hotels and restaurants	3.67	5.75	4.62	4.70	6.40	5.47
Transport, storage and communication	7.39	6.16	6.83	3.83	4.20	4
Railways	0.63	2.67	1.56	–4.53	–0.04	–2.49
Transport by other means	7.39	6.68	7.07	4.19	4.43	4.30
Storage	—	—	—	7.02	4.43	5.84
Communication	12.18	2.67	7.86	15.37	4.43	10.39
Financial intermediation, real estate and business activities	5.42	7.13	6.20	5.34	9.56	7.26
Banking and insurance	0.63	2.67	1.56	4.08	5.45	4.70
Real estate, ownership of dwelling, business services	12.18	10.78	11.54	6.52	12.54	9.26
Community, social and personal services	–1.33	1.38	–0.10	–2.04	3.90	0.66
Public administration and defence	0.63	–5.44	–2.13	–0.38	–1.80	–1.03
Other services	–1.94	3.22	0.41	–2.95	6.62	1.40
Total	0.65	2.65	1.56	2.27	4.41	3.24

Source: Computed from unit-level records of NSS 50th, 55th, and 61st Rounds.

In the industry sector, employment in the construction industry grew the fastest, particularly in rural areas. In the service sector, employment growth was highest in rural and urban areas in the dynamic new sectors of communications, finance, and business services. In this sector, too, the rural–urban differential was striking, with communication and banking and insurance showing much faster growth in employment in urban areas. It would appear that the new and modern industry with rapid export growth potential was growing more rapidly, not only in terms of GDP but also in terms of employment in urban areas.

Share of Rural in Total Income and Employment

The NAS does not report the rural–urban composition of net domestic product (NDP) on a yearly basis. It generally reports the rural composition only when there is a series change in the GDP estimation. We, therefore, were able to find estimations of the share of rural in total NDP for the years 1970–1971, 1980–1981, 1993–1994, 1999–2000, and 2004–2005. The rural share of total NDP at factor costs is presented in Table 2.

At the aggregate level share of rural area in the NDP has been shrinking from 62 per cent in 1970–1971 to 54 per cent in 1993–1994 and it has reduced further to 48 per cent 2004–2005. Agriculture, forestry, and fishing are confined almost entirely to the rural areas, and these sectors have declined only marginally, as may be expected, over the period 1970–1971 to 1999–2000. Thereafter agriculture increased its share by around 2 per cent in 2004–2005, while forestry and fishing continued their previous declining trend during the same period. Within industry, the share of rural manufacturing in total NDP rose from 25 per cent to 42 per cent between period of 1970–1971 and 2004–2005.The share of utilities increased from 39 per cent to 45 in 1999–2000 and then declined to 33 per cent. Within rural manufacturing, the share of rural income in both the organized and unorganized sectors appears to have risen. The share of income from construction in rural areas remained more or less constant.

Table 2
Share (%) of Rural in Total NDP at Factor Cost, 1970–2005

	Sector	*Rural as % of total*				
		1970–1971	*1980–1981*	*1993–1994*	*1999–2000*	*2004–2005*
1	Agriculture, forestry and fishing	96.23	94.89	93.94	93.25	94.04
1.1	Agriculture	96.91	95.24	94.80	93.83	95.50
1.2	Forestry and logging	88.16	96.62	96.78	94	91.67
1.3	Fishing	76.33	70.35	66.41	79.24	73.65
2	Mining and quarrying	61.01	54.75	65.88	42.39	66.28
3	Manufacturing	25.79	31.84	29.77	41.56	42.52
4	Electricity, gas and water supply	39.81	40.02	37.88	45.44	33.25
5	Construction	43.22	45.62	45.11	43.32	45.46
6	Trade, hotels and restaurants	18.18	30.34	30.45	27.06	40.90
6.1	Trade	*	*	30.75	26.26	41.03
6.2	Hotels and restaurants	*	*	25.36	35.9	39.52
7	Transport, storage and communication	22.81	22.99	34.29	29.3	33.40
7.1	Railways	26.36	29.52	33.83	30.98	30.98
7.2	Transport by other means	16.13	17.84	32.33	28.43	38.29
7.3	Storage	**	16.67	30.99	31.18	13.97
7.4	Communication	35.82	38.66	40.97	30.76	17.03
8	Financing, insurance, real estate and business services	43.18	37.61	28.18	23.62	26.93
8.1	Banking and insurance	19.31	15.7	16.37	14.52	14.82
8.2	Real estate, ownership of dwellings and business services	48.41	49.98	39.9	32.07	35.81
9	Community, social and personal services	39.8	39.08	41.71	29.16	28.18
9.1	Public administration and defence	42.2	34.28	40.34	19.91	16.11
9.2	Other services	37.86	42.85	42.8	36.25	36.28
	Net domestic product (1–9)	62.35	58.91	54.27	48.09	47.98

*included in Item 6; **included in Item 7.2; Data from different years pertain to different NAS series.

Source: National Accounts Statistics (NAS) (2007, 2010).

The sectoral transformation in income is more prominent in the service sector. Among the traditional service sectors trade, hotel, and restaurant maintained its share at around 30 per cent from 1980–1981 to 1999–2000 and then drastically jumped to 41 per cent in 2004–2005. The other traditional services such as railways retained their contribution to the rural income since 1980–1981. Rural share of other transport services fluctuated growing sharply in 2004–2005. The share of storage sector declined continuously to 14 per cent.

The dynamic and new service sectors that we identified earlier showed a marked decline in their share in income in rural areas. The share of the communication sector in NDP in rural areas declined from 35 per cent to 17 per cent in 2004–2005, the lowest level since 1970–1971. The share of banking and insurance declined from 19 per cent to 14 per cent during 1970–1971 to 2004–2005 and that of real estate and business services declined from 48 per cent to 36 per cent during 1970–1971 to 2004–2005 (Table 2). Other personal services, such as education and health, showed a significant decline in their share in income in rural areas, falling from 42 per cent in 1980–1981 to 36 per cent in 2004–2005 and the share of public administration and defence declined to 16 per cent from 34 per during the same period. Except trade, hotel–restaurants, and transport, share of other service segments have either declined or remained unchanged.

This raises questions about the nature of the structural transformation occurring in India. Is this new IT-led communication and service industry mainly concentrated in urban areas? Does this imply that rural India is not sharing the fruits of the new service sector-led growth of the economy?

A similar shift in employment in the service sector is also noted. The share of employment in manufacturing and traditional services such as trade and hotels and restaurants remained more or less the same during the period from 1993–1994 to 2004–2005 (Table 3).

Table 3

Share (%) of Rural in Total Employment, 1993–2005

Sector	*1993–1994*	*1999–2000*	*2004–2005*
Agriculture and allied	95.8	96.6	96.1
Mining and quarrying	64.2	67.1	65.1
Manufacturing	51.6	51.5	49.6
Electricity	41.8	48.2	46
Construction	57.7	57.4	64.9
Industry	53.3	53.6	54.6
Trade, hotels and restaurants	44.2	38.2	42.5
Trade	44.5	37.9	43
Hotels and restaurants	41.8	40.3	39.5
Transport, storage and communication	38.9	43.8	46.5
Railways	19.3	24.6	27.2
Transport by other means	43.5	48.2	51
Storage	0	0	0
Communication	41.8	37.2	35.2
Financing, insurance, real estate and business services	24	24.1	22
Banking and insurance	29.7	25.5	23
Real estate, ownership of dwellings and business services	17.4	22.9	21.4
Community, social and personal services	43.9	44.9	41.8
Public administration and defence	34.2	35.5	31.5
Other services	47.7	49.2	45
Services	42.4	40.7	41.5
Total (all)	78.2	76.5	74.9

Source: Computed from unit-level records of NSS 50th, 55th, and 61st Rounds.

The share of employment in rural areas in the dynamic sector of communications fell from 42 per cent to 35 per cent, and that of banking and insurance fell from 30 per cent to 23 per cent, in the same period (Table 3). It would appear that the share of both income and employment in the new sectors led by dynamic export-oriented growth was restricted to urban areas.

Hence, we would argue that the benefits of this rapid growth in more productive and high-income-earning sectors were not obtained in rural areas.

IT Revolution in Rural India

The analysis of the growth in exports, incomes, and employment in the Indian economy has led us to believe that the most dynamic segments of the economy are the IT-led sectors of communications, banking and insurance, and business and professional services. The latter include both ITES and BPOs. We also found that these segments were growing faster in urban areas compared to rural areas.

A recent paper argued that the IT labour market has been deepening and thickening (Basant and Rani, 2004). Labour market deepening occurs through extension and penetration into new areas, when diversity in the demand and supply of skills is enhanced. With increasing specialization and expanding scale, the demand for skills in specific segments grows, which is referred to as thickening. To what extent have these processes in the IT-related skilled labour market growth occurred in rural areas?

The number of IT workers has been growing (Table 4). IT workers can be classified on the basis of occupation and industry. The overall share of IT workers in rural areas was very low, being 11 per cent in 2004–2005; it has been declining since 1993–1994. Furthermore, the distribution of IT occupations into computing machine operators, data processing operators, and system analysts/programmers shows a striking difference in the nature of the work performed by IT workers in urban and rural areas. In urban areas, nearly a third of IT workers were professionals even in 1993–1994, while they accounted for nearly 9 per cent in rural areas in 2004–2005. IT workers in rural areas were employed as less qualified data processing or machine operators (Table 5).

The lack of diversity in IT-related occupations in rural areas as compared to urban areas is also noted in the classification by industry groups. The variety of industries in which IT workers were engaged in rural areas was restricted to manufacturing, business services, public administration, and, more recently, trade and communications (Table 6). Furthermore, while the proportion of IT workers in the manufacturing sector in rural areas increased, the proportion of those in the business service sector declined. Of course, some new areas of IT penetration were noted in 2004–2005 in rural areas.

Table 4

Distribution of IT Workers by Occupation in Rural Areas (% Rural of Total)

Occupation	*1993–1994*	*1999–2000*	*2004–2005*
System analysts and programmers	0	1.1	3.2
Data processors	56.4	1	16.5
Computing machine operators	7.9	9.6	14.7
Total	26.6	5.5	11.4

Source: Computed from unit-level records of NSS 50th, 55th, and 61st Rounds.

Table 5

Distribution (%) of IT Workers by Occupation in Rural and Urban Areas

Occupation	*Rural*		
	1993–1994	*1999–2000*	*2004–2005*
System analysts and programmers	0	4.6	8.9
Data processors	91	4.6	28.6
Computing machine operators	9	90.8	62.5
Total	100	100	100
	Urban		
System analysts and programmers	36.3	24.5	34.5
Data processors	25.5	26.1	18.7
Computing machine operators	38.2	49.4	46.8
Total	100	100	100

Source: Computed from unit-level records of NSS 50th, 55th, and 61st Rounds.

Table 6

Distribution of IT Workers (%) by Industry and Area, 1993–2004 (to add 64th Round data)

Sector	*Urban*			*Rural*			*Rural as % of Total*		
	1993–1994	*1999–2000*	*2004–2005*	*1993–1994*	*1999–2000*	*2004–2005*	*1993–1994*	*1999–2000*	*2004–2005*
Mining			0.2	0.4			100		
Manufacturing	26.5	20.6	11.3	12.6	42.1	29.2	14.8	10.5	25.1
Electricity, gas, Water supply	1.8	0.3	0.3	—	2.9	—	—	33.5	—
Construction	0	1.7	0	—	—	—	—	—	—
Trade	3.7	8.3	2.7	—	—	6.4	—	—	23.3
Hotels and restaurants	0.1	0	0.8	—	—	—	—	—	—
Transport	2	2.8	1.8	—	6.4	—	—	11.6	—
Post and tele-communication	3.4	0.3	1	—	—	1.8	—	—	19
Banking	17.7	9.8	6.1	—	—	—	—	—	—
Insurance, pension funding	1.8	0.9	2	—	—	—	—	—	—
Computer and computer related	—	38.8	62.7	—	—	37	—	—	7.1
Business services	26.4	3.1	3.1	80.2	25.5	14.8	52.6	32	37.8
Public administration and defence		3.2	2.6	6.8	0.8	2.6	100	1.5	11.6
Education	—	7.1	4.1	—	8.5	8.2	—	6.4	20.6
Health and social work	—	1	0.4	—	13.8	—	—	44	
Recreation	—	1.4	—	—	—	—	—	—	
Other community, social, and personal service activities	16.5	0.7	0.9	—	—	—	—	—	—
	100	100	100	100	100	100	26.73	5.45	11.44

Source: Computed from unit-level records of NSS 50th, 55th, and 61st Rounds.

Overall, it appears that the process of labour market deepening and thickening occurred mainly in urban areas. The transformation of the IT sector or the movement of IT workers into varied industries, in rural areas continued to be limited.

Conclusion

The most dynamic sector in the last decade globally has been the service sector. India is said to have outpaced a number of countries with its growth in the service sector, powered by software and BPO services. A large share of the export growth in the country is also fuelled by the growth of the service sector. We identified communications, banking and insurance, and business services as the most dynamic segments of the service sector. It appears that the share of both income and employment in these new sectors was restricted to urban areas. Thus, much of this high-productivity, high-income growth of the service sector has not created a structural transformation in rural India. The IT and BPO revolution is considered the engine of the recent growth of the service sector. However, we noted that the rural workforce has not gained from the labour market deepening in the IT sector. We, therefore, argue that the benefits of rapid economic growth in the more productive and high-income-earning service sectors were not obtained in rural areas.

Notes

1. An abridged version of the paper was published in *Economic and Political Weekly* (June 25, 2001, Vol. XLVI, Nos. 26, 27, pp. 196–200).
2. Computed from unit-level records of NSS (National Sample Survey) 50th, 55th and 61st Rounds.

References

Banga, Rashmi (2006). 'Statistical overview of India's trade in services', *Trade in Services and India: Prospects and Strategy*, editor Chanda, Rupa. New Delhi: Centre for Trade & Development (Centad) and Wiley India, pp. 15–49.

Basant, Rakesh, and Rani, Uma (2004). 'Labour market deepening in India's IT: An exploratory analysis', *Economic and Political Weekly* 39(50), 5317–5326.

Chanda, Rupa (2007). 'Services', *The Oxford Companion to Economics in India*, editor Basu, Kaushik. New Delhi: Oxford University Press.

Dasgupta, Sukti, and Singh, Ajit (2005). *Will Services be the New Engine of Economic Growth in India?* Working Paper No. 310, Centre for Business Research, and Faculty of Economics, University of Cambridge. http://www.cbr.cam.ac.uk/pdf/WP310.pdf.

Li, Shantong, Wang, Yan, and Zhai, Fan (2003). 'Impact of service sector liberalization on employment and output: A CGE analysis' (first draft 17 September 2003). http://siteresources.worldbank.org/INTRANETTRADE/Resources/WBI-Training/ServiceLibinChina.pdf.

Planning Commission (2008). *Report of the High Level Group on Services Sector*. New Delhi: Government of India.

Reserve Bank of India (November, 2006). *Monthly Bulletin*. New Delhi: Government of India.

4

Jobless Growth and Need for Employment Policy in India

Trupti Shah and Aswini Trivedi

'Employment is the main source of livelihood and self-fulfilment for most women and men. It is critical to the way women and men live and view their lives. A well-nurtured and productive labour force contributes towards a dynamic economy and equitable society. Lack of access to employment, that is decent and remunerative, lowers self-esteem and leads to denial of basic needs of the individual and the family, and can lead to social instability.

It is, therefore, important to work towards the goal of decent and remunerative work for all women and men seeking such work, in conditions of freedom, equity, security and human dignity' (NEP, 2008: 2).

The above quote from the preamble of the National Employment Policy's (NEP) draft, which was formulated in 2008 but not yet passed by the Parliament of India, rightly describes the significance of decent employment. The document for the 11th Five-Year Plan reiterates that 'the generation of productive and gainful employment, with decent working conditions, on a sufficient scale to absorb our growing labour force must form a critical element in the strategy for achieving inclusive growth'.[1]

The question arises whether there are adequate steps taken or planned to have definite impact on the employment scenario or not? The fact that India does not have employment policy even after more than 60 years of planned development itself is an evidence for the approach of the planner towards the issue of employment.

As per the recent economic survey 2010–2011, 'The Indian economy has emerged with remarkable rapidity from the slowdown caused by the global financial crisis of 2007–2009. With growth in 2009–2010 now estimated at 8.0 per cent by the Quick Estimates released on 31 January 2011 and 8.6 per cent in 2010–2011 as per the Advance Estimates of the Central Statistics Office ... the Indian economy is poised to further improve and consolidate in terms of key macroeconomic indicators'.

The other side of the reality is that the consistent high growth rate in the Indian economy since the last few years and the fast paced recovery in the face of world financial crises is not reflected in the employment data for the economy. The comparison between the growth rate of various sectors and the growth rate of employment in them challenges the underlying assumption of the Indian planners that investment will automatically generate employment. The lack of connection between growth and employment in the economy is particularly a cause for great concern due to emergence of double-digit food inflation.

Not only the number of employment generated is insufficient but also the quality of employment is a major concern (NCEUS, 2009). In spite of the growth story of India as an 'emerging economy' of the world, more than 90 per cent of the working population is forced to rely on the unorganized sector for livelihood, thanks to the non-existence of effective employment policy. Thus, there is a need to argue for an effective employment policy and examine the efficacy of draft employment policy in the context of current economic scenario.

An effective employment policy should consider the lessons learnt from historical experiences and incorporate the analysis about the root cause of the problem. The analysis of employment and unemployment situation among social groups such as male, female, SC, ST, OBC, and others in rural and urban areas of India suggests the differential impact of the economic growth on these groups. Hence, there is an urgent need for a group specific policy intervention.

This paper analyses the historical experience of the employment–unemployment situation in pre- and post-independent India and the data from various rounds of NSSO in pre- and post-reform period including recent data from 64th round, to understand the impact of economic reforms on the employment situation.

Historical Perspective on the Employment Issue

The employment problem in the Indian economy reflects the interplay of major historical forces such as the process of development of industrial capitalism in pre- and post-independence India with the socio-political structures of gender and caste.

The industrial capitalism introduced through the process of colonization affected the employment patterns in several ways, which have had a lasting effect on the quantity and quality of the employment of women and other marginalized groups such as SCs, STs, and others which is haunting the economy today. With the introduction of the market economy, the dichotomy between productive and unproductive work was introduced. All those activities carried out by women and marginal communities for self-consumption, which were necessary for subsistence but not for sale in the market, were termed as 'unproductive'. The policies of export–import, tax, and revenue were imposed for the benefit of British manufacturing industries in such a manner that it ruined the cottage industries run by artisan families in the various parts of India.

Ashok Mitra,[2] Acharya, and others described the process as 'de-industrialization' or 'peasantization' of the Indian economy. They conclude that the development of the economy had almost been frozen at the early 20th century level. The result was a fall in demand for labour which affected women the most. The consequence was that only non-remunerative and unrecognized occupations stayed with women and thus agriculture has been the only expanding source of employment for females.

Thus, poverty, unemployment, illiteracy, and ill-health were major challenges before the nation at the time of independence but the transfer of power from British rulers did not change the structure of administration or economy radically. The strategy of planned development in the 'mixed economy' was adopted for economic growth. The introduction of the public sector along with private enterprise was said to be the principal mechanism of redistribution. But it gave rise to a 'mixed economy' in which the market principles continue to be dominant (Banerjee et al., 1988). Capital-intensive industrialization took place during this period. Though lip service was paid to the development of small-scale sector and village industries, they were never considered as an inherent part of the planning model. The model did not incorporate unorganized or informal sector in the mainstream process of economic development. 'The neglect of the unorganised sector was no doubt a factor contributing to the deterioration in the condition of women workers in the period since that sector in India has always employed more than 90 per cent of them' (Banerjee, 1998: 11). On the one hand, women were losing their traditional work and skills because the traditional sector was losing out to the modern sector of the economy; on the other hand, the planning exercise failed to recognize women's role as productive workers in the economy. Though on the eve of India's independence, women constituted almost 30 per cent of the workforce of the country, women were not viewed as workers or producers but as a weaker section of society because of the patriarchal ideology behind the planning. The report of the Committee on the Status of Women in India highlighted the fact that 'the transition to a modern economy has meant the exclusion of an increasing number and proportion of women from active participation in the productive process' (GoI, 1974: 365).

The capital-intensive industrialization without employment growth in urban areas and the 'Green Revolution' without land reform in rural areas accentuated the disparities between rich and poor. The hope that benefits of economic growth would trickle down to the poorer sections of society was not realized. To pacify the discontent of the masses, a shift from economic growth to minimum needs and target approach was adopted in the planning during the 1970s, but 'removal of poverty' remained more in the nature of a political slogan. It failed in changing the direction and thrust of the economic processes towards decreasing poverty, inequality, and unemployment.

Thus, in both urban and rural areas, this process of marginalization or casualization has been observed by several scholars. The process has resulted in more and more people taking recourse to the informal sector for their survival. Visaria and Minhas (1991) have rightly observed regarding employment and unemployment in 1990s that 'the poor in India cannot afford to remain unemployed for an extended period of time such as even a week. They have little choice except to take up whatever work, even casual, is available to them, irrespective of the quantum of return'. This observation is truer for women, because apart from the fact of being poor, they are also responsible for the survival of their household especially in the present context of male-dominated society.

The dominant trend in economic thinking attributed this failure of unemployment to the inefficiency of the public sector over bureaucratization and restrictions on the market forces. The debate about planning versus market was initiated in the 1980s (Banerjee et al., 1988).[3]

Economic Reforms and Supremacy of Market Forces

The Indian government in 1991 officially adopted a new economic policy also known as *Economic Reforms* or *Structural Adjustment Programme*. However, as noted by several economic analysts, 'India had began a process of "adjustment" quietly since the beginning of the 1980's' (Shah et al., 1994: WS–39). With the introduction of Structural Adjustment Programme (SAP), the focus of the economy changed. 'Liberalization', 'privatization' and 'globalization' became the terminology of development plans instead of 'planning', 'public sector', and 'self-reliance'. Even the rhetoric of poverty eradication, equity, etc., were done away with and 'efficiency', 'market forces', 'export promotion', and 'foreign direct investment' (FDI) have became some of the buzz words in the economic debate.

As a result of the new economic policy and Industrial Policy 1991, foreign direct investments are welcomed in the name of capital formation and need for high-tech production process to compete in the world market. To make production and sales more efficient, bureaucratic processes are simplified and steps to abolish 'license-permit raj' have been taken for the benefit of investors. On the other hand, workers in large companies, both in the public and private sectors, are pushed to accept voluntary retirement schemes. Labour laws are changed or by-passed to make 'hire and fire' policies easier for the employers and to restrict the rights of workers and trade unions (Papola and Pais, 2007).

How does this policy tackle the problem of unemployment since the production processes are capital-intensive and do not generate new employment in significant ways, and labour policies do not protect even existing employment? According to the proponents of this policy, employment will be generated through self-employment and the informal sector. The proposal is to reduce the gap between the formal sector workers and informal sector workers.

The Initial Debates

Economic reforms have remained controversial since its introduction in 1991. The long-term effect of the various policy changes has triggered off the debate about its implication on the working and living conditions of the poor and all the marginal groups in the economy.

The supporters of the policy have argued that SAP would introduce internal and external competition and would reduce the wasteful use of scarce resources and improve international competitiveness. According to their argument, the NEP will not affect the poor but it would affect the 'organized interests groups' of the economy (Tendulkar, 1991). The strong supporters of economic reforms were in favour of leaving everything to the mercy of market forces (Kamath, 1992).

There was an extensive debate on the impact of economic reforms on women. It is claimed that economic reforms affect women as producers as well as consumers. Lynn Bennett,[4] argued that 'market forces have great potential to influence gender ideology and increase the perceived value of women'. In fact, Devaki Jain (1993) and her colleagues were in favour of converting the crises into opportunity. They suggest a wide safety net, by way of expanded public distribution system and employment programmes and an entry policy before launching an exit policy to save the poor and women from shouldering the entire burden of structural adjustment. Renana Jabvala (1994) suggested several strategic steps to empower women in the people's sector and bring them into the mainstream of economic reforms and development. According to her, if supported, these women would create a model of development worthy of being followed by others.

The arguments against the reforms were also not homogeneous. Some were against the reforms as it is contrary to the Nehruvian policy of self-reliance and self-sufficiency of the economy and it is a sell-out of the country to the World Bank and IMF; but they could not recognize the fact that economic reforms were also demanded by the Indian corporate sector. There is a strong argument that because of structural adjustment, the spending on social sectors and anti-poverty programmes would decrease and the poor will be doubly affected.

The impact on women's employment was the most debated issue and subject matter of various scholarly works. The thesis of feminization of workforce, marginalization of women and stagnation were put forward by several scholars. Varghese (1993), Singh (1994), and others in their study argued that development has led to marginalization of women in India. Deshpande (1993, 1994) put forward the 'feminization' hypothesis. Initially, she argued that the processes of deregulation and feminization have taken place in India and the trend would accentuate in the future, though in her later article she suggested that the feminization of the labour force in urban India is very less and marginal compared to other countries. According to Banerjee (1997), the process which led to the feminization in other countries has not taken place in India and there is no evidence that it will take place in the future. Dreze (1997), while comparing the various positions on the marginalization and feminization hypothesis, suggested that there may be case for a 'stagnation' hypothesis. He stresses the need to go beyond the overall rate of work participation and recommends examining detailed patterns of female employment in different types of activities.

Several authors[5] has analysed the impact on the household sector with the help of social accounting matrices and vulnerable sector approach. Ranadive (1994) argued in her paper that the household sector would act as a buffer during the transitional period of economic reforms. And further due to certain specific gender-related circumstances within the household, it is women who act as the buffer.

The common concern emerging from these studies focus on the privatization and withdrawal of the state from the provision of various social sectors such as health, education, and food subsidy which will force women to work more for meeting the needs of family survival both in the household and in the labour force. Both the supporters and opponents of the Economic Reform were agreed on one point that the increase in employment or livelihood opportunities for women and other marginalize groups will be mainly in the informal sector of the economy.

The Current Scenario: What Do the Data Indicate?

Over the years NSSO had comprehensively assessed the labour market situation in different rounds from time to time. Latest employment–unemployment survey was conducted during July 2007–June 2008 and released in May 2010.[6] This section deals with NSSO data of different rounds in percentage forms and brings out employment pattern of rural–urban and male–female employment and connects them with employment pattern among social groups.

During 1983 to 1987–1988, employment declined for rural and urban areas for both genders except 0.1 per cent increase in urban female employment. From 1987–1988 to 1993–1994 employment is increased by 1.4 per cent and 1.5 per cent for rural and urban males. It increased by 0.5 per cent for rural female and 0.3 per cent for urban females. But it could not be sustained and in the next round (1999–2000), employed male and female in both rural and urban areas declined (Table 1).

Table 1

Worker Participation Rates according to Usual Status (ps + ss) (in %)

NSS round	*Rural male*		*Rural female*		*Urban male*		*Urban female*	
	%	*%Δ*	*%*	*%Δ*	*%*	*%Δ*	*%*	*%Δ*
38th (1983)	54.7		34		51.2		15.1	
43rd (1987–1988)	53.9	–0.8	32.3	–1.7	50.6	–0.6	15.2	0.1
50th (1993–1994)	55.3	1.4	32.8	0.5	52.1	1.5	15.5	0.3
55th (1999–2000)	53.1	–2.2	29.9	–2.9	51.8	–0.3	13.9	–1.6
61st (2004–2005)	54.6	1.5	32.7	2.8	54.9	3.1	16.6	2.7
64th (2007–2008)	54.8	0.2	28.9	–3.8	55.4	0.5	13.8	–2.8

Source: NSSO Report Nos. 515 and 531.

Computed on the basis of Statement 5.1, NSSO Report 515, p. 93 and Statement 11, NSSO Report 531, p. 47.

Figure 1

Worker Participation Rates according to Usual Status (ps + ss) in (% & %Δ)

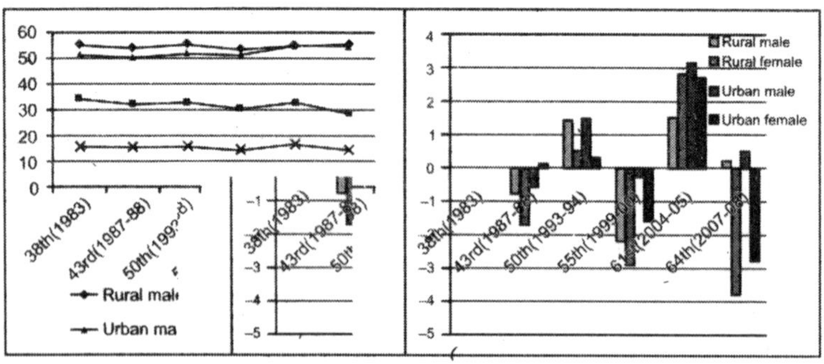

Computed on the basis of Statement 5.1, NSSO Report 515, p. 93 and Statement 11, NSSO Report 531, p. 47.

According to Sundaram (2001a, 2001b), between 1993–1994 and 1999–2000, there has been a significant decline in the crude worker–population ratios in all the four population segments resulting in a slower growth of workforce relative to the growth in population and an absolute reduction in the number of women workers in rural India which is just offset by a rise in the number of urban women workers. It recovered in next round, i.e., 2004–2005. The usual employment in urban areas rose by 3.1 per cent for urban male and 2.7 per cent for urban female. In rural areas as well it increased by 1.5 per cent and 2.8 per cent for rural male and female, respectively.

Rangrajan and others infer from the NSSO 61st round that the reversal of the declining trend in employment growth rate which increased from an annual 0.98 per cent in the period 1993–1994 to 1999–2000 to 2.89 per cent in the period 1999–2000 to 2005–2005. They predicted that 'with a growth rate of 9.1 per cent the workforce would become equal to the labour force, by 2009'. But they also conclude that the bulk of the increase in employment has happened in the informal sector. This trend is a cause for concern as the relatively low wage and lack of social security translates into the phenomenon of the working poor. In other words, the congruence of labour force and workforce by itself does not guarantee an elimination of poverty (Rangrajan et al., 2007). The reversal of declining trend observed by them is not sustainable. Results of female employment in 2007–2008 concerned the policy makers as there was a decline by 3.8 per cent and 2.8 per cent in rural and urban females' employment. However, in the rural and urban areas, male employment increased marginally by 0.2 per cent and 0.5 per cent, respectively.

The *usual status* approach, with the long reference period of 365 days, adopted for classification of the population is unable to capture changes in the activity pattern caused by seasonal fluctuations. But, the estimates obtained by adopting the Current Weekly Status (CWS) and Current Daily Status (CDS) approaches are expected to reflect the overall effect caused by intermittent changes in the activity pattern during the year. The latter reflects under employment.

According to the CWS, in rural areas both male and female employment declined by 0.7 per cent and in urban areas it increased marginally by 0.1 per cent for females from 1983 to 1987–1988. Employment situation improved in 1993–1994 across regions and gender wise as well but declined during 1999–2000 period. During 1999–2000 to 2004–2005, employment grew from 51 per cent to 52.4 per cent and 25.3 per cent to 27.5 per cent for rural male and female, respectively. In urban areas too employment increased from 50.9 per cent to 53.7 per cent for urban male and from 12.8 per cent to 15.2 per cent for urban female. Despite various schemes by the government, CWS employment declined for females in rural and urban areas during 2004–2005 to 2007–2008. It increased marginally for male workers in rural and urban areas in 2007–2008.

CDS employment increased from 1983 to 1993–1994 in rural and urban areas for male and female workforce. It declined in 55th round, i.e., during 1999-2000. It again increased in next two rounds, i.e., 61st and 64th rounds, except decline in female employment in 64th round for rural and urban areas. According to CDS basis, 48.2 per cent male were employed in rural areas in the 38th round, which increased substantially in the 43rd and 50th round, but started declining and finally reached to 49 per cent in 2007–2008. Female employment kept fluctuating for different rounds and finally in 2007–2008 declined. For urban males, it increased from 47.3 per cent in 1983 to 52.9 per cent in 2007–2008 (Table 2).

Table 2

Worker Participation Rates according to Current Daily Status (%)

NSS round	*Rural male*		*Rural female*		*Urban male*		*Urban female*	
	%	*%Δ*	*%*	*%Δ*	*%*	*%Δ*	*%*	*%Δ*
38th (1983)	48.2		19.8		47.3		10.6	
43rd (1987–1988)	50.1	1.9	20.7	0.9	47.7	0.4	11	0.4
50th (1993–1994)	50.4	0.3	21.9	1.2	49.6	1.9	12	1
55th (1999–2000)	47.8	−2.6	20.4	−1.5	49	−0.6	11.1	−0.9
61st (2004–2005)	48.8	1	21.6	1.2	51.9	2.9	13.3	2.2
64th (2007–2008)	49	0.2	18.7	−2.9	52.9	1	11.3	−2

Computed on the basis of Statement 5.10, NSSO Report 515, p. 91 and Statement 11, NSSO Report 531, p. 32.

Source: NSSO Report Nos. 515 and 531.

Figure 2

Worker Participation Rates according to Current Daily Status (% and %Δ)

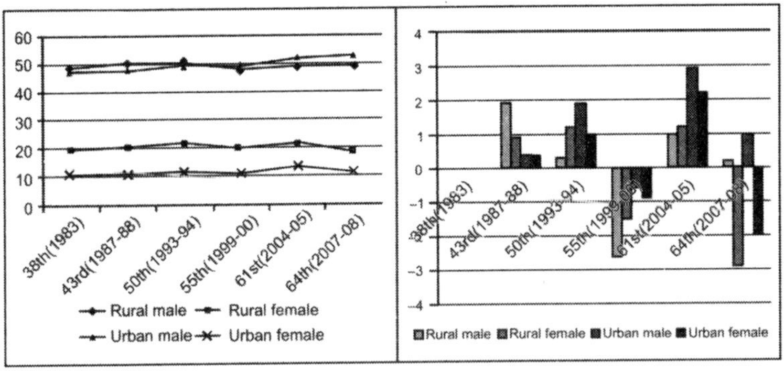

Computed on the basis of Statement 5.10, NSSO Report 515, p. 108 and Statement 11, NSSO Report 531, p. 47.

Table 3

Worker Participation Rates according to Usual Status (ps + ss) among Different Social Groups

	Rural male			*Rural female*		
NSS Round	*ST*	*SC*	*Others*	*ST*	*SC*	*Others*
38th (1983)	58.8	55.1	54	47.8	38.1	31
43rd (1987–1988)	56.7	53.8	53.5	45.4	35.8	29.4
50th (1993–1994)	59.1	55.4	54.7	48.2	35.5	29.7
55th (1999–2000)	55.8	53.1	52.7	43.8	32.5	26.6
61st (2004–2005)	56.2	54.5	54.4	46.4	33.3	30.5
64th (2007–2008)	56.8	54.3	54.6	39.7	30.7	26.6
	Urban male			*Urban female*		
NSS Round	*ST*	*SC*	*Others*	*ST*	*SC*	*Others*
38th (1983)	53.1	49	51.4	25.5	20.5	13.9
43rd (1987–1988)	50.4	49.2	50.9	22.5	21.3	14
50th (1993–1994)	52	50.5	42.3	23.4	19.9	14.5
55th (1999–2000)	48	50.3	52.3	20.4	18.5	12.8
61st (2004–2005)	52.3	53.7	55.2	24.5	20	15.7
64th (2007–2008)	51	55.8	55.5	20.4	16.7	13.1

Computed on the basis of Statement 30, NSSO Report 531, p. 78 and Statement 32, NSSO Report 531, p. 80.

Source: NSSO Report Nos. 516 and 531.

Figure 3

Change in Worker Participation Rates among Different Social Groups acccording to (ps + ss) (%Δ)

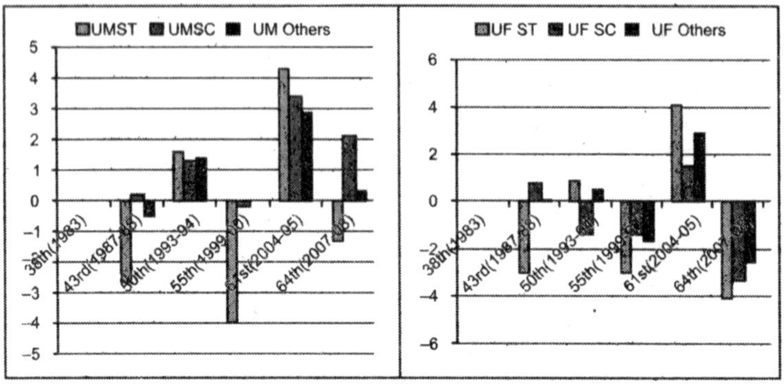

Computed on the basis of Statement 32, NSSO Report 531, p. 80.

It can be seen that after the fall in usual employment for rural and urban areas for both genders across social groups in 1999–2000, there was some increase in male and female employment for SC, ST, and others in rural and urban area in the 61st (2004–2005) round but subsequently female employment across all social groups and in rural and urban areas showed a decline in 2007–2008. SC employment declined in rural male but showed increase by 2.1 per cent for urban male. For others, usual employment increased marginally by 0.2 per cent and 0.3 per cent for rural and urban male. For urban males, employment among STs increased by 0.4 per cent and declined by 1.3 per cent for urban male.

It is important to interpret the low worker participation rates (WPR) for women. The low WPR does not mean lower contribution of women in the economy and household but the limitation of the data collection system and concentration of women in the lowest segment of the informal sector which keeps them invisible.[7]

Unemployment

A comparison between the different estimates of unemployment shows that the CDS estimate of unemployment rate being the broadest is the highest. The higher unemployment rates according to CDS approach compared to the weekly status and usual status indicates a high degree of intermittent unemployment. The unemployment rates for the urban areas in the usual status approach are higher for male and female compared to rural areas. It is highest among urban female. For rural male, it remains approximately the same or almost 2 per cent from 1983 to 2007–2008 except 2.8 per cent in 1987–1988.

Figure 4

Usually Unemployed (in %)

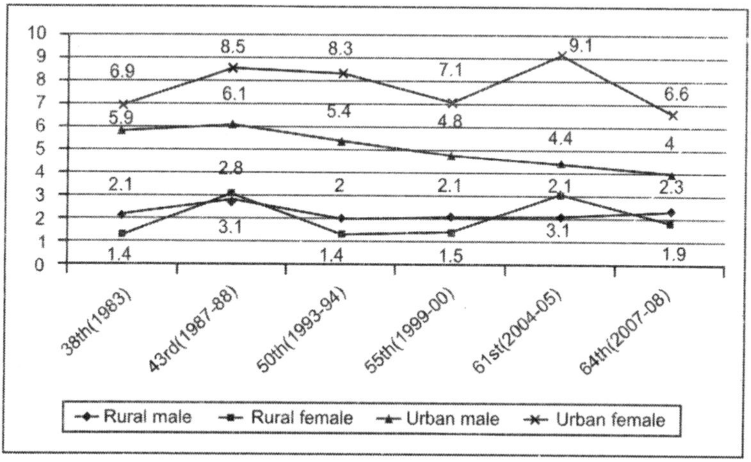

Computed on the basis of Statement 6.2, NSSO Report 515, p. 108 and Statement 22 and 23, NSSO Report 531, p. 67 and 69.

Urban male unemployment increased from 5.9 per cent in 1983 to 6.1 per cent in 1987–1988 afterwards it started declining and reached to 4 per cent in 2007–2008.There are lots of variations among urban female unemployment, according to usual status female unemployment rates in urban area were 6.9 per cent and increased to 8.5 per cent in 1987–1988; thereafter, it started declining and reached 7.1 per cent in 1999–2000 and during 1999–2000 to 2004–2005, it rose by 2 per cent and later declined to 6.6 per cent, i.e., a 2.5 per cent decline. In rural areas, the female unemployment rate stood at 1.4 per cent in

1983 and increased to 3.1 per cent in 1987–1988. Then there was a decline in unemployment rates which increased to 3.1 per cent in 2004–2005 which again declined to 1.9 per cent in 2007–2008. These data show that usual unemployment is high in urban and rural areas.

Figure 5

Unemployment according to Current Daily Status

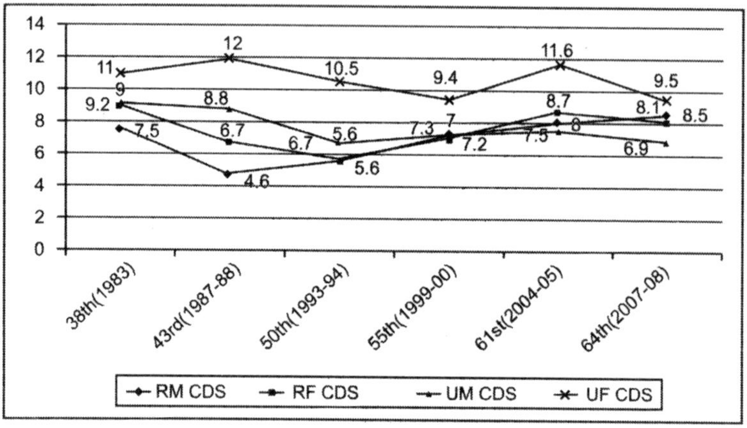

Computed on the basis of Statement 6.2, NSSO Report 515, p. 171 and Statement 23, NSSO Report 531, p. 70.

For 2007–2008, rural areas show female unemployment rate at 8.1 per cent in CDS compared to 8.5 per cent for males. Whereas in the urban areas, female unemployment rates in the CDS was 9.5 per cent which was 2.5 per cent higher compared to male unemployment rate. According to CWS unemployment estimates, rural male unemployment ranged between 3 per cent and 4.2 per cent in various rounds from 1983 to 2007–2008. Unemployment rates for rural male were highest at 4.2 per cent in 1987–1988 and it also showed the highest unemployment rates at 4.4 per cent for rural females as per the CWS during 1999–2000 to 2004–2005. CWS unemployment for rural female increased from 3.7 per cent to 4.2 per cent in 2004–2005 but which further declined to 3.5 per cent in 2007–2008.

For urban areas, female unemployment rate was higher than male unemployment rates for 64th rounds, for urban male it declined from 5.2 per cent to 4.7 per cent on CWS bases.

According to CWS unemployment rates for urban female, further decline from 9 per cent in 2004–2005 to 6.5 per cent in 64th rounds. On CDS bases, unemployment rates have declined from 61st to 64th rounds. Over the years, unemployment rate has kept on fluctuating and ranged from 6.7 per cent to 12 per cent.

The unemployment rates among STs, SCs, and others are compared. Others also include OBC from 1983 (38th round) to 2007–2008 (64th round). Among rural males, usual unemployment for STs, SCs, and others has increased between the years 2004–2005 to 2007–2008. Unemployment rates declined among rural female by 0.6 per cent for SC and 0.8 per cent for ST between the years 2004–2005 and 2007–2008. For rural female among the STs, it increased marginally by 0.1 per cent. But, over the years, the percentage of unemployed has increased or more or less remained the same from 1983 to 2007–2008.

Table 4

Unemployment Rates according to Usual Status (ps + ss) for Social Groups (%)

	Rural male			*Rural female*		
NSS Round	*ST*	*SC*	*Others*	*ST*	*SC*	*Others*
38th (1983)	0.5	1.2	1.6	0.1	0.5	0.8
43rd (1987–1988)	0.7	1.6	2.1	1.4	3.1	2.2
50th (1993–1994)	0.8	1.2	1.6	0.3	0.4	1
55th (1999–2000)	1.1	1.8	2.3	0.5	0.6	2.2
61st (2004–2005)	1.1	1.7	2	0.4	1.4	2.9
64th (2007–2008)	1.4	2	2.3	0.5	0.8	2.1
	Urban male			*Urban female*		
NSS Round	*ST*	*SC*	*Others*	*ST*	*SC*	*Others*
38th (1983)	4.3	5.1	5.1	1.5	2.9	5.5
43rd (1987–1988)	4.3	5.6	5.1	2	3.6	6.7
50th (1993–1994)	4.7	4.6	3.9	1.7	4.4	6.9
55th (1999–2000)	4.4	5.1	4.8	2.8	3.1	7.7
61st (2004–2005)	2.9	5.5	3.7	3.4	4.6	8.5
64th (2007–2008)	5.4	4.4	3.9	2.6	3.6	6.1

Computed on the basis of Statement 3.18, NSSO Report 516, pp. 39–40 and Statement 31, NSSO Report 531, p. 64.

Source: NSSO Report Nos. 516 and 531.

In urban areas, unemployment rates have declined for SCs by 1.1 per cent and 1 per cent for both male and female, respectively, during 2004–2005 and 2007–2008. For STs, the unemployment rates have increased by 2.5 per cent for males and reduced by 0.8 per cent for females. For others (including OBCs), the unemployment has increased by 0.2 per cent for urban males and declined by 2.4 per cent for urban females. Female unemployment has increased in urban areas for all social groups, i.e., SCs, STs, and others.

The data on categories of employment show that self-employment status was dominant for both males and females in both rural and urban areas. In rural India, more than half of the usually employed were self-employed, i.e., 55 per cent among males and 58 per cent females were self-employed in 2007–2008. In urban areas, the corresponding figures were 43 per cent and 42 per cent for males and females, respectively. In urban areas, the share of regular workers has increased for women. Kundu (1997: 450) cautioned that this should not be interpreted as a growing capacity of the urban economy which is to absorb women and show a reduction in gender biases; because in several urban sectors, regular female workers are paid less than the casual male workers. He calls this process 'organized informalization' of the labour market. According to him, 'the system of having on the one hand, contract labour and subcontracting of jobs in the formal sector, and a growth of employment (often on a regular basis) in low-productivity tertiary activities on the other, are the other manifestations of this process'.

Regular wage/salaried employees were relatively lower among females compared to males. In rural area, 9 per cent males and 4 per cent females were regular wage/salaried. Whereas in urban areas, these figures were 42 per cent and 38 per cent, respectively. Thirty-six per cent of males and 38 per cent of females were casually employed in rural areas. The corresponding figures were 25 per cent of male workers and 20 per cent of female workers in urban areas. The share of casual workers was higher among rural labour compared to urban labour force.

Figure 6

Rural WPR for Various Employment Categories, according to (ps + ss)

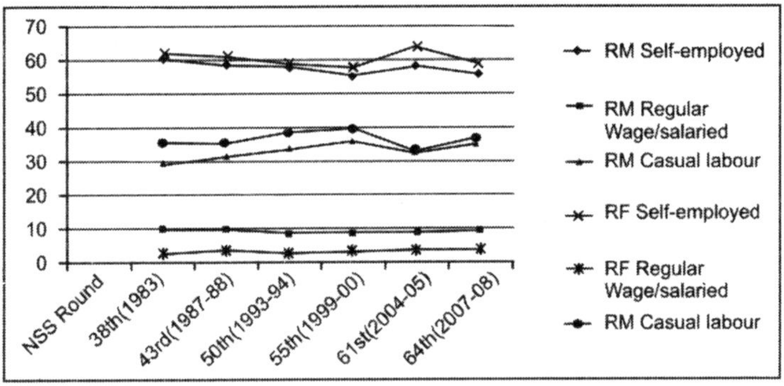

Computed on the basis of Statement 3.18, NSSO Report 516, p. 45.

Figure 7

Urban WPR for Various Employment Categories (%) according to (ps + ss)

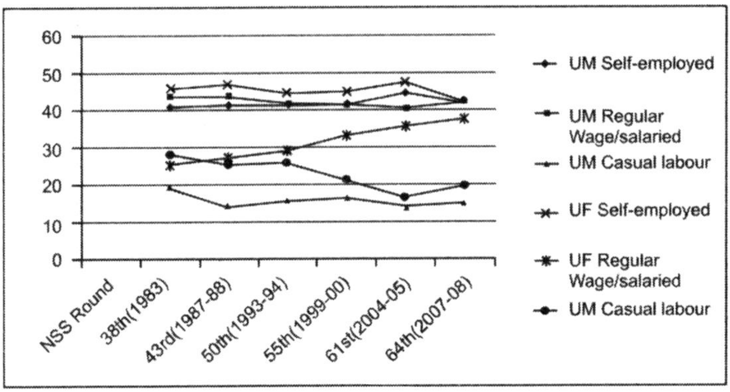

Computed on the basis of Statement 14, NSSO Report 531, p. 54.

Self-employment has declined for urban males and females by 2.1 per cent and 5.4 per cent, respectively. In rural areas, it declined by 2.7 per cent for males and increased by 0.4 per cent for females during 2004–2005 to 2007–2008. Proportion of regular wage/salaried employees has increased in rural and urban areas. For rural India, it increased by 2.6 per cent and 0.4 per cent for males and females, respectively. Corresponding figures are 1.4 per cent and 2.3 per cent in urban area during 2004–2005 to 2007–2008.

In recent article, Kundu and Sarangi (2007) examined the nature of 'formalization' of informal activities in terms of increase in the regular workers and self-employed compared to casual workers and conclude that 'even the regular workers have not benefited from the process linked to globalisation'. According to them, 'urban poverty can partly be attributed to lack of growth and partly to growth itself which is responsible for the emergence of new kinds of labour relations and accentuation of inequality'.

In spite of the abysmal situation on the employment front, there is no specific employment policy in India. There is no dearth of information and analysis on this front as there are several in-depth reports of the working group and commissions appointed by the government itself. Some of the important reports are the 'Shram Shakti' (1998), Report of the National Commission on Labour (2002), Various Reports of the National Commission for Enterprises in the Unorganized Sector.[8] In their final report published in 2009, The National Commission for Enterprises in the Unorganized Sector concluded that 'Though the population suffering from extreme poverty and living below the so called official poverty line (approximately ₹ 12 per day per capita consumption in 2004–2005) came down significantly from 1993–1994 onwards, they seem to have moved only marginally above the poverty line and about 77 per cent of them were stuck below the expenditure on average of ₹ 20 per day per capita. We described these people as 'poor and vulnerable', as against the remaining 23 per cent of middle class and higher income groups who seemed to have captured most of the benefits of the high income growth' (NCEUS, 2009).

Their analysis of the characteristics of this poor and vulnerable group shows that they contain about 88 per cent of SCs/STs, 80 per cent of OBCs, and 85 per cent of the Muslim population of this country. Most of the population of this group were also either illiterate or without even primary education, and also suffer from malnutrition. These groups emerge as a sort of a coalition of socially discriminated, educationally deprived, and economically destitute, whereas less than one-fourth of the population enjoyed a high rate of growth or had the purchasing power. It is important to note that these vulnerable poor are not unemployed but the 'working poor' of the economy.

The question is whether the draft for NEP under consideration since 2008 reflects the rich information, analysis, and suggestions generated during the above-mentioned exercises?

The NEP Draft

A draft NEP is under consideration since 2008. We have analysed the version provided on the web site of the Ministry of Labour and Employment. The objective of the NEP as mentioned in the draft is to provide a framework towards the goal of achieving remunerative and decent employment for all women and men in the labour force. More specifically it aims at:

1. Accelerating employment growth in the organized sector and
2. Improving the quality of jobs (in terms of productivity, earnings, and protection of workers) in the unorganized sector.

At the same time, the draft policy admits that 'this document, however, concentrates mainly on the productive employment generation aspects, and signals a number of related issues for which separate policies need to be considered'. Who will prepare these policies and how is not clear from this draft. Though it talks about acceleration of employment in the organized sector, any specific mechanism for that is not suggested. The suggestions about macro-economic policies such as fiscal and monetary polices and trade policies are that employability of the project may be an added criteria to give additional incentives to the projects.

The draft emphasizes on the sector-focused strategies. It suggests adopting employment as a major goal of development and aiming at faster growth of sectors with high employment potential. The sectors for high employment potential such as agriculture, manufacturing, construction, retail trade, and ICT are to be given special treatment from employment viewpoint.

Some of the suggestions for policy changes include the following:

- Changes in the labour market policies with the aim at changing labour regulations and special programmes for employment and improving labour market information.
- Changes in the policies for micro and small enterprises by removing constraints they face in increasing productivity and creating decent work condition through cluster development and organization of industry and workers.
- Skill development through matching training with demand, standard and certification, linkage with education system, and other programmes are included.
- A section in the draft on women workers and their special concerns includes suggestions on gender-sensitive macro policies, identifying sectors with significant participation of women and development of facilitating structures, organization, and empowerment.
- A section on the vulnerable workers, defined as the segment of workers at a distinct disadvantage arising out of their helplessness in terms of local distress, distress-induced migration, working children, workers with physical challenges, or those in bonded-like conditions.

As per the implementation and monitoring, two major tools suggested in the policy are as follows:

- Employment Audit (EA)
- Employment Impact Assessment (EIA)

It is suggested that 'a suitably empowered institutional mechanism needs to be constituted to oversee employment outcomes of macro economics and sectoral polices' and data systems and monitoring mechanisms should have annual rounds of the household NSSO employment and unemployment to improve coverage of employment data by Annual Survey of Industries (ASI) and Directorate General of Employment and Training (DGET).

Conclusion

The overall picture that has emerged from the NSSO rounds (between the 1983 and the latest 2007–2008 estimates) of employment and unemployment is that the rate of employment generation during the years of high growth rate is very poor. The historical trend in the planning policy which views growth as a major objective and employment as incidental to it is not changed even after acceptance of the fact that growth has not generated employment in all these years.

The idea that the declining trend in employment is reversed on the basis of the 61st round is not sustained in the 64th round. Whatever jobs are created in the formal or informal sectors for the masses do not have quality to provide secure livelihood and self-fulfilment or human dignity for most women and men as reflected in the draft of NEP or 'decent working conditions' which can lead to inclusive growth as describe in 11th Five-Year Plan.

The draft of NEP recognizes the severity of the problem but is not treating the root cause of the problem. It talks about generating employment through the following:

1. Accelerating employment growth in the organized sector.
2. Improving the quality of jobs in the unorganized sector.

But it fails to understand the relationship between the two.

'The current policies are based on the view that it would be unwise to interfere with growth process to make it more employment intensive as this might disrupt the growth process and slow down the pace of growth'. Thus, attention is focused on government interventions outside the growth process for attaining employment objective (Ghosh, 2010).

The trend of growth process remains the same, which means that the organized sector would continue to expand at a faster pace and continue to have relatively jobless growth. But the growth in the markets for organized sector may be at the cost of unorganized sector. The policies based on the idea that the concern for employment can be separated from the concern for economic growth will promote further widening of the huge gap that already exists between small minority of formal employees and a vast majority of informal workers.

The special employment programmes such as MGNREGA is needed in the short run and also needs to be expanded as mentioned in the policy and reports of other commissions as it may alleviate poverty for a while, but it cannot replace productivity-enhancing investments in the unorganized sector for its sustainable impact on employment and incomes. What is required is to increase employment intensity of economic growth (Ghosh, 2010).

The unabated growth of the organized sector in fact is not just jobless but may turn out to be a 'job-killing growth' in the long run. If we have realistic EIA of the large projects in the organized sector as suggested in the NEP, it may turn out to be a job-killing growth in reality. The huge amount of natural resources including land, surface water, and ground water used in such projects is more than the resources required for an entire village. Most of them are used as free goods or taken from the local people at throwaway prices. The owner of the land which has been taken by industries or governments for such projects may get the 'market price' for the land, but what about agricultural labourers and unpaid household labour working on the land? What about the loss of livelihood for the forthcoming generations from the land? If we consider the livelihood loss of the farmer, agriculture labourer, fisher folk, and many who may not have the ownership of resources but their livelihood depends on it, then many projects may turn out to be 'job killing', i.e., 'livelihood destructing growth' rather than just contributing to jobless growth. Further research and EIA is required to elaborate this point.

Notes

1. 11th Five-Year Plan in the chapter on *Employment Perspective and Labour Policy* (p. 63).
2. See Mitra (1979, pp. 52–53) and Acharya (1992, pp. 23–39).
3. See Banerjee and Ghosh (1988, p. 105).
4. See Bennett (1988).
5. Some of them were Ghosh, (1994), Kumar (1993), Dietrich (1993), Shah et al (1994), George. (1993).
6. This was a smaller round compared to the quinquennial rounds but larger than the yearly rounds and according to the experts, the results can be good to look at the trend at national level though state-wise comparison may not give good estimates.

7. Several studies including one of the authors, Shah Trupti's thesis on informal sector, point to the fact that underestimate of women is about 40 per cent to 70 per cent in the employment data. Please see Hirway (2002).
8. Several reports were prepared by the National Commission for Enterprises in the Unorganised Sector, Government of India, New Delhi. Between 2006 and 2009, the final report was 'The challenge of employment in India: An informal economy perspective', National Commission for Enterprises in the Unorganised Sector, April 2009.

References

Acharya, S. (1992). *Women and Work-changing Scenario in India*, editors Sharma, A.N., and Singh, S. Patna: Indian Society for Labour Economics.

Banerjee, D., and Ghosh, A. (1988). *Economy, Society and Polity – Essays in the Political Economy of Indian Planning*, editor Bagchi, A. Kolkata: Oxford.

Banerjee, N. (1998). 'Whatever happened to the dreams of modernity? – The Nehruvian era', Paper presented at the IAWS Seminar, Baroda.

Banerjee, N. (1997). 'How real is the bogey of feminisation?', *Indian Journal of Labour Economics* Vol. 40(3), 427–438.

Bennett, L. (1988). *Women, Poverty and Productivity in India*. Washington, DC: Economic Development Institute of World Bank.

Deshpande, S. (1993). 'Feminisation through flexible labour in India: Evidence and future prospects', in *The New Economic Policy and Women*. Kolkata: Indian Association of Women's Studies, pp. 72–87.

Deshpande, S. (1994). 'Adjustment policies and women's access to employment in urban India: Past experience and likely future challenges', *Women and Globalisation*, editors Rajput, P., and Swarup, H.L. New Delhi: Ashish Publishing House, pp. 235–256.

Dietrich, G. (1993). *Women and the New Economic Policy*. New Delhi: Fredrich Ebert Stifing (FES), pp. 9–13.

Dreze, J. (1997). 'Introduction', *Indian Journal of Labour Economics* 40(3), pp. 421–426.

Editorial (2010). *Economic and Political Weekly* XLV(39), September 25, 2010.

George, J. (1993). *Gender, Structural Adjustment Programme and the Household*. New Delhi: FES, pp. 47–53.

Ghosh, J. (1994). 'Gender concern in macro economic policy', *Economic and Political Weekly*, April 30.

Ghosh, A.K. (2010). 'India's employment challenge', *The Indian Journal of Labour Economics* 53(4), pp. 571–586.

Hirway, I. (2002). 'Employment and unemployment situation in 1990s: How good are NSS data?', *Economic and Political Weekly*, May 25.

Jabvala R. (1994). 'Women workers under structural adjustment: Some issues and strategies for India', *Women and Globalisation*, editors Rajput, P., and Swarup, H.L. New Delhi: Ashish Publishing House, pp. 167–186.

Jain, D., et al. (1993). 'Can we convert the crisis into an opportunity?', *The New Economic Policy and Women*. Kolkata: Indian Association of Women's Studies, pp. 11–35.

Kamath, A. (1992). 'Exit policy-need for bold initiatives', *The Economic Times*, January 6.

Kumar, A. (1993). *Impact of the NEP on the Household Sector in Women and the New Economic Policy*. New Delhi: Fredrich Ebert Stifing (FES), pp. 1–7.

Kundu, A. (1997). 'Trends and pattern of female employment in India: A case of Organised informalisation', *The Indian Journal of Labour Economics* 40(3), pp. 439–452.

Kundu, A., and Sarangi, N. (2007). 'Dynamics of labour market under globalisation: Changing characteristics of informal employment in India', *The Indian Journal of Labour Economics* 50(2), pp. 201–206.

Mitra, A. (1979). *Changes in Economic activities of Male and Female in India 1911–61*. New Delhi: ICSSR.

Papola, T.S., and Pais, J. (2007). 'Debate on labour market reforms in India: A case of misplaced focus', *The India Journal of Labour Economics* 50(2).

Ranadive, J. (1994). 'Gender implications of adjustment policy programme in India – Significance of the household', *Economic and Political Weekly*, April 30.

Rangrajan, C., Iyer Padma, K., and Seema. (2007). 'Revisiting employment and growth', *ICRA bulletin 'Money & Finance'*, September.

Shah, N., Gothoskar, S., Gandhi, N., and Chhachhi, A. (1994). 'Structural adjustment, feminisation of labour force and organisational strategies', *Economic and Political Weekly*, April 30.

Singh, G., Sharma, S.P., and Bhardwaj, P. (1994). 'Structural adjustment and marginalisation of female workers in India', *Women and Globalisation*, editors Rajput, P., and Swarup, H.L. New Delhi: Ashish Publishing House, pp. 257–270.

Sundaram, K. (2001a). 'Employment-unemployment situation in the nineties–some results', NSS 55th round survey', *Economic and Political Weekly*, March 17.

Sundaram, K. (2001b). 'Employment and poverty in 1990s – Further results', NSS 55th round, *Economic and Political Weekly*.

Tendulkar, S. (1991). 'Economic reform: Hostage of interest groups', *The Economic Times*, September 16.

Varghese, N.V. (1993). *Women and Work: An Examination of the Female Marginalisation Thesis in the Indian Context*, editors Sharma, A., and Singh, S. Patna: Indian Society for Labour Economics.

Visaria, P., and Minhas, B.S. (1991). *Evolving an Employment Policy for the 1990s: What do the data tell us?* Ahmedabad: The Gujarat Institute of Area Planning.

Government Reports

Economic Survey 2010–11.

Employment and Unemployment Situation in India. NSS Report No. 531, July 2007–June 2008.

Employment and Unemployment Situation in India, 2004–05. NSS Report No. 515, September 2006.

Employment and Unemployment Situation among Social Groups in India 2004–05. NSS Report No. 516, October 2006.

Government of India (1974) *Towards Equality: Report of the Committee on the Status of Women in India*.

Government of India (1988). 'Shramshakti', Report of the Committee on Self-employed Women and Women in Informal Sector, New Delhi.

Ministry of Labour and Employment (2002). *Report of the National Commission on Labour*. New Delhi: Government of India.

National Commission for Enterprises in the Unorganised Sector (2009). *The Challenge of Employment in India: An Informal Economy Perspective*. Government of India, Academic Foundation, New Delhi.

National Employment Policy (NEP). First Draft, 1 August 2008 as on the website of the Labour Ministry.

The Planning Commission, Government of India, 11th Five-year Plan.

5

Employment Scenario in Post-Reform India

Social Security Dimensions

Manjira Dasgupta and Paramita Saha

Employment and Social Security Issues

Security considerations and employment benefits form an important aspect of conditions for employment. In the absence of secured employment, for a majority of the population in developing countries such as India, social security (SS) issues assume even greater significance. In its various connotations, the term 'social security' (alternatively, social assistance, safety nets, or social protection) is generally taken to mean a system of 'collective care' to meet conditions of adversity. This notion of SS developed primarily in the context of advanced economies with high degree of industrialization and a majority of employment in formal wage labour. SS, then, means providing the workers assured employment with income protection safeguards against potential contingencies.

This conventional meaning needs modification when we consider a developing country, where most of the population is engaged in informal labour outside the purview of formal labour market. Even in formal sectors, workers may be informally employed without any social protection. A four-fold classification of the workforce may be possible with workers in both organized and unorganized sectors being either formally or informally employed (Table 1). There is also evidence that globalization has resulted in increasing informalization of the labour market in India (Table 2). Moreover, a significant section falling under the nomenclature of 'informal workers' is self-employed so that the concept of 'worker protection' remains inapplicable. In addition, the conventional definition of work in terms of labour force participation, adopted by the ILO, is restrictive and excludes the majority of care and labour reproductive activities, usually performed by women (Saith, 2008).

Table 1

Proportion of Informal Workers in India (2007)

Sector/workers	*Informal/unorganized worker*	*Formal/organized worker*
Informal/unorganized sector	99.6	1.4
Formal/organized sector	46.6	53.4
Total	92.4	7.6

Source: NCEUS (2007: 4).

In such a context, the significance of SS has to reach beyond the provision of safeguards against contingencies, as ensuring the minimum conditions of survival with dignity at the basic level becomes the overriding security need.

From the perspective of a developing country, a wider view of SS is warranted (Dreze, 1991; Sen, 2002), distinguishing its protective and promotional aspects. While the former is concerned with ensuring basic minimum living standards, the latter emphasizes capability enhancement.

Others with similar concerns have distinguished between basic social security (BSS) and contingent social security (CSS) (Kannan, 2004). Thus, 'social security (SS) may be viewed in a developing country context in terms of a basic social security (BSS) to meet deficiency and a contingent social security (CSS) to meet adversity' (Kannan and Pillai, 2007: 6).

Defined thus, BSS denotes the fulfilment of the minimum developmental needs for human existence, comprising the fundamental dimensions of food, housing, health, and education security, with the indispensable aspect of income and employment security underlying all of this. Contingent social security (CSS), viz., protection against contingencies designed on the basis of work status can benefit only a small proportion of workers engaged formally. For the rest, basic security needs with its protective and promotional role bring forth the centrality of employment assurance.

The World Commission on the Social Dimension of Globalization in 2004 mooted the idea of BSS floor which contains a base of social and economic rights that are outside the realm of SS and are formulated as a set of guarantees rather than as defined benefits. Even within BSS floor, income security to the vulnerable category of working-age persons who are either unable to find employment or underemployed remains crucial in addition to universal access to health, education, and nutrition for children, and income security for the elderly and disabled.

Protection and promotion of human and physical capital remain the overriding development concerns in developing countries such as India. Policies that protect human capital include better access to clinics and hospitals, better nutrition, better health support, health insurance policies, improved access to schools, universal primary education, and so forth. Policies aimed at employment creation, labour-intensive investments, and promotion of rural development are identified as crucial in protection of physical capital. It is imperative that the focus of SS policies in developing countries is integrated with overall development strategy.

This paper, organized in four sections, seeks to present an overview of the present SS structure and initiatives in India and argues that the SS coverage remains very thin despite the existence of several schemes. While the first section notes the conceptual development of SS in developing country context, the next section deals with the contingent aspect of SS in India. The third section takes up initiatives towards BSS, focusing on its employment aspects. The last section presents the overall concluding remarks and discusses further research.

CSS in India

Two crucial issues relating to CSS in the Indian context are that of unorganized sector security on one hand and the pension reforms in the face of an ageing population on the other hand.

Figure 1 clearly brings out the stark contrast between organized employments vis-à-vis the vast proportion engaged in unorganized labour.

Figure 1

Extent of Informal Sector in India (2008–09)[1]

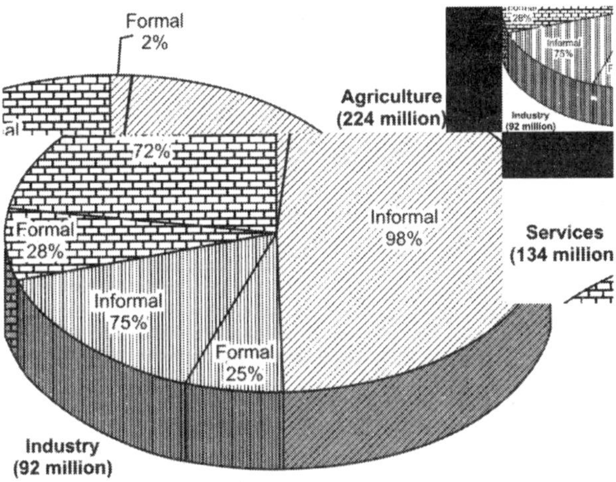

Source: "Modified Current Weekly Status employmentes" in *The Challenge of Employment in India Report*, National Commission for Enterprises in the Unorganized Sector, April 2009.

As Table 2 depicts post-reform, unorganized sector employment has continued to grow much more rapidly, while employment in the organized sector has lagged behind in absolute terms and shrunk the ratio of total workforce. All this clearly emphasizes the need for particular attention to the designing of security measures for the vast unorganized sector.

The 2009 NCEUS report on the findings of the National Commission for Enterprises in the Unorganized Sector (NCEUS) summarizes as follows:

'... The entire increase in the employment in the organized sector (over the post-reforms period) has been informal in nature, i.e., without any job or social security. (...) this can be termed as *informalization of the formal sector* (emphasis added), i.e., employment increase consists of regular workers without social security benefits and casual or contract workers again without the benefits that should accrue to formal workers'. (NCEUS, 2009: 7)

Table 2

Workers in Organized and Unorganized Sectors, 1987–88 to 2004–05

Year	*Number (million persons)*			*% of total workforce*		
	Organized	*Unorganized*	*Total*	*Organized*	*Unorganized*	*Total*
1987–1988	25.4	301.8	327.2	7.8	92.2	100
1994–1995	27	348.8	375.8	7.2	92.8	100
1999–2000	27.8	371.2	399	7	93	100
2004–2005	29.1	410	439.1	6.6	93.4	100

Source: Rajan (2010).

In India, for an overwhelming majority of the population, the means of old-age sustenance comes from informal systems such as earnings and transfer from their children or other family members; sources that are increasingly becoming unreliable with the changing social and demographic realities. This coupled with gradual informalization of the formal sector implies that there is little scope of resource transfer for supporting increasing number of elderly population (Table 3). It therefore becomes 'essential that policymakers correctly anticipate the course of the transition so that adequate counter measures are in place at the appropriate time. (...) without guidance, encouragement and support, most Indian workers will not save sufficiently for their old age and the capacity of the State and the labour market to face the challenges is likely to become even more limited' (Swarup, 2008: 12).

As Swarup (2008) pointed out that the potential deterrents posed by poverty and unemployment in providing tax financed state pension for every citizen attaining old age may have conceivably resulted in the adoption of a pension policy based on financing through employer and employee participation for the organized sector (except for government servants). This has, however, left the vast majority of the workforce in the unorganized sector without access to formal channels of old-age economic support.

Table 3
Population Ageing in India (1950–2050)

Year	*Population (60+) (in million)*	*Percentages of total population*	*Growth rate (%)*	
			Total population	*60+ population*
1950	19	5.6	2	2
1975	38	6.2	2.1	2.9
2000	77	7.6	1.5	2.7
2025*	169	12.5	0.8	3.2
2050	324	20.6	0.4	2.2

Note: United Nations (2002). World Population Ageing (1950–2050); *medium variant.

Source: Panigrahi (2009).

CSS for the Organized Sector: A Brief Overview

Formal SS provisions available for organized sector workers relate to public and private sector employees. Provisions for the former are in most cases not legislatory but constitute a part of service conditions without involving employee contributions. Public/Government sector employees enjoy SS provisions that generally include entitlement to highly subsidized medical care, pay-protected leave in sickness, insurance in case of death in harness, pension and gratuity on retirement, and life pensions for survivors.

SS coverage applying to employees in the organized private sector, on the other hand, is essentially legislatory in nature with their diverse limitations. The CSS measures available in India are mostly central laws applicable to all states with provision for state-level extensions wherein two categories can be distinguished, which as follows:

(a) *Those that are run administratively and routinely enforced:* These cover the Employees' State Insurance Act, 1948, and the Employees' Provident Funds and Miscellaneous Provisions Act, 1952, both financed through joint contributions of employers and employees. The Acts on Welfare Funds for unorganized workers may also be placed in this category, although their statutory cover is much weaker.

(b) *Self-enforcing where the aggrieved can seek redress through courts or other competent authorities:* This includes the Workmen's Compensation Act, 1923, the Maternity Benefit Act, 1961, and the Payment of Gratuity Act, 1972 – all three putting the employers in a position of liability in case of non-compliance. These also constitute the array of non-contributory CSS schemes available for the organized sector.

The various acts currently covering organized sector employees and the contingencies to which they apply are listed in Table 4.

The Employees' State Insurance (ESI) Act, 1948 and the Employees' Provident Fund (and Miscellaneous Provisions) (EPF & MP) Act, 1952 constitute the contributory schemes under organized sector CSS.

The Employees State Insurance (ESI) scheme provides a composite insurance cover comprising health care and cash benefits in sickness, maternity, and disability or death. Its coverage, as at the end of fiscal year 2003, was almost 7.86 million employees and close to 31 million beneficiaries. Administered by the Employees' State Insurance Corporation, the scheme is financed through the Employees' State Insurance Fund raised through contribution by employers and employees and grants/donations from Central and State Governments, local authorities, and any other body.

Although widely acclaimed from the design aspect in its comprehensiveness and wide reach, the limitations of the ESI lie at the implementation level and in the often questionable quality of medical care provided.

Table 4
List of Acts for CSS Cover

Contingency	*Acts covering the contingency*
Death	(i) Workmen's Compensation Act, 1923
	(ii) Employees' State Insurance Act, 1948
	(iii) Employees' Family Pension Scheme, 1971/Employees' Pension Scheme, 1995
Disablement	(i) Workmen's Compensation Act, 1923
	(ii) Employees' State Insurance Act, 1948
	(iii) Employees' Pension Scheme, 1995
Funeral	(i) Employees' State Insurance Act, 1948
Lay-off, retrenchment, and closure	(i) Industrial Disputes Act, 1947
Maternity	(i) Employees' State Insurance Act, 1948
	(ii) State Maternity Benefit Acts
	(iii) Central Maternity Benefit Act, 1961
Old age	(i) Coal Mines Provident Fund and Bonus Scheme Act, 1948
	(ii) Employees' provident Funds and Miscellaneous Provisions Act, 1952
	(iii) Assam Tea Plantations Provident Fund Scheme Act, 1955
	(iv) Seamen's Provident Fund Act, 1966
	(v) Payment of Gratuity Act, 1972
Sickness	(i) Employees' State Insurance Act, 1948

Source: Kannan and Pillai (2007).

The EPF & MP Act provides for setting up compulsory provident funds for employees in factories and other establishments engaged in 180 industries/classes of establishments employing 20 or more workers. The coverage as of March 2004 was 3.70 lakh establishments with above 40 million subscribers.

For the organized sector employees, excluding government employees, the basic structure of pension and other retirement benefits has been outlined in the EPF & MP Act. This Act is administered by the Employees Provident Fund Organization (EPFO). Under this Act, the further three schemes in force are as follows, the first two being essentially old-age income schemes:

(a) *The Employees' Provident Fund Scheme, 1952:* An individual account defined contribution (DC) scheme wherein both the employee and employer contribute to the fund at the rate of 12 per cent of the employee's pay. The EPFO scheme enjoys an 'EEE' tax structure.

(b) *Employees' Pension Scheme, 1995:* Marking a major change in 1995, whereby part of the DC EPF scheme was converted to a defined benefit (DB) scheme in the form of Employees' Pension Scheme. Applicable to the workers who entered into employment after 1995, the EPS is based on a contribution rate of 8.33 per cent from the employee which is augmented by an additional contribution of 1.16 per cent by the government. The scheme provides for a lifetime pension to the spouse in the event of death of a member. Frequent use of the pre-mature withdrawal provision available in this scheme by members often leads to reduced old-age income benefit at retirement.

(c) *Employees' Deposit Linked Insurance Scheme, 1976:* Other voluntary pension schemes available for general public are essentially DC schemes offered by Life Insurance Companies (supervised by IRDA) and mutual funds (regulated by SEBI), but these schemes cover a very small segment of the total population. Total coverage under these pension plans is about 1.6 million.

The other popular scheme, Public Provident Fund (PPF), is also a DC scheme managed by the government. Coverage under the PPF is about 3.5 million.

Pensions and Recent Initiatives: A Brief Discussion[2]

Vis-à-vis the internationally familiar 'three-pillar system' of old-age pensions, the Indian scenario presents a very much restricted version (Figure 2).

Pillar I, i.e., standardized state-financed pension with its basic thrust on poverty removal has very limited coverage in India, consists of (i) the NSAP for the aged destitute, and (ii) pension for government employees through the PAYG scheme or the DB scheme.

Pillar II, that is, mandatory occupational pension system with employee and employer contributing towards the pension, covers workers in the organized sector through a DC-cum-DB scheme.

Pillar III is a voluntary, private-funded system, including individual saving plans, insurance, etc. India presents a very much restrictive form through PPF, superannuation schemes, and personal pension plans through annuity providers as indicated in the preceding section.

The main source of financing of pensions in India has traditionally been through employer and employee participation, resulting in the coverage being restricted to the organized sector, leaving the vast majority of the workforce in the unorganized sector without access to formal channels of old-age financial support. Only about 12 per cent of the working population in India is covered by some form of retirement benefit scheme, making limited coverage one glaring problem of the old-age income security system (Swarup, 2008).

Even with this limited coverage, sustainability of the existing system has been repeatedly brought into question. Total pension liability on account of the Central Government employees increased at more than 21 per cent CAGR during the 1990s, while the comparable rate for the State Government was 27 per cent per annum (Swarup, 2008). Fragmented regulatory framework, lack of individual choice and portability, and lack of uniform standards, coupled with high incidence of administrative cost and low real rate of returns, have all resulted in making the present system unsustainable.

The Civil Servants' Pension (CSP), a DB scheme based on the PAYG (pay-as-you-go) system for employees of Central Government recruited up to 31st December 2003 and employees of State Governments recruited up to notified dates, is an unfunded scheme. There has been no attempt at building up pension assets through contribution or any other provision. The scheme is indexed to wages and inflation. Its main problem is one of fiscal stress that has increased with improving life expectancy. The fiscal stress at the sub-national level has been more acute with instances of State Governments failing to make timely payment of pension benefits.

Figure 2
The Pension Structure in India

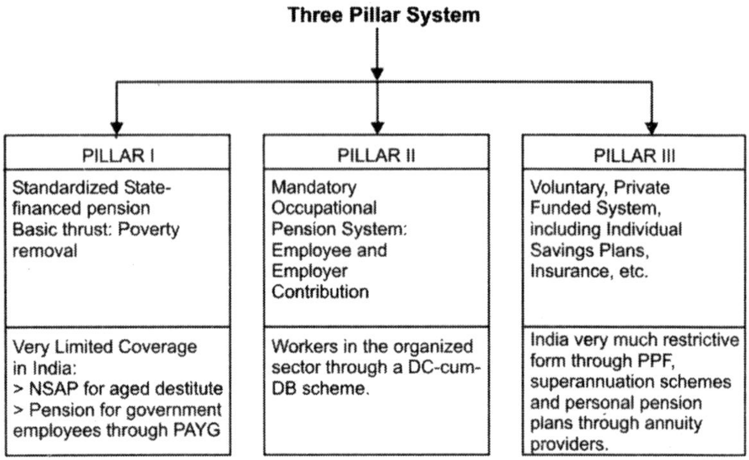

Source: Based on Swarup (2008).

Evidently, the existing system of pensions which leaves more than 88 per cent of the Indian workforce uncovered is unlikely to act as a SS umbrella for the ageing Indians. Even for those that the system covers, the DB is strictly not guaranteed. Increase in life expectancy, evolution of nuclear family systems and rising expectations due to increase in per capita income, education, etc., are some of the factors that led to the long-overdue introduction of the *New Pension System (NPS/'National Pension System'* (as it is currently termed), based on DC and funded liability. Spread of NPS is seen by many as the direction in which the pension reforms need to move to find a viable and sustainable solution to the problem of old-age income security.

A 2001 projection by a GoI-appointed group of experts estimated the projected growth of the pension market (which includes pensions, provident funds, and other small savings, i.e., NSC, NSS) at about ₹ 4,064 billion by 2025. This relates to the normal growth of economy in terms of growth in income and population and does not consider the significant increase in coverage that would arise because of reforms in the insurance and pension sectors. A more conservative estimate is that the pension market will be worth about ₹ 1,808 billion by 2025 (Swarup, 2008)

The Pension Fund Regulatory and Development Authority (PFRDA) was set up in October 2003 and the NPS, introduced in December 2003, has been later extended to all citizens of India from July 2008. To enhance the popularity of the NPS, investments made to the NPS have been extended tax deduction under Section 80C. However, incentives notwithstanding the number of subscribers opting for NPS till February 7, 2011 was less than ₹ 40,000.

The key features of the NPS may be summarized as follows:

- Shift from the DB to a DC regime.
- Facilitating portability of labour force.
- Offering voluntary participation to unorganized workers.

The measures and recent steps envisaged in the NPS for unorganized workers' SS are indicated in the following section.

Finally, efforts to introduce the PFRDA Bill in Parliament in March 2005, and again in 2009, have failed to succeed so far. The polity is deeply divided on the crucial issues.

CSS for the Unorganized Sector[3]

As of Census 2001, the proportion of employees in the government sector directly coming under the CSS umbrella, along with those in the private sectors covered by the comprehensive EPF scheme, together represented only 15 per cent of the working population (Kannan and Pillai, 2007). This means that about 85 per cent of Indian workers went without any significant income protection. The fact that this latter uncovered section includes about 42 per cent of workers in the organized private sector itself with the remaining spilling over into the unorganized sector, coupled with the earlier amply demonstrated evidence of the increasing informalization trend clearly brings out the enormity of the situation.

While Indian planners have consistently stressed the importance of SS for the unorganized sector workers, the first major move towards addressing this need was the initiation of a *National Social Assistance Programme (NSAP)* in 1995. Originally intended for the rural poor, the scheme was extended later to casual and self-employed workers in rural and urban areas.

The following basic principles/models are at the base of CSS initiatives at the unorganized level:

- *Growth Poles* – a strategy of building rural infrastructure that generates significant 'spread effects' – proposed for the Indian case by the NCEUS, under the chairmanship of Dr Arjun Sengupta.

The NCEUS also recommended a minimum package of contributory SS covering the entire unorganized sector.

- *Welfare Funds Model* – at the base of central- and state-level SS measures – is typically a tripartite model consisting of representatives of workers, employers (where identifiable), and the government. The fund is managed by a government-appointed board. Contributions from workers–members of the board, employers (usually through a cess), and the government form the basis of defined SS coverage extended to workers. Employees are, however, not required to make specific contributions.

Among SS initiatives already undertaken at the state level, Kerala topped the list in 2005–2006 with the largest number of Welfare Funds (24) catering to about 64 per cent of informal workers in the state. Tamil Nadu has also succeeded in partially extending Welfare Funds coverage to unorganized sector workers, while Maharashtra, Gujarat, Karnataka, Madhya Pradesh, and Andhra Pradesh have successfully established Welfare Boards for selected categories of workers. West Bengal, followed by Tripura, has initiated statutory SS provision for unorganized sector workers through Provident Funds. Although contingencies such as accidental death and injury, maternity, and some financial assistance for education of children are covered, the benefits are limited by the lack of medical provision.

At the central level, five welfare funds, financed out of the cess levied under the respective Cess/Funds Acts, were functioning under the Ministry of Labour around 2007. These include the following:

1. The Mica Mines Labour Welfare Fund Act (1946)
2. The limestone and Dolomite Mines Labour Welfare Fund Act (1972)
3. The Iron Ore, Manganese Ore and Chrome Ore Mines Labour Welfare Fund Act (1976)
4. The Beedi Workers Welfare Fund Act (1976)
5. The Cine Workers Welfare Fund Act (1981)

These schemes provide for housing, medical assistance and reimbursements, SS, education, and recreational facilities to the concerned workers. The Fund for the beedi workers is the relatively active one among all these.

In addition to the Welfare Funds, a few subsidized Group Insurance Schemes (GISs) under the LIC are implemented by the Centre and directly by various departments, prominent among which are the Landless Agricultural Labourers Group Insurance (LALGI) and the GISs for the weaker sections. An array of new and affordable insurance policies are also available now for the poor and the low-income families, such as the Rural Group Life Insurance Scheme (1995), the Jan Arogya Policy (1996), and Personal Accident Policies – as a fall-out of the recommendations of the Committee on Reforms in the Insurance Sector (1994) that recognized the immense potential offered by rural India for insurance business. Mention may be made of the Varishtha Pension Bima (2003), exclusively targeted at unorganized sector workers aged 55 years and older and fully financed by the investment of the beneficiary (annual return 9 per cent in the form of monthly pension) and implemented by the LIC, and the Janashree Bima Yojana (2000), meant for BPL urban and rural poor and those at the margin.

The Unorganized Sector Workers Social Security Scheme launched by the Central Government in 2002 for unorganized and self-employed workers drawing an income not exceeding ₹ 6,500 per month, included an Old-Age Pension Scheme, Personal Accident Insurance, and Medical Insurance. However, the lack of any statutory backing resulted in only limited coverage. This scheme is now virtually defunct.

In accordance with NCEUS stress on SS provision for unorganized workers, the 2007 Budget proposed offering death and disability cover to the rural landless through the LIC via 'Aam Admi Bima Yojana' (AABY). By the end of March 2007, around 50 per cent of the rural landless households were expected to be covered by this.

The community-based Universal Health Insurance Scheme (UHIS) was launched by four public sector general insurance companies in 2003 and redesigned in 2004–2005 exclusively for BPL persons and families.

Worker-group-specific initiatives:

(a) *Scheme for handloom weavers and artisans:* offering thrift fund, personal and group insurance, a pension plan and insurance for power loom weavers.

(b) The significant introduction of Umbrella Legislations for the Welfare of Construction Workers (1996) – the latter group being one of the largest segments of workers in the unorganized sector.

NSAP, 1995

Intended for providing protective SS to the very poor, the NSAP is the first national cash transfer programme in India, although such a programme was already in existence in some states. Funded entirely by the Centre, the programme includes the following:

1. *National Old Age Pension Scheme (NOAPS):* Eligibility: age above 65 years and 'destitute'. The initial financial assistance of ₹ 75 per month per beneficiary was increased to ₹ 200 per month. The coverage, as of 2005–2006, was nearly 73 lakhs.
2. *National Family Benefit Scheme (NFBS):* Eligibility: BPL households in the event of death of primary breadwinner of the family. Applicant should be aged between 18 and 65 years. This scheme includes a lump sum assistance of ₹ 10,000 and covered 2.11 lakhs as of 2005–2006.
3. *National Maternity Benefit Scheme (NMBS):* Meant for pregnant women aged 19 years and above in BPL households for up to the first two live births, this scheme has

been later transferred from the Ministry of Rural Development to the Department of Health and Family Welfare. Cash benefits (₹ 1,300 for rural and ₹ 800 for urban households) are provided for antenatal care and institutional care. In all this, the Gram Panchayats and Municipalities play an important role in identifying beneficiaries, monitoring programmes, and disbursing funds.

At the State Government level, apart from the statutory provisions mentioned earlier, a system of monthly pensions to various categories of destitutes are in operation. Here also, Kerala offers a wide spectrum of pension schemes.

There are, finally, well-known initiatives at the various NGOs and self-financed social insurance schemes.

NPS and the Unorganized Sector – the 'Swavalamban' Scheme (2010)

The impetus to inclusive growth received significant boost in the Central Government Budget 2010–2011 with the launching of the co-contributory Pension Scheme 'Swavalamban'. The objective was 'encouraging unorganized sector subscribers to voluntarily save for safe, secured and dignified life in old age'. The contribution of the Central Government would be ₹ 1,000 per annum, available for the current financial year and three years thereafter. The government contribution period has been later extended to five years in the Budget 2011–2012 and exit norms from the scheme have been eased.

While the move has been lauded for its exemplary intentions, with expected benefits envisaged to reach around 10 lakh NPS subscribers of the unorganized sector, the need to generate sufficient invested resources for sustaining the laudable initiatives is being increasingly felt.

BSS: Employment Guarantee Initiatives in India

Employment and income security as embodied in the BSS measures are best achieved through labour market interventions combining employment and social protection because these are found to be more effective and fiscally affordable than traditional pure social welfare programme such as unemployment insurance. Employment guarantee schemes within the framework of public works can act as important instrument of cash transfers and provide employment-based safety nets for livelihood protection, consumption smoothing, and income stabilization. Labour-based infrastructure programmes lead to growth and development through creation of assets, livelihood promotion, and income enhancement.

Public works ensuring employment and income have been an important component of the Indian safety net, with programmes both centrally sponsored and state specific. The successive central employment schemes implemented are listed in the following text. While changes in programmes have been frequent, much of the development has been re-branding rather than fundamental reform. The more recent policy shift has been from scheme-based provision of works to a legislatively backed 100-day rural-employment guarantee under The Mahatma Gandhi National Rural Employment Guarantee Act (MGNREGA).

- *Jawahar Rozgar Yojana (JRY, from 1989 to 1999)*: A CSS targeted to BPL households in rural areas, with preferences for SC/ST and women, and 80:20 financing split between centre and states. The wage/material ratio was 60:40 and DRDA/ZP, the main implementing agencies through line departments and GPs.
- *Employment Assurance Scheme (EAS – from 1993 to 2001)*: A CSS initially focused on 261 districts and gradually extended to nationwide rural coverage by 1997. EAS committed to 100 days of lean-season employment for up to two adults per rural family and was also financed on an 80:20 central and state split. As with JRY, the wage/material ratio was 60:40 and DRDA/ZP, the main implementing agencies through line departments and GP.

In 1999, JRY was restructured into the *Jawahar Gram Samidhi Yojana* (JGSY), with the main difference being that creation of demand-driven community infrastructure moved from being a secondary objective to the primary objective, with rural-employment generation conversely becoming the secondary objective.

From 2001, the EAS and JGSY were merged into *Sampoorna Grameen Rozgar Yojana* (SGRY), which had a target of 100 days employment (per rural household). Financing is split 75:25 between the centre and the states, and (Panchayati Raj Institutions (PRIs) have in principle been given an increased implementation role.

In late 2004, the *National Food for Work Programme* (NFFWP) was introduced in 150 backward districts, with a massive increase in funding to ₹ 5,400 crores in the 2005–2006 budget.

The Ministry of Rural Development, Government of India, initiated a holistic and integrated development scheme, viz. National Rural Employment Guarantee Scheme, which came into force during February 2005, in 200 backward districts of India. During 2007, the scheme was extended to another 130 districts and since April 2008, this scheme covers all other districts of India. This is the largest employment programme ever started in the country with a huge public investment. The focus of the scheme is to provide 100 days wage employment to rural households who wish to work and ask for work. The act has been renamed as the MGNREGA on 2nd October 2009.The scheme has been universalized for all persons living in rural areas instead of being available only for the families 'below poverty line'. The Central Government provides 90 per cent share of funds for the scheme. It also compensates various states if a fund crunch affects employment generation. The NREGA marks a paradigm shift from all precedent wage employment programmes. The significant aspects of this paradigm shift are captured as follows:

(a) NREGA provides a statutory guarantee of wage employment in a rights-based framework.
(b) There is a 15 days' time limit for fulfilling the legal guarantee of providing employment and the legal mandate of providing employment in a time-bound manner is underpinned by the provision of unemployment allowance.
(c) The Act is designed to offer an incentive structure to the State for providing employment as 90 per cent of the cost

for employment provided is borne by the Centre. There is a concomitant disincentive for not providing employment as the states then bear the double indemnity of unemployment and the cost of unemployment allowance.

(d) Unlike the earlier wage employment programmes that were allocation based, NREGA is demand driven. Resource transfer under NREGA is based on the demand for employment and this provides another critical incentive to states to leverage that Act to meet the employment needs of the poor.

(e) NREGA has extensive inbuilt transparency safeguards.

(f) Various CSS measures are also provided under the scheme.

These are as follows: (i) if any injury occurs to any persons employed under the scheme, he or she shall be entitled to free of charge medical treatment; (ii) if a person employed under the scheme dies or become permanently disabled by accident arising out of and in course of employment, he shall be paid by the implementing agency an ex gratia payment at the rate of ₹ 25,000; and (iii) facilities of safe drinking water, shade for children and periods of rest, first-aid box with adequate material for emergency treatment for minor injuries, and other health hazards connected with the work being performed shall be provided at the work site.

Several observations with regard to the impact and implementation of MGNREGA are available now. For example, a bare 3.2 per cent of registered needy households in 200 of India's poorest districts managed to get the guaranteed 100 days of employment in a year (Jha et al., 2008). The average employment provided was 18 days per needy household. Another assessment (Biswas, 2007) draws attention to the unevenness in its implementation. Emphasizing that while a total estimated expenditure of $4.5 billion was expected to generate 2 billion days of employment, the actual was about 1 billion, and the benefits varied across different states. With the passing years, performance seems to have improved.

There is evidence of quite a sharp increase in both the number of total person-days generated and per household, under this scheme. Thus far, it has provided some employment to more than 50 million households, and nearly 2.6 billion person-days of employment have been generated. The enhanced wage earnings have contributed to strengthening the livelihood resource base of the rural poor in India, reduced distress migration, and become an extremely important buffer against both the employment shocks generated by the economic crisis (as migrant workers returned home to their villages) and the drought that swept across large parts of the country in the summer of 2009 (UNCTAD, 2010) and thus has ensured social protection in both BSS and CSS sense.

Table 5

Households having 100 Days Employment under MGNREGA (during 2009–10)

Proportion of households having 100 days employment			
<1%	*1–10%*	*10–20%*	*>20%*
Manipur	Goa	Karnataka	Andhra Pradesh
Puducherry	West Bengal	Madhya Pradesh	Rajasthan
Lakshadweep	Punjab	Uttar Pradesh	Sikkim
Arunachal Pradesh	Andaman & Nicobar Islands	Tamil Nadu	Nagaland
Dadra & Nagar H	Maharashtra		Tripura
	Mizoram		
	Uttaranchal		
	Meghalaya		
	Kerala		
	Haryana		
	Orissa		
	Assam		
	J&K		
	Gujarat		
	Bihar		
	Jharkhand		
	Chhattisgarh		
	Himachal Pradesh		

Source: MGNREGA website downloaded on 20 February 2011.

However, the basic objective of providing 100 days' assured employment per rural household remains a distant dream. Table 5 categorizes the states in India on the basis of proportion of households employed for 100 days among those households who got employed during 2009–2010. It is evident that in most of the states, less than 10 per cent of the households received employment for 100 days. Only in five states, more than 20 per cent of households got employment for 100 days. The highest proportion (37%) is recorded in Tripura.

If the total number of households were to get employment for 100 days, the required number of person-days to be generated far exceeded the total number of person-days actually generated in all the states (Table A1 in Appendix), with the shortfall estimated above 46 per cent at the national level.

Much improvement is necessary with respect to implementation of the programme. Data reveal that a huge amount of available funds remained unspent during 2009–2010 (Table A1 in Appendix). Better implementation is likely to generate expected benefits not only as SS cover but also by inducing growth stimulus via income and demand generation, and boosting of farm income.

Concluding Remarks and Further Research

To conclude this brief survey of the SS scenario in India, some reference is in order to the limitations of the diverse CSS provisions made available at the unorganized sector level. Various difficulties are perceived as having often impeded the progress of the schemes and resulting in limited usefulness to the intended beneficiaries. To highlight a few major ones are as follows:

- The lack of a comprehensive legislatory framework leading to difficulties in administration and dispute settlements.
- The extreme fragmentation of schemes resulting in difficulty of monitoring and implementation.
- Rigidity of the extremely localized eligibility and other requirements that often stand in the way of necessary flexibility in interpretation and sensible intervention.

The foregoing discussion on the NPS, however, makes it clear that it is precisely these problems that the concerted reform efforts seek to address. The ongoing efforts at extending the pension system to include unorganized sector workers would make it possible to bring them under a homogeneous scheme that would enable better administration and monitoring.

Pension reforms initiated in the recent years need to be taken forward immediately if India's relative demographic advantage over similarly placed economies is to be capitalized on. The need to educate the population financially and the need to develop the right attitudes towards saving and income-planning however pose daunting challenges. 'Creating awareness about these reforms and gaining the confidence of the people to encourage them to be a part of this movement is the single most important challenge faced by policymakers today' (Swarup, 2008 :16).

Coming to the BSS initiatives, the need for better implementation of the Employment Guarantee Programs has been amply demonstrated. The large proportion of unutilized funds (Table A1 in Appendix) is a case for concern.

Further Research

Finally, a few areas and concerns that are of particular relevance to this review need to be highlighted. Given the compulsions faced by governments in developing economies in today's globalizing world, and the fast disappearing traditional social safety nets in the post-global financial crisis scenario, designing and ensuring safety nets for the vulnerable still remain the overriding need facing us without which any efforts at growth/development is likely to backfire. However, what are the implications of the recent crisis for the envisaged SS reforms in India? A number of researchers are actively studying the implications of the crisis on a global level, and we feel there is a need to closely examine the proposed pension reforms in India in this context in view of the inherent 'policy risk' vis-à-vis 'market risks' involved.

The second question is whether the growth implications of increasing informalization are apparently inevitable concomitants of India's development journey (Mazumdar, 2010)? The evidence is far from unanimous owing to the lack of statistical documentation of this vital yet under-represented or unrepresented dimension of the economy (UNESCAP, 2010). At the same time, as policies are being designed to provide safeguards, on one hand, and integrate the informal into the formal sector on the other hand, there is a pressing need of properly assessing the contribution of the informal sector to the economy.

Notes

1. Although closely related, the concepts (in-)formal and (un-)organized are different from each other from a strictly definitional aspect. However, the terms are used interchangeably for the present purpose since this does not affect the main thrust of the present paper. For a detailed discussion of the concepts; see Sharma, R., and Chitkara, S. (CSO, India 2006). 'Informal Sector in the Indian System of National Accounts', Expert Group on Informal Sector Statistics (Delhi Group), New Delhi, May, http://www.mospi.gov.in/GDP%2006.doc; p. 5.
2. The brief account of the salient features of the Indian pension system is based on Swarup (2008) with updating in light of subsequent developments on the economic and policy front.
3. CSS measures upto 2007 have been extensively detailed and referred in Kannan and Pillai (2007).

References

Biswas, S. (2007). 'India job scheme disappointing', *BBC News*, 10 November cited in Jha et al. (2008).

Dreze, J. (1991). 'Public action for social security: Foundations and strategy', *Social Security in Developing Countries*, editors Ahmed, E., Dreze, J., Hills, J., and Sen, A. Oxford: Clarendon Press.

ILO (2010). *World Social Security Report 2010/11: Providing Coverage in Times of Crisis and Beyond*. International Labour Organization.

Jha, R., Gaiha, R., and Shankar, S. (2008). *National Rural Employment Guarantee Programme in India – A Review*, ASARC Working Paper 2008/01.

Kannan, K.P. (2004). *Social Security, Poverty Reduction and Development: Arguments for Enlarging the Concept of Social Security in a Globalizing World*. Extensions of Social Security Papers, ILO, Geneva, p. 21.

Kannan, K.P., and Pillai, V.N. (2007). *Social Security in India: The Long Lane Treaded and the Longer Road Ahead Towards Universalization*, Munich Personal RePec Archive (MPRA) Paper 9601, July 2008.

Mazumdar, D. (2010). *Employment and Inequality Outcomes in India*. New Delhi, India: University of Toronto and Institute of Human Development.

National Commission for Enterprises in the Unorganised Sector (NCEUS) (2007). *Report on Conditions of Work and Promotion of Livelihoods in the Unorganized Sector*, New Delhi, August.

NCEUS (2009). *Skill Formation and Employment Assurance in the Unorganized Sector*. New Delhi: NCEUS, May 2009, Accessed Feb. 2011. www.nceus.gov.in

Panigrahi, A.K. (2009). *Determinants of Living Arrangements of Elderly in Orissa: An Analysis*, Working Paper 228, ISBN 81–7791–184–8, Institute for Social and Economic Change, Bangalore.

Rajan, S.I. (2010). *Demographic Ageing and Employment in India*. ILO Asia-Pacific Working Paper Series, International Labour Organization.

Saith, A. (2008). 'Towards universalizing socio-economic security: Strategic elements of a policy framework', *Indian Journal of Human Development* 2(1).

Sen, A. (2002). *India: Development and Participation*. New Delhi: Oxford University Press.

Swarup, D. (2008). *Pension Reform in India – A Social Security Need*. Chairman's Address, PFRDA.

UNCTAD (2010). *Trade and Development Report*. New York/Geneva: United Nations, pp. 154.

UNESCAP (2010). *Interregional Cooperation on the Measurement of Informal Sector and Informal Employment*. http://www.unescap.org/stat/isie/index.asp.

World Commission on the Social Dimension of Globalization (2004), p. 110.

Appendix

Table A1

Proportion of Households having 100 Days Employment and Shortfall in Person-days Generated (State-wise) 2009–2010

States	*Per cent of households employed in households demanding employment*	*Per cent of households employed 100 days among those who got employment*	*Per cent of shortfall in person- days generated*	*Fund unspent (% of available fund)*
Andhra Pradesh	100	22.66	34.33	6.34
Arunachal Pradesh	93.87	0.40	75.09	21.62
Assam	99.91	6.10	65.71	21.22
Bihar	100	6.85	72.45	17.92
Chhattisgarh	100	7.94	48.59	41.7
Gujarat	100	6.50	63.35	21.75
Haryana	100	5.65	62.25	24.18
Himachal Pradesh	99.63	9.71	42.71	7.66
Jammu & Kashmir	95.39	6.36	61.70	11.02
Jharkhand	99.96	7.83	50.51	28.01
Karnataka	97.49	12.61	43.33	20.38
Kerala	99.84	4.56	64.46	20.24
Madhya Pradesh	99.99	14.40	44.34	33.15
Maharashtra	99.99	3.83	53.62	48,11
Manipur	100	0.02	26.84	1.17
Meghalaya	99.32	4.48	87.40	15.61
Mizoram	100	3.92	5.44	2.52
Nagaland	100	31.80	12.60	1.77
Orissa	98.71	5.92	60.37	6.06
Punjab	99.72	2.83	71.62	28.32
Rajasthan	100	23.22	31.03	21.27
Sikkim	100	23.33	20.10	37.51
Tamil Nadu	100	17.39	45.33	26.95
Tripura	99.82	37.16	20.17	24.18
Uttar Pradesh	96.75	14.53	35.09	13.49
Uttaranchal	100	3.96	65.07	18.84
West Bengal	99.73	2.07	55.41	9.28
Andaman & Nicobar Islands	98.56	3.23	71.33	19.1
Dadra & Nagar H	100	0.64	81.28	32.03
Goa	99.86	1.83	71.98	60.85
Lakshadweep	100	0.39	72.84	23.13
Puducherry	100	0.31	77.53	27.34

Source: MGNREGA website downloaded on 20 February 2011 and authors' calculation.

Table A2

Households having 100 Days Employment and Person-days Generated (State-wise) 2009–2010

States	*Households demanding employment*	*Households got employment*	*Households employed for 100 days*	*Person-days generated (in lakhs)*
Andhra Pradesh	6,158,493	6,158,493	1,395,537	4044.3
Arunachal Pradesh	72,606	68,157	276	16.98
Assam	2,139,111	2,137,270	13,0457	732.95
Bihar	4,127,330	4,127,330	282,797	1136.88
Chhattisgarh	2,025,845	2,025,845	160,851	1041.57
Gujarat	1,596,402	1,596,402	103,752	585.09
Haryana	156,410	156,406	8837	59.04
Himachal Pradesh	499,174	497,336	48,283	284.94
Jammu & Kashmir	352,287	336,036	21,360	128.71
Jharkhand	1,703,243	1,702,599	133,296	842.47
Karnataka	3,626,437	3,535,281	445,930	2003.43
Kerala	957,477	955,976	43,596	339.71
Madhya Pradesh	4,714,916	4,714,591	678,717	2624
Maharashtra	591,611	591,547	22,630	274.35
Manipur	418,564	418,564	101	306.18
Meghalaya	302,537	300,482	13,453	37.86
Mizoram	180,140	180,140	7059	170.33
Nagaland	325,242	325,242	103,436	284.27
Orissa	1,416,560	1,398,300	82,710	554.09
Punjab	272,684	271,934	7702	77.17
Rajasthan	6,522,264	6,522,264	1,514,420	4498.1
Sikkim	54,156	54,156	12,633	43.27
Tamil Nadu	4,373,257	4,373,257	760,689	2390.75
Tripura	577,540	576,487	214,218	460.22
Uttar Pradesh	5,667,644	5,483,434	796,929	3559.23
Uttaranchal	522,304	522,304	20,664	182.41
West Bengal	3,489,363	3,479,915	72,123	1551.68
Andaman & Nicobar Islands	20,634	20,337	657	5.83
Dadra & Nagar H	3741	3741	24	0.7
Goa	6613	6604	121	1.85
Lakshadweep	5192	5192	20	1.41
Puducherry	40,377	40,377	125	9.07

Source: MGNREGA website downloaded on 20 February 2011 and authors' calculation.

Part II

Growth and Employment Scenario in Gujarat

6

Changing Scenario of Agriculture and Rural Employment in Gujarat

Challenges and Opportunities

R.C. Popat

There has been a significant growth in the agriculture sector in Gujarat in the last five years and it is very rightly described as an agrarian miracle in Gujarat after 2000 (Shah, T. et al., 2009). Gujarat has set the example for other states in the agriculture sector which has achieved a 9.6 per cent growth rate. This has been thought to be unbelievable because even at national level, the growth in agriculture has never crossed the apex line of 4 per cent growth rate, though currently it has been limited to only an average rate of 2.9 per cent since 2000.

However, this achievement is not enough. The Gujarat Government has been determined, as a matter of policy, to achieve successful growth in agriculture in the coming years and to establish the state as the forerunner of a second-generation Green Revolution in the country.

Since enhancement of employment in this sector is the fundamental aspect of the poverty reduction programme, the issues related to agricultural employment bear considerably high weightage in the study of agricultural development. With the transformation of this sector in Gujarat, the development of agricultural labour has undergone a drastic change especially after 2000. This paper aims at a comprehensive study of this aspect of agriculture in Gujarat.

Pre-reform Scenario

Production and Productivity

Agriculture in Gujarat prior to 1991 has very little at its credit. Agricultural practices during the pre-reform period were a traditional activity with no level of professionalism. The method and techniques applied were age old. Innovations and technological research were not the main focus for Gujarat agriculture. Knowledge used was generally traditional except for improved varieties of seeds especially of wheat and cotton. Improved practices and updated knowledge were also popularized under the Green Revolution in 1967–1968. Only 29 per cent of gross cropped area (GCA) was fortunate to have irrigation facilities, while the rest of the 71 per cent of cultivated land was left to the mercy of irregular and uncertain monsoons.

The production and productivity of agriculture in Gujarat were significantly lower. Land productivity of 14 major crops taken together was 34 per cent lower in pre-1990 period than in 2009. Similarly, annual average growth rate during the same period moved up by almost 3 per cent only.

Labour Force

Labour force in the pre-reform period faced an unfavourable imbalance of demand and supply factors. However, it is very difficult to have an exact estimation of the demand for labour in agriculture, because agricultural production is not a continuous process like in industrial manufacturing. For different crops and different operations, the number of workers required varies from time to time. Besides, labour requirement was not the same for single crop and double crop cultivation. Moreover, there was no mathematical relationship between the number of labourers required and the total cultivated area. Even with these limitations, demand for agricultural labour in the pre-reform period could roughly be estimated at 27 million per year for 74 lakh hectares GCA in pre-1990 period.

On other hand, the supply and demand aspects were clearly balanced. Once again an accurate calculation of the supply of labour supply in the agricultural sector is practically impossible. However, some workable calculations have been made, allowing room for some uncertainties and assumptions.

The average population in two decades (1971–1991) in Gujarat was 373 lakhs (320 lakhs in 1971 and 426 lakhs in 1991). Considering that 70 per cent of the population subsisted on agriculture, it was not surprising that around 60 lakh families were dependent on it. An average of three persons out of five in each family was actually working on farms as active farm workers. Thus, the estimated supply of labour force in agriculture was about 180 lakhs. Consequently, 67–70 per cent of the demand for labour force was available from the family members of the land owners itself. Only 30 per cent was required to be hired as casual labourers. The unfortunate fact being that landless workers were easily available at low wage rates.

Moreover, the agricultural sector suffered from labour pressures on the farm land. Because of inadequate employment outside the farms in rural Gujarat, increased labour force – because of the expansion of family size – was forced to rush to the farms for the livelihood. Consequently, it created the problem of disguised unemployment in the agricultural sector.

Thus, the main features of the state of affairs in the area of agricultural labour force in Gujarat before 1990 could be summarized as follows:

1. Largest part of agricultural labour force came from among the family members of land-owning families which included female workers.
2. Questions of wages thus were hardly raised.
3. Labour force was easily available.
4. Regular workers comprised 70 per cent, while the remaining 30 per cent were casual workers during the harvesting period for crops such as groundnut and cotton.
5. Casual workers were paid wages as low ₹ 50 per day (i.e., for 8 hours a day).
6. Migrant labour constituted of a small proportion of the total labour force.

Change in Scenario after 1991

The situation in agricultural labour especially in the post-reform period has undergone a sea change. It is mainly due to the drastic structural changes in the agricultural sector that has taken place in Gujarat after 1991, especially after 2001. We will first look at these trends before examining the situation of labour in the state.

· As mentioned earlier (see 'Introduction'), agriculture in Gujarat has seen a phenomenal growth since 2001. The average annual growth rate of agriculture moved from 3 per cent to 3.5 per cent before 1991 and achieved an optimum growth of 9.6 per cent in 2001–2009 (Bagchi, A. et al., 2004). Not only in this respect, but the post-reform period witnessed an overall transformation of the agricultural system as a whole in Gujarat. The driving factors of this transformation can be traced out as follows (Shah, T. et al., 2009).

Endogenous Factors

These factors are supported by a number of extrogenous factors, which shall be discussed in the following section. Some of these endogenous factors have played a pivotal role in increasing agricultural production after 1991. A few examples are as follows:

(a) There has been a remarkable increase in the production of cotton, wheat, and the value of the livestock as well as in milk production. Table 1 reflects this growth.

Table 1

Annual Average Growth of Major Crops in Gujarat (%)

Sector		*1991–1992 to 1999–2000*	*2000–2001 to 2007–2008*
Total	Food grains	7.3	11.8
	Wheat	12.8	24
	Cotton	10.5	35
	Fruits and vegetables	8.6	14.4
	Livestock	5	6.6
	Milk	4.9	6.9
Total agriculture and live stock		5.4	11.2

Table 1 shows an increase in the average annual growth rate of food grains from 7.3 per cent to 11 per cent during 1991–2000. And 8 per cent during 2000–2008, the production rates of wheat and cotton during the same period have increased respectively to 24 per cent from 12.8 per cent and to 35 per cent from 10.5 per cent. Similarly, the production of fruits and vegetables has also increased remarkably.

Cotton crops in the state have contributed significantly in the overall agricultural growth after 2000. The percentage of cotton in the gross value of the output of agriculture has increased from 9.4 per cent in 1999–2000 to 15.6 per cent in 2006–2007, while the food grain production decreased to 13 per cent from 16 per cent during the same period.

(b) There has been a significant increase in the GCA in Gujarat during the post-reform period from 74 lakh hectares in the pre-reform period to 80.6 lakh hectares in 1990–2000 and 88 lakh hectares in 2007–2008. Despite 2009–2010 being a drought year, the GCA did not reduce to below 82.5 lakh hectares. The GCA in the post-reform period has increased to 19 per cent as compared to the pre-reform period. Even in the post-reform period, an increase in the GCA has been more considerable as compared to earlier years. For example, the area under food crops jumped to 47.11 lakh hectares in 2007–2008 from 36.6 lakh hectares in 2004–2005 which augmented the total food production to 55 per cent from 51.53 lakh metric tonnes in 2004–2005 to 80 lakh tonnes in 2007–2008.

Extrogenous Factors

Along with these endogenous factors, some extrogenous factors have played a crucial role in agricultural growth during the post reform period. Credit for this growth should be attributed to the following major factors:

(a) *Rainfall:* Nature had been rather kind to Gujarat during this period. On an average the rainfall in Gujarat during the period from 2002 to 2007 has been about 47 per cent of the normal rainfall received in the state. Mainly the rain deprived areas are the southern and central Gujarat. In northern Gujarat and Saurashtra Kutch, the rainfall received is about 85 per cent of the normal rainfall. In other words, except for central and southern parts of Gujarat, the average rainfall had been quite favourable to increased agriculture during 2002–2007 in three-fifth parts of the state.

(b) *Market environment:* The high minimum support price announced by the central government from time to time for cotton, wheat, and other crops has provided a strong incentive to the Gujarat farmers in increasing production. Especially the high prices for cotton have played a crucial role in agricultural growth, since The Cotton Corporation of India has a sizeable procurement operation in this state. Moreover, export demands for Gujarat cotton has also increased significantly. Consequently, Gujarat has emerged as the largest cotton-producing region in India and a major cotton supplier to China.

(c) *Bt cotton:* A dramatic increase in cotton production and structural change in crop patterns in recent years must be attributed to the popular use of Bt cotton seeds after 2004. Taking a lead from the Monsanto Company who introduced this seed to the Indian farmers, local companies in north Gujarat have now come forward producing Bt cottonseeds on large scales. Mansa town in Mehsana district has been the hub of Bt cottonseed. Local increased production has made it available at very reasonable prices to the farmers. In place of ₹ 1,600 per packet of 450 gm of Monsanto seeds, the local seeds are available at ₹ 650 which is less than half the cost of the foreign seeds. The introduction of Bt cottonseeds has revolutionized cotton crop.

(d) *New experiments:* Encouraging measures by the state government with the profound political will for faster agricultural growth in Gujarat in recent years have provided great incentives to educated, progressive, and foresighted farmers to make new experiments in the crops of fruits and vegetables. Numbers of new varieties of fruits and vegetables have been invented by Gujarat farmers. Reliance Industries Ltd. at Jamnagar, for example, has developed 137 new types of mango fruit in their orchards. Though this experiment is in the initial stages only, it has definitely generated hope for a rapid increase in the production of fruits and vegetables in coming years. It is evident from the fact that the production of this crop has increased at the rate of 14.4 per cent during 2000–2008 instead of 8.6 per cent during 1991–2000.

Other Factors

Along with these endogenous and exogenous factors, other factors not included in the above list such as the encouragement by the state government at the policy level, immense political will for exemplary agricultural growth in the state, growth of infrastructural facilities, and improved market access as well as new dimensions of irrigation system have contributed much more than the factors discussed above. These factors have provided strong and valuable support to the amazing agrarian growth in the state in recent years.

(a) *Market factors:* A number of measures taken by the state government to improve farmers' access to better markets have been the effect of enhancement of agricultural activities in the state. With amendments in Agricultural Produce Marketing Committee Act, farmers feel comfortable to sell their produce directly to the local as well as to export markets and industries at the worthwhile price without the interference of intermediaries. Similarly, the government has pursued an aggressive policy of diversification where high-value crops such as fruit, vegetables, spices, and others are concerned. The government offers a direct capital subsidy of ₹ 2.5 lakhs to the farmers to set up green houses along with 25 per cent relief in electricity duty. As a result of this, horticulture production in Gujarat has increased by 108 per cent between 2001 and 2006.

Moreover, the government has pursued the policy of encouraging the corporate sector to invest in retail chain malls of agro-based production and get their supply directly from the farmers. Recently, the government has decided to confer the status of industry to the agriculture sector with the implementation of Index-A which provides direct entrepreneurship to the farmer in all agricultural operations from sowing to marketing. It is expected that this step will not only help increase agricultural production but also increase farm and non-farm employment on a large scale in rural Gujarat.

(b) *Technical and credit support:* In the last six years, the BJP government has taken steps to provide technical- and finance-based support to the agricultural sector. For example, four subordinate centres at the agriculture university have been converted into four independent agricultural universities with full resources and finance. Similarly, celebration of the annual Krishi Mahotsav lasting a full month every year has worked as a unique extension model which brings together agricultural scientists, agro-industrialists, input suppliers, co-operatives, banks as well as local- and state-level political leaders together on one platform to exchange knowledge and views about new dimensions in agricultural development.

Likewise, providing credit cards and soil health cards to each farmer has opened up new horizons for a scientific cultivation.

(c) *Irrigation:* Total irrigation facilities could be extended to about 48 per cent of gross cultivated area in 2007–2008 from about only 29 per cent in 1990–1991. This has been possible by canal irrigation facilities increased through the Sardar Sarovar Project, Mahi Canal Project, Ukai Kakrapar Project, and the Daman Ganga Project. These projects have mainly extended their benefits to central, north, and south Gujarat. Saurashtra Kutch regions have not been the beneficiaries so far. Saurashtra region is irrigated mainly by locally situated medium-sized dams, Bhadar Dam and thousands of check dams at village level. Whatever the case may be, the fact is that increased irrigation facilities have undoubtedly increased agricultural production.

(d) *Ground water management:* Since the time of the Keshubhai Patel government, the state of Gujarat has actively undertaken unconventional initiatives in ground water management with a view to fill up the gap of Narmada water for irrigation in Saurashtra and Kutch regions. Rain water harvesting and ground water recharge at decentralized levels with the active involvement of NGOs and the participation of the people were the main themes of the campaign under the Sardar Patel Sahkari Jal Sanchay Yojana. By the end of 2008, nearly 5 lakh works were taken in the following manner:

1. Check dams (with the participation of the people)	113,738
2. Bori bandhs	55,917
3. Farm Ponds	2,400,199
4. Check dams (constructed by the Gujarat Government)	62,532

Production has thus been raised to almost 1.5 times in impacted regions.

Besides this, the Narendra Modi government has pioneered a new programme of micro-irrigation, i.e., drip irrigation to be popularized among farmers throughout the state. The government has established a corporate-level unit called the Gujarat Green Revolution Company for this purpose. This micro-irrigation scheme is capable of saving 70–90 per cent of water as compared to canal irrigation.

The Gujarat Government has also implemented the Jyoti Gram Yojana since 2003. This rural electrification scheme assures 24 × 7 supply of electricity to households of all 18 lakh villages of the state and uninterrupted supply of power to each farm for eight hours a day. This Yojana has successfully overcome road blocks to smooth irrigation programmes in Gujarat.

The whole agricultural scenario has changed in Gujarat after 1991; the clear impacts of these changes are evident in the overall improvement in all aspects of agricultural development, e.g., gross cultivated area, land productivity, agricultural production, and crop pattern.

The gross cultivated area has increased to 80.6 lakh hectares in 1999–2000 and 88 lakh hectares in 2007–2008 from 74 lakh hectares before 1991. Land productivity in terms of rupee value per hectare (at 1999–2000 prices) has increased from ₹ 15,000 in 1990–1991 to ₹ 22,000 in 1999–2000 and ₹ 30,000 in 2007–2008. That means that land productivity has certainly doubled after 1991. Similarly, the annual average growth rate of the total agricultural production which was less than 3 per cent in the pre-reform period has increased to 17 per cent in 2007–2008. Finally, the composition of Gujarat's farm economy has also been transformed in terms of crop patterns as presented in Table 2.

Table 2
Changing Crop Pattern in Gujarat Agriculture

Crops	*Pre-reform period (average)*	*1999–2000*	*2006–2007*
Total food grains	16.2	15.8	12.9
Cotton	7.8	9.4	15.6
Cash crops other than cotton (including ground nut)	30.5	27.4	25.8
Fruits and vegetables	4.6	9.9	12.5
Total livestock	22.5	22.7	22.4
Total others	18.4	14.8	10.8
Total	100	100	100

The above-mentioned data reveal that the main crop in Gujarat which was groundnut has been replaced in recent years by cotton. In 2010 Kharif season, it is estimated that the sowing of groundnut would be reduced by 33 per cent this year and that of cotton and castor seeds would increase, attracted by the higher market price of these crops. Similarly, the higher market yield has tempted the farmers to grow more vegetables and fruits than in other years.

The transformation of Gujarat's agriculture has helped prepare the foundation of our forthcoming analysis regarding the changing scenario of agricultural labour in recent years.

Agricultural Labour: Changing Scenario

In recent years, especially after 2001, agricultural labour has undergone a considerable change in respect to both supply and demand (Pradhan, A.K. et al., 2001).

Demand Side

With technological improvements in agriculture and the increase in the gross cultivated area, there has been a remarkable increase in the demand for workers, both regular and casual, in Gujarat's agriculture. As per a rough estimation, this sector needs almost 3.5 crore workers including farmers as landowners, family members of farmers as regular workers, and landless casual workers. Against this estimate, only 2.77 crores workers were working on farms during 2009–2010. The remaining 73 lakh workers are supposed to be migrant workers.

Moreover, the qualitative nature of demand for agriculture workers has also undergone a change in the last decade. The use of new technology, application of new techniques and methods in farming operations, creation of new varieties of fruits and vegetables, skilled use of pesticides as well as popularizing micro-irrigation techniques, etc., are now required from skilled labour force.

Just as in industry and service sectors, the requirement of skilled farm hands has also taken place in farm employment. Agriculture workers with specialization in different operations such as sowing, irrigation, spraying pesticides, harvesting, and others are now in demand. In the same way, crop-based specialization of labour has also been a new and important factor that has entered into the demand for skilled workers.

Supply Side

The supply of agricultural labour, against increasing demand, has been declining during the post-reform period mainly in the last decade. It is a reverse condition of imbalance between the demand and supply factors in comparison to the pre-reform situation.

Agricultural employment in Gujarat has been steadily decreasing as in the following:

1981	68.64 per cent
1991	56.30 per cent
2001	52.20 per cent
2011 (projected)	46.74 per cent

This list includes land owners, female workers, and landless workers as well. At the same time, a percentage share of casual workers in total population has increased in urban sector, while it has decreased in the rural sector as shown in the following:

Year	*Urban sector*	*Rural sector*
1981	18.3	34.8
2001	24.9	34.5
2011 (projected)	30.5	28.3

It is very clear from the above data that the structure of employment in Gujarat in the last decade has moved away from primary sector to tertiary sector even from the manufacturing sector of industry.

The main reasons for workers moving away from agriculture can be traced to the following developments in the rural economy of Gujarat.

1. There has been an accelerated flow of rural–urban migration in Gujarat. Rural–urban population ratio which was 70:30 in 1991 is decreased to 66: 34 in 2001 and is estimated to be 58:42 in 2011. This means that in each decade about 4–5 per cent of the rural population has migrated permanently to large urban cities. Reasons for migration may be economic, for instance in the search of employment opportunities or non-economic such as socio-cultural purposes, but it has put a definite adverse impact on the availability of labour in the agricultural sector.
2. With the establishment of large-scale industries or in SEZs just 15–20 km away from large cities, newer opportunities of employment have been generated in neighbouring areas of villages. Consequently, agricultural labourers shift generally to industrial labour. Establishment of industries such as Reliance Industries Ltd. and Essar Ltd. in Jamnagar, Nano Plant of Tata in Sanand, SEZ in Dahej, and others, are some of the examples of such shifts.

3. The National Rural Employment Guarantee Act (NREGA) of the Central Government has serious adverse effects on the supply of agriculture labourers since 2004. Casual workers in agriculture are now not ready to work on farms at lower rates when they are guaranteed ₹ 100 per day under NREGA. It has forced the Gujarat Government to raise the minimum wage rates for agricultural workers. Thus, the minimum wage rate has doubled from ₹ 50 to ₹ 100 per day from July 2008. This has increased the labour cost from ₹ 600 per acre to ₹ 1200 per acre.
4. NREGA has also decidedly affected the supply of migrant workers in agriculture. The flow of workers coming from other districts of south Gujarat to central and north Gujarat and Saurashtra Kutch regions as well as from other states such as Bihar, Rajasthan, and others during the harvesting period has declined considerably as these labourers get an employment in their home states at the attractive wage rate of ₹ 100 per day under NREGA. Subsequently, these workers are not available even at ₹ 200 per day in these regions. Large farmers have a hard time as some crops are chiefly dependent on specialized migrant workers only.

   The situation in Punjab and Haryana has been worse when compared to Gujarat. This year, during paddy sowing, farmers had to coax and cajole migrant labour and additional facilities such as furnished quarters, water cooler, TV sets, and fresh cooked food in the seasonal labour camp were offered. Despite these privileges, workers were not ready to work on farms since they got lighter work at higher wages in the NREGA. Labourers now dictate the terms of work when once they begged for work from door to door.
5. Recently implemented central government schemes such as the food guarantee scheme also discourage agricultural workers from toiling in farms for the whole entire day since under this scheme food is assured.
6. Education opportunities in rural Gujarat have turned the employment from farm to non-farm jobs. The young generation from farmers' families is moving away from the hard

work expected on farms to white collar jobs in urban areas because of the improved education they get.

7. Urbanization effects on rural areas of the state also play their role in creating scarcity of agricultural labour. Villages have come closer to large cities, thanks to the impact of economic reforms and revolution in information technology. Evidently, young rural youth and workers in villages attracted by the glitter of the urban lifestyle prefer to enjoy urban facilities rather than toil on farms and in villages.

All these factors have brought the present scenario of agricultural employment to a delicate imbalance. The demand for agricultural workers have not only increased remarkably after 1991 but has diversified also, from illiterate and unskilled labour to educated, skilled, and specialized workers for different farm operations.

The nature of agriculture employment now is not only confined to cultivation work on the farm only, but also has extended very far to other non-farm jobs. The sale of Bt cotton and seeds at reasonable prices, counselling to farmers for loans and subsidies as well as a scientific approach in agriculture, mechanical workings of tools and equipments, providing expert knowledge and active guidance in local marketing and the export of agricultural products, and providing technical services for micro-irrigation as well as for water storage facilities in farms, etc., are all new but inevitable dimensions opened up in agricultural employment in recent years.

As we can see, the demand for agricultural employment has thus become multi-dimensional since the last decade. But the supply of labour on the other hand has suffered from an acute shortage due to various factors. Agricultural growth in the state has suffered immensely because of restricted access in the agricultural employment front.

What Is the Way Out?

Confronting and finding a solution to these problems is a challenge before the Gujarat Government. The State Government needs to fight on two fronts, on one hand to solve water scarcity and on other hand, shortage of manpower in the agricultural sector.

Regarding water scarcity problems, the development of water-saving techniques in agriculture is the most needed solution. The campaign of decentralized irrigation facilities through Sardar Patel Sahkari Jal Sanchaya Yojana pioneered in Saurashtra and Kutch regions has proved to be the most effective way of groundwater storage for irrigation. This campaign needs to be widely adopted all over the state with the target of 100 per cent irrigation in the state.

On other hand, the present canal irrigation techniques consume huge water resources for irrigation and have to be replaced by micro-irrigation techniques as soon as possible. Not only this, but by going one step ahead, porous techniques of irrigation, recently developed by Israel, brings in the technique of almost waterless irrigation which is urgently required for Gujarat. If this advancement is made possible, Gujarat State will be the first state in India to create an irrigation revolution in the country.

Regarding labour scarcity problems, an effective and result-oriented action plan to retain agricultural workforce needs to be implemented. An increase in wage rates for agriculture labour in 2008 is the first step in this direction and the proposed 'Rurban' (rural urbanization) scheme of the Gujarat Government should be the next step towards this goal.

Some policy-level suggestions to solve these problems are made in the following section:

1. NREGA scheme of the Central Government should be linked up with agricultural employment in Gujarat. Only non-farm jobs are offered under this scheme at present, but it requires to be extended to farm jobs also. It will help provide workforce to the agriculture sector.
2. Micro-irrigation or drip irrigation techniques have not been whole heartedly adopted by farmers because of some technical and financial problems. Small and medium farmers hesitate in adopting this technique because they find it costly. Its installation costs about ₹ 1,600 per acre despite the subsidy extended by the government, which is too high for the farmers. It is suggested that the government

should bear 100 per cent of the expenses of installing the micro-irrigation system in all farms under 15 acres. Considering that such farms are 80 per cent of the total land holdings and 48 per cent of these are under irrigation, the government will be required to spend about ₹ 1,200 crores to meet this expense. Since it is a one-time expenditure, the government should have no problems in going in for this scheme.

3. Porous techniques of irrigation, when and if adopted in Gujarat, shall require the use of a specific type of soft rubber hose pipe with micro pores through which the water is percolated to the roots of the plants. Such pipes are not produced locally at present. The import of these pipes is costly, thus affecting the cost of irrigation per hectare. Hence, the State Government should take the initiative and encourage local production of such pipes through considerable subsidy as well as budgetary incentives to the manufacturers.
4. As discussed earlier, the agriculture sector currently requires skilled manpower to work on farms. To meet this demand, all four agriculture universities in the state should be advised to implement effective manpower planning and training and prepare skilled graduates with such knowledge that is required by the agriculture sector. Work on these farms for a prescribed period of time should be a mandatory requirement for these expert graduates.

Conclusion

The agriculture sector in Gujarat is passing through revolutionary changes after breakthroughs in economic reforms, especially in the last decade. Where labour is concerned, the demand side has been stronger and multi-sphered, while the supply side has been weak for a number of reasons if we compare it to the pre-reform period.

Certain policy-level measures have also been suggested to overcome the problems confronted and avail of the advantages of the momentum which the agriculture sector has seen in the state in the last number of years.

References

Bagchi, Amiya, Das, Panchanan, and Chottopadhyaya, Sadhan (2004). 'Growth and structural change in Gujarat economy, 1970–2000', *Economy and Political Weekly* Vol. 28.

Pradhan, A.K., Pandya, J.G. and Gosai, S.P. (2001) *Employment and Human Resource Development Challenges and Opportunities*. Ahmedabad: SPIESR. *Anveshak* Vol. 31, No. 1–2, June–December 2001, Bi-annual Journal of Sardar Patel Institute of Economic and Social Research (SPIESR).

Shah, Tushaar, Gulati, Ashok, Hemant P., Shreedhar, Ganga and Jain, R.C. (2009). 'Secrets of Gujarat's agrarian miracle after 2000', *Economic and Political Weekly*, December, 26.

——. *Agriculture Performance in Gujarat Since 2000*. New Delhi: IWMI and IFPRI.

Further Studies

Labour Bureau of India: Different Survey Reports – 2001 to 2007.

Government of Gujarat:

- Socio-economic survey – 2007–2008 and 2009–2010.
- Irrigation in Gujarat; Director of Economics and Statistics.
- District-wise Area, Production and yield in Gujarat (2009); Director of Agricultural Development.

7

Quality and Employability Aspects of Rural Labour Force in Gujarat

Niti Mehta

Gujarat is one of the most industrialized and fast growing states in the country. During the 10th Five-Year Plan, the state grew annually at a rate of 10.4 per cent, considerably higher than the national average of 7.6 per cent per annum. Gujarat contributes nearly 6.5 per cent of the country's gross domestic product. The state has experienced rapid industrial growth in the post-reform period triggered by good physical infrastructure, productive labour force, and a prolonged record of a pro-business government. The liberalization process seems to have benefited the state more than other states. There is a high level of urbanization (nearly 38%) and the state is relatively more urbanized than rest of the country. Gujarat as it bifurcated from Bombay state made a clear choice in according priority to productive activities particularly the industrial sector, vis-à-vis creation of social overhead capital. A long coastline also helped urban-based development processes.

A major constraint in the growth is the inadequacy of natural resources, which are also unevenly distributed and managed inefficiently. Soils in Gujarat are generally rich but the cost of cultivation of food grains is relatively high. In addition, the state has limited mineral base. Its water resources are scarce and the regional variation in the availability of rainfall is very high. Energy resources in the state are limited. The state also faces severe problems of environmental degradation in several regions, which is reflected in declining vegetation, soil erosion, deforestation, waterlogging, and increased salinity of land and water.

The state is also characterized by large spatial imbalances in the levels of development. Development is biased in favour of areas having proximity to the urban corridors, which also attract the largest magnitude of investment flows. Industrial development in the state is specialized in nature and concentrated in certain pockets. The remote hilly areas in the east and to the south have witnessed little growth per capita of income or employment. Regional imbalances are glaring and growing. The development gains have trickled down unevenly among rural and urban areas, developed and backward pockets, and scheduled and non-scheduled sections of the population. Education and health care facilities face problems of delivery and access. The selective path of development in the state has thus posed major impediments to distributive justice. For this reason, the effective use of human resources for realizing the full potential of the economy requires careful analysis of the economic structure.

In the ongoing dynamic macro-economic situation, this paper highlights the employability aspect for the rural workforce. Unfortunately, we have not dealt with the education profile of the workforce (such data are available only for 2001). The same holds good for information on the level of education or dropout rates. The latter's relevance is far greater for the education system, rather than the employment aspect per se. We have concentrated instead on the extent to which the rural labour force has the capability for full time employment. Second, we have paid particular attention to the rural workers who are fully employed in the non-primary sectors of the economy. Such sections of the labour force are considered to possess a higher scale of intrinsic employment quality and capability. Third, we look at the extent to which the workers have shifted and/or have the ability to engage in urban jobs. The recent growth process has not been employment augmenting type in urban areas and hence entry to the urban labour markets is highly restricted. It is possible that shift to urban jobs is an outcome of distress factors pushing workers out from the rural areas. Under such conditions, the displaced eke out a living from inhospitable conditions, but display considerable enterprise in seeking fortunes outside the rural environment. The extent to which such influences occur vary depending on locational factors and hence in this paper we proceed with the analysis by forming typologies of districts.

In the next section, we trace the economic growth experience of Gujarat. It also profiles the resource base of the selected districts and the state at large. The section deals with commodity production, specifically cropping patterns, output, and productivity aspects. An attempt is made to establish a relationship between the resource base with commodity production aspects. This at present is done by simple correspondence, rather than rigorous analysis. In the third section, we trace the employment processes at the state and district levels. Since time series analysis for all districts would become far too unwieldy, we confine our discussions to a cross-section of selected districts. Employment shared by broad categories of primary, secondary, and tertiary sectors is arrived at for the state and the districts. At the district level, this analysis is done for two points of time, i.e., 1998 and 2005. We would like to state at the outset that given the limitations of data, our conclusions need to be treated with caution. The broad conclusions deserve to be strengthened with detailed analysis backed by field studies. Unfortunately, at present, no systematic information has been generated that could help in resolving the main issues addressed in this paper. The final section culls out broad relations between output and employment aspects and also highlights the forces shaping the employment patterns across different categories of districts. Finally, the policy conclusions follow.

Growth Experience and Nature of Output

In the 1980s, in terms of growth profile, Gujarat lagged behind the nation in nearly all sectors. In the 1990s, the state grew at 8.1 per cent per annum – this was in fact the highest recorded growth among the major states. In the 2000s, the overall economy grew at 7.8 per cent per annum (Table 1). With regard to the pattern of inter-sectoral growth, the agriculture sector grew negatively in the 1980s and continued to decline in the 1990s. However, official statistics reveal a high growth in agriculture since the early years of the 2000s, averaging at 8.6 per cent per annum. The sectoral share of agriculture has risen from 14.5 per cent to 15.3 per cent, even though the output from allied activities to agriculture is dwindling. Allied activities are growing at 1 per cent per year. A large proportion of the population is still dependent on agriculture, where the fall in its relative share to total labour force was not as steep as that in output. The relative sectoral product per worker (RSPW) for primary sector, a crucial variable in this respect, had declined from 0.61 (1983–1984) to 0.43 (1993–1994) and further to 0.35 (1999–2000) (Kashyap and Mehta, 2007). It is heartening to note that the index based on estimates of NSDP in 2006–2007 revealed some improvement of the RSPW for the primary sector at 0.40, perhaps due to decline in the labour force in agriculture. Improvement in RSPW implies improvement in labour productivity in primary sector and reduction in rural–urban inequalities. Favourable weather conditions in the present decade have led to the upswing in the rate of agricultural growth in Gujarat. Efforts of the government by way of improved extension services and increase in small irrigation projects in hitherto dry regions may also have contributed to reversal of the long drawn process of agriculture stagnation in the state (Gulati et al., 2009).

The liberalization process had considerable impact on the state's economy. The secondary sector experienced growth acceleration to 8 per cent in the 1990s, though in the 2000s the pace somewhat decelerated to 7.2 per cent per annum. Manufacturing that grew at 8.3 per cent throughout the 1980s and 1990s also faced a slow down at 7.4 per cent after 2000. The tertiary sector witnessed a similar growth pattern in the 1990s, with transport, storage, communications, business, and insurance sub-sectors recording the fastest growth. Even during the 2000s, the tertiary sector grew fastest at 8.5 per cent per annum. The highest growth was recorded in sub-sectors involving trade, hotels, and transport, etc. Undoubtedly, the 2000s has seen the revival of the primary sector in terms of output growth, but inter-sectoral growth variations persist, pointing towards an unbalanced nature of economic growth in the state. Nonetheless the widening disparity that marked the primary and non-primary sectors during the 1990s has possibly narrowed in the early part of the 2000s, responding to a high growth in agriculture output.

Table 1

Share of Economic Activity in Gross State Domestic Product (%)

Sectors	*1999–2000*	*2006–2007*	*Annual growth*
Agriculture	14.5	15.3	8.6
Allied activities	1.6	1	1
Mining and quarrying	2.5	1.9	3.8
Primary sector	*18.6*	*18.2*	*7.5*
Manufacturing and repairs	30.8	29.9	7.4
Electricity, gas and water	2.7	2.6	7.1
Construction	5.8	5.3	6.6
Secondary sector	*39.2*	*37.8*	*7.2*
Trade and hotels	12.2	16.6	12.6
Transport, storage and communications	6.4	8.9	13
Financial, banking and real estate	6.6	5.8	5.8
Other services	16.9	12.6	3.4
Tertiary sector	*42.2*	*44*	*8.5*
Total	100	100	7.8

Source: Statistical Abstract of Gujarat State, 2009.

We now look at the resource base for the districts and relate with the overall economy. Table 2 examines the agro-climatic features, extent of irrigation development and input use in the selected districts. These districts represent two categories of agricultural conditions in Gujarat – one where food grains dominate the cropping pattern and the other having a highly diversified crop sector. For representing the varied agro-climatic and socio-economic conditions prevailing in

Table 2

Resource Profile of the State and Districts

District	*Agro-climatic region*	*Climate*	*Rainfall (mm)*	*TE 2005–2006 (%)*				*Cropping intensity*	*2003*	*2008–2009*
				% of NIA		*NIA*	*GIA*		*Tractors/ 00ha*	*NPK (kg/ha)*
				Surface	*Ground*	*to NSA*	*to GCA*		*NSA*	*NSA*
Category 1: Food grain-based agriculture										
Anand	Middle Guj	Semi arid	904	46.5	53.5	99.3	81	157.7	3.2	221
SK	North Guj	Arid to semi arid	735	14.7	85.3	36.3	38.2	119.2	2.2	149
Category 2: Diversified agriculture										
Surat	South Guj	Semi arid to dry subhumid	974	66.2	33.8	58.2	58.5	112.3	1.7	230
Valsad	South hills	do	1793	39.8	60.2	39.6	40.5	109.4	0.6	118
Amreli	Saurashtra	Semi arid	537	6.2	93.8	21.6	22.9	106.7	1.2	101
Gujarat				*21.1*	*78.9*	*36.9*	*38.5*	*116.5*	*1.5*	*112*

Gujarat, the districts selected are Anand and Sabarkantha under Category 1 and Surat, Valsad, and Amreli under Category 2, each belonging to different agro-climatic sub-regions of the state. Time series comparison across districts has been done to observe the changes in the cropping patterns. Output and productivity aspects are also highlighted.

Table 2 shows the resource profile. In Gujarat during TE 2006, around 37 per cent of the sown area was irrigated, that led to a cropping intensity of 116.5 per cent. Groundwater irrigated roughly 79 per cent and surface sources 21 per cent of the total area cultivated. Anand, located in the middle Gujarat region is a highly developed district agriculturally with almost the entire cultivated area under irrigation, chiefly by underground sources. Surface irrigation is dominant here. Agriculture in the district is highly mechanized as seen from the above state-level tractor usage. Abundant availability of water has led to intensive use of fertilizers. All these factors have contributed to exceedingly high cropping patterns in the Anand district. Sabarkantha belonging to the northern arid sub-region has poorly developed irrigation (36%), mainly through ground water sources, leading to much lower cropping intensity and fertilizer consumption. Agriculture here is not as mechanized as in Anand.

In Surat (southern plains region), 58 per cent of the sown area is irrigated, which is considerably higher than the state average. Agriculture here is more mechanized than other districts of this category. High capital intensity in agriculture is reflected in fertilizer use that is much above the state average. Here surface irrigation, notably canals account for 66 per cent of the total irrigated area and has led to cultivation of highly water-intensive crops. Valsad belonging to the southern hills region has irrigation mostly through underground sources. Amreli in Saurashtra has poorly developed irrigation facilities, largely through wells and tube wells. Agriculture practiced in these two districts is rudimentary and use of purchased inputs is very limited. Scarcity of water has led to low cropping intensity in these two districts.

Table 3

Cropping Pattern in Gujarat and Selected Districts, TE 1983 to 2004

District	*Year*	*Total cereals*	*Total pulses*	*Total food grains*	*Ground-nut*	*Total oilseeds*	*Sugar-cane*	*Cotton*	*Others*
Category 1: Food grain-based agriculture									
Kheda*	TE 1983	59.2	4.4	63.6	3.9	6.3	0.1	7.1	22.9
	TE 1988	61.5	4.8	66.3	1.7	4.5	0.1	3.5	25.6
	TE 1993	61.8	4.7	66.4	1.6	6	0.1	2.4	25
	TE 1998	63.1	4.6	67.7	1	6	0.2	1.9	24.1
	TE 2004	61.5	3.6	65.1	0.2	5.3	0	2.7	27
Sabar-kantha	TE 1983	45.9	9.3	51.9	10	13.9	0.2	23.1	10.9
	TE 1988	46.5	14.6	61.1	6.5	12.7	0.1	18.9	7.2
	TE 1993	49.9	18.9	68.7	3.8	18.8	0.1	3.8	8.6
	TE 1998	50	16.5	66.4	4.4	17	0.1	5.5	10.9
	TE 2004	41.5	14.9	56.4	7.5	16.5	0	6.8	20.2
Category 2: Diversified agriculture									
Surat	TE 1983	43.8	13.8	57.5	4.3	5	11.7	6.8	19
	TE 1988	42.3	14.1	56.3	3.3	3.7	16.4	3.7	19.8
	TE 1993	38.2	12.8	50.9	5.8	6.1	23.7	1.4	17.9
	TE 1998	36.7	10.4	47.1	4.9	5.2	29.5	1.2	17
	TE 2004	32	8.5	40.5	4.1	4.4	25.7	1.1	28.3
Amreli	TE 1983	30.7	1.4	32.1	61.4	65.3	1.6	4.8	-3.9
	TE 1988	25.9	0.6	26.5	59.4	62.5	1.2	4.3	5.5
	TE 1993	21.9	0.8	22.7	56.6	65.1	1.2	5.8	5.3
	TE 1998	19.5	1.6	21.2	50.3	58	1.2	15	4.6
	TE 2004	11.3	2	13.3	51.4	59.2	0	18	9.5
Valsad	TE 1983	43.1	11.1	54.3	0.5	1.4	2.8	0.5	41.1
	TE 1988	41	9.8	50.8	0.2	1	5.4	0	42.9
	TE 1993	39	8.7	47.7	0.2	0.9	8.9	0	42.5
	TE 1998	36.8	7.5	44.3	0.3	1.1	12.6	0	42.1
	TE 2004	35.6	6.5	42	0.1	0.7	12.3	0	44.9
Gujarat	TE 1983	40.3	7.9	46.3	19.8	24.7	1	14.1	14
	TE 1988	40.7	8.4	49.2	17.8	23.7	1.3	12.4	13.4
	TE 1993	35.6	8.7	44.3	17.6	26.7	1.6	10.7	16.7
	TE 1998	32.8	8.1	40.9	16.6	26	2.1	14	17
	TE 2004	27.3	7	34.3	17.9	26.9	1.8	15.4	21.5

*Includes Anand and Kheda.

Source: Directorate of Agriculture, GoG.

Cropping pattern in the state is dictated by resource availability – water (irrigation and rainfall), soil type, and climate. Table 3 depicts the changes in cropping pattern for the districts belonging to the two categories of agriculture. Overall, Gujarat is predominantly a non-food crop economy. The share of food grains has been declining continuously and giving way to commercial crops such as oilseeds, cotton, and 'other crops' notably fruits, vegetables, flowers, spices, medicinal, and fodder crops combined. Cropping pattern in Anand and Sabarkantha is dominated by food crops. However, a distinction needs to be made between the two districts. In Anand, since TE 1983, share of food grains has remained nearly stagnant at 64–65 per cent of the gross cropped area. Crop diversification is thus of halting nature, even though the category of 'other crops' has gained in TE 2004 over TE 1983. Share of cereals has remained constant, but cultivation of pulses has declined in recent times. However, within the category of cereals the finer ones, mainly rice and wheat, are continuously replacing the coarser cereals and pulses. Sabarkantha which belongs to the dry region and the tribal eastern tract of the state, agriculture is largely food grain based. It is quite likely here that small and marginal farmers grow food mainly for household consumption and enter into exchange only to meet meagre non-food requirements, thereby depicting tenets of subsistence agriculture. Among the food grains, there is dominance of pulses and coarser cereals such as maize. The cultivation of wheat has been significantly growing lately. Cash crops notably groundnut and 'other crops' are also expanding acreage, while the area under cotton has declined significantly in the district.

The remaining three districts have commercialized agriculture (Category 2) with varying degrees and nature of crop diversification. In Amreli, this highly diversified nature is manifested in oilseeds, mostly groundnut cultivation which dominates the cropping pattern, though the latter is slowly giving way to *rabi* oilseeds. Cotton cultivation has made significant strides in the district. In Surat, the abundant availability of canal water has prompted considerable expansion of area under sugarcane cultivation. 'Other crops' too have gained importance. These crops together with sugarcane accounted for 54 per cent of the gross cropped area in the district during TE 2004. The area under food grains has been shrinking continuously in Surat; this phenomenon has also been noted in Valsad. Sugarcane on the other hand has gained prominence. Nearly 45 per cent of the district's cultivated area was under 'other crops', mainly fruits, vegetables, and flowers that have a large urban market. More areas are now under cultivation of 'other crops', thus reflecting the deflection from traditional cropping practices. However, many factors have influenced the change in this direction, foremost being infrastructure, facilitating exports, value addition, and cost of production.

Output levels of major crops and their growth in the recent past show that food grains have shown buoyancy in the less developed districts such as Sabarkantha. In contrast, fruits, vegetables, flowers, and other commercial crops have forged ahead at a high rate in Valsad and Amreli. It could be due to the growing market demand for such crops in the proximate urban centres and possibly due to global demands. However, this aspect is not reflected in Surat. The district had experienced high growth in some commodities in the past and has perhaps reached near stagnation, while Valsad, Amreli, and Anand had the scope to avail of emerging opportunities in the non-rural areas.

In all the districts, there are considerable gaps in the yields achieved and the maximum recorded for the state and even the country. This is so for nearly all the crops, and particularly true for irrigated rice, wheat, maize, pulses, groundnut, sugarcane, and cotton. This indicates that agriculture, whether food grain dominant or diversified, is marked by deficiencies in production. There is nonetheless considerable scope for enhancement in the yield levels of all major crops cultivated across the cross-section of districts in the state. It indicates the need for better management of land and water resources and improvement in input use in nearly all the regions. Improvements in productivity are desired to increase profitability and to narrow the gap between agricultural and non-agricultural incomes. Agriculture in the state still holds the key for productive employment for the majority of the workforce especially in the rural sector. Labour productivity is significantly tied to output levels besides labour absorption in the primary sectors. Developments in agriculture have also been historically linked to decline in rural poverty and ushering in prosperity and growth in rural areas.

In the above context, recent studies (Joshi, 1995; Hashim et al., 2000) to ascertain yield gap across states of the country and their sub-regions offered important insights. It has been shown that between triennium ending 1989 and 1996, across the state sub-regions and for selected crops where the yield levels surpassed the maximum achievable yield, in most cases there was a rise in fertilizer consumption and irrigation development. Also in cases where the narrowing of yield gap was more than 10 per cent, both factors seemed to play a major role. The worrying feature was that in large areas of food crops, yield gaps had either widened or a very slow progress was seen over the 7-year period towards raising the productivity levels. Moreover, it was noted that the yield gap analysis requires updating over recent years. Technological enhancement however is imperative to diminish the existing yield gaps. Without technological change, labour can only be absorbed into agriculture at falling labour productivity levels and conditions may arise leading to 'agricultural involution', particularly where employment generation in non-farm sector is tardy.

Notwithstanding that employment elasticity with reference to agriculture is not very high and is in fact falling, it does not negate the possibilities for enhancing opportunities for employment in agriculture. The process of labour absorption in agriculture sector is already strained and productive employment may become restricted due to rising capital labour substitution. While land constraint compounds the issue of reducing labour intensity in agriculture, the green revolution through expansion of gross cropped area (GCA) and cropping pattern shifts towards labour-intensive crops saved the overall employment situation. Technological changes and diversification towards labour-intensive crops can achieve high rates of labour absorption associated with rising labour productivity. However, this would still lead to employment generation but of a lower order. Also, past experience shows that in developed regions land augmenting technological change eventfully gives way to labour-saving technologies (greater mechanization), causing a fall in the labour absorption. In this context, faster generation of non-farm employment opportunities for rural workers assumes relevance. We shall next examine employment changes in rural Gujarat in the recent two decades.

Changes in Rural Workforce Composition

Availability of remunerative employment is the most important determinant of material well-being. The main features of the employment scene in Gujarat and the changes in the decades of 1990s and 2000s assume importance in this respect. The real challenge that the state economy faces is how to remain on a high growth trajectory and usher in a people-centred development process. Equitable growth process is essentially related to the associated labour use pattern. The decade of the 1990s coincided with the onset of the liberalization process in the Indian economy and would be dealt with along with developments in the 2000s. Table 4 captures changes in worker participation by region and sex during 1991 to 2007–2008.

Table 4

Worker Participation Rates in Gujarat, 1991 to 2007–08

	1991			*2001*			*2007–08*		
	Male	*Female*	*Total*	*Male*	*Female*	*Total*	*Male*	*Female*	*Total*
Main worker									
Rural	54.4	17.7	36.5	50.3	18.8	35	59.6	24.4	42.5
Urban	50.9	6	29.5	52.3	7.1	31.2	59.1	9.9	36.4
Total	53.2	13.7	34.1	51.1	14.6	33.6	59.4	18.8	40.1
Marginal worker									
Rural	0.5	17.9	9	5.1	19.7	12.2	0.6	11.5	5.9
Urban	0.2	1.2	0.7	1.6	2.2	1.8	0.2	3.2	1.6
Total	0.4	12.2	6.1	3.8	13.3	8.3	0.4	8.3	4.2
Total worker									
Rural	54.9	35.6	45.5	55.5	38.5	47.2	60.2	35.9	48.4
Urban	51.1	7.2	30.2	53.9	9.3	33	59.3	13.1	38
Total	53.6	26	40.2	54.9	27.9	41.9	59.8	27.1	44.3

Source: For 1991 and 2001, Census of India; for 2007–2008, estimated as described in Annexure 1.

Information for 1991 and 2001 is obtained from the Population Census. Workforce for the year 2007–2008 is estimated by applying the NSSO worker participation rates (WPR) to the projected population for the state. Detailed methodology used to arrive at the district-level workforce estimates is given in Annexure 1. Workforce estimates for the year 2007–2008 are approximations and hence there is need to view them with caution.

It may be noted as follows:

(a) Between 1991 and 2001, the percentage of main workers in rural areas fell by nearly 6 percentage points (from 70% to 64%). The fall in total number of workers was less steep at 3.4 per cent, as during this period the proportion of marginal workers in the rural population rose from 9 per cent to 12.2 per cent (Table 4).

(b) During 2001 to 2007–2008, the fall in workers in the rural areas is only by 1 per cent. However, the decline in the proportion of the total rural workers (from 70.5 per cent to 66%) was quite steep, largely contributed by the sharp fall in marginal workers in rural areas (as percentage of rural population marginal workers declined from 12.2 to 6). Despite the falling share of rural workers in the total workforce, in absolute terms, almost 1.8 million workers were added in rural areas during 2000s. (This scenario is the reverse of the 1990s when, in absolute figures, the increase was of far more rural workers.) In rural areas, the absolute numbers of marginal workers also fell, while the increase in total rural workers was due to the addition of main workers. In urban Gujarat, only 0.1 million marginal workers, as against nearly 3.8 million main workers, were added. The evidence suggests a definitive shift towards urban jobs along with declining marginalization of rural workers.

(c) The above trends are reflected in WPR (Table 4). In the 1990s, WPR fell steeply for rural males, but there was a sharp rise in the WPR of rural male marginal workers. Also notable was the rise in female participation rates in all categories (rural, urban, main, and marginal). For the total number of workers, the WPR rose in 2001 (from 40.2% to

42%). This was in contrast to the picture at all-India level, as labour force participation rates had gone down for all age groups, in both rural and urban areas (Kashyap and Mehta, 2005).

(d) The 2000s presented a different picture. For rural male main workers, the WPR rose sharply (50.3–59.6%), but there was a fall in the WPR for rural male marginal workers (5.1–0.6%). The WPR of rural (male + female) marginal workers also fell very steeply from 12.2 per cent to 6 per cent in 2007–2008. With regard to female WPR, there was an increasing trend in rural main workers (14.6–18.8%), this was true in urban areas too. Female marginal WPR in rural areas declined sharply (19.7–11.5%) which caused the overall decline in female marginal WPR. However, the female urban WPR rose quite substantially from 9.3 per cent to 13.1 per cent. It is obvious that the latest trends suggest a reversal of trends from the earlier decade.

Table 5

Changes in Workforce Composition for Typologies of Districts (1991 to 2007–08)

District	*Rural*			*Urban*		
	1991	*2001*	*2007–2008*	*1991*	*2001*	*2007–2008*
Category 1: Food grain-based agriculture						
Anand						
Main workers	79	75.6	74.4	21	24.4	25.6
Marginal workers	96.9	88.8	78	3.1	11.2	22
Total workers	82	78.4	74.8	18	21.6	25.2
Sabarkantha						
Main workers	91.5	90.4	86.9	8.5	9.6	13.1
Marginal workers	98.8	97.4	95.7	1.2	2.6	2.3
Total workers	93.1	92.5	91	6.9	7.5	9
Category 2: Diversified agriculture						
Surat						
Main workers	56.4	43.2	42.2	43.6	56.8	57.8
Marginal workers	95.8	85.8	74.6	4.2	14.2	25.4
Total workers	60	47.2	43.6	40	52.8	56.4

Cont'd...

...*Cont'd*

Amreli						
Main workers	79.7	80.1	79.1	20.3	19.9	20.9
Marginal workers	93.5	93.9	87.4	6.5	6.1	12.6
Total workers	81.9	83.1	80.1	18.1	16.9	19.9
Valsad						
Main workers	82.7	73.4	72.3	17.3	26.6	27.7
Marginal workers	97.3	94.2	89	2.7	5.8	11
Total workers	85.4	78.1	74	14.6	21.9	26
Gujarat						
Main workers	70.2	65.3	64.1	29.8	34.7	35.9
Marginal workers	96.1	91.8	85	3.90	8.20	15
Total workers	74.1	70.6	66.1	25.9	29.4	33.9

Source: Same as Table 4.

An analysis of workforce composition data suggests that as the globalization forces take root, the opportunity set in rural Gujarat is changing. Workers staying in rural areas also have increasing access to full time employment. However, there are sections of workers unable to eke out a living in the rural areas, such as landless labourers, marginal farmers, and artisans. They are becoming part of the ever increasing marginal workforce brigade in the urban areas. Again distress factors are actively operational in the rural areas. Such a process is also strengthening in urban areas where informalization is forging ahead.

We will now look at the regional picture and the main features of workforce composition and variations among the selected districts. We first list the changes in the districts having food-grain-oriented cropping pattern, that is Sabarkantha and Anand. This is followed by employment accounting in the diversified agriculture districts of Amreli, Surat, and Valsad (Table 5).

- *Sabarkantha:* The proportion of rural total workers has declined from 1991 onwards. The decline is steeper for rural main workers (by 4.6 percentage points) resulting in increased marginalization of workforce in this less developed district. In absolute terms, additions to the total workforce of 0.09 million in rural areas were noted between 2001 and 2007–2008. Absolute numbers of marginal workers increased despite a declining rural proportion as the share of population, marginal workers increased from 10.7 per cent (1991) to 18.5 per cent (2007–2008). Thus, the marginalization process witnessed in the 1990s had strengthened further in the 2000s. It is seen that workers are moving out of the overburdened primary sector to urban areas in search of livelihood opportunities, either as part time or as full time workers.

- *Anand:* Despite having an agriculture based predominantly on food grain cultivation, the nature of economy in Anand is distinct from the tribal and less developed Sabarkantha district. During 1991 to 2001, the percentage of rural main workers fell by 3.4 percentage points, but the fall in the total number of workers was steeper. This was so as a proportion of marginal workers in the rural areas declined steeply by 8 percentage points. As in the rest of Gujarat, the process of marginalization of rural labour force vis-à-vis urban in Anand has notably reversed in the 2000s. Second, the absolute numbers of marginal workers in rural areas also fell steeply, their share in rural population falling from 11 per cent to 5.1 per cent. Urban areas are seemingly more attractive in terms of employment, though the quality of jobs is deteriorating. Migration of workers from the surrounding districts may also lead to increased informalization of workforce in urban centres of the district.
- *Amreli:* In the 1990s, the proportion of rural main workers remained unchanged, though the proportion of rural workers had increased. In absolute terms, additions to the rural workforce were more pronounced in the category of marginal workers than main workers, following the macro trends. In the 2000s, estimates show that while the proportion of rural main workers remained constant, the fall in total workers was far steeper (by 2.9 percentage points), contributed by a downward slide in the proportion of rural marginal workers. Even in absolute terms, their share in rural population registered reduction from 11.4 per cent to 9 per cent in 2007–2008. The trends clearly suggest that agriculture is overburdened and further jobs are not being

generated in rural areas, leading to migration towards urban employment. However, workers staying back have greater access to full-time employment opportunities.

- *Surat:* The district belongs to the southern plains region with a diversified agricultural pattern and developed secondary and tertiary sectors. The 1990s was marked by a fall in rural main workers by 13.2%. During this period, the proportion of rural marginal workers also declined steeply indicating large-scale shift of workers to urban locations. Additions to the urban workforce were more pronounced in the category of main workers. During the 2000s, the percentage of rural main workers remained stagnant but the share of marginal rural workers continued to fall sharply (from 85% to 74.6%) along with their absolute numbers, indicating that marginalization in rural areas was on the wane. It is a positive sign that the share of marginal workforce in rural and urban populations has nearly halved in Surat district.
- *Valsad:* This district belongs to the golden corridor in Gujarat having proximity to urban and industrial centres. By 2001, the proportion of rural main workers declined from 83 per cent to 73 per cent and not much change was reported thereafter. The share of total rural workers continued its downward trend by nearly 11.4 per cent in the last 17 years indicating a shift of workers to urban centres. The share of rural marginal workers in the rural population has halved from 13.4 per cent to 6.1 per cent and urban areas show a picture of enhanced marginalization of the spill over from the workforce.

Evidence on the regional patterns can be summarized by noting that the percentage of rural workers in the total workforce was high in some of the less developed districts, such as Sabarkantha and Amreli. It was also relatively high in developed districts such as Valsad and Anand. But the difference lies in that in developed districts the proportion of urban workforce was forging ahead rapidly. It was already very high in Surat, which was possibly due to the city of Surat having job opportunities in the textile, diamond polishing, and other secondary/tertiary sectors. Regions having progressive and diversified agriculture and those with larger degree of urbanization witnessed a decrease in the extent of marginalization of the workforce in their rural locations. However, a shift towards urban jobs does not necessarily indicate secure livelihoods. What about occupational structure? We will now examine the available, though highly limited evidence for Gujarat as well as the five representative districts. This is shown in Tables 6–8.

Table 6

Industrial Distribution of Rural Workforce (Main Workers), 1991 and 2001

	1991				*2001*			
	Cultivators	*Agriculture labour*	*HHI* workers*	*Other workers*	*Cultivators*	*Agriculture labour*	*HHI* workers*	*Other workers*
Category 1: Food grain-based agriculture								
Anand	35.6	39	2.5	23	23.8	42.7	2.2	31.4
Sabarkantha	53.4	24.4	1.7	20.5	38.7	28.7	1.5	31.2
Category 2: Diversified agriculture								
Surat	34.2	40	1.5	24.3	25.1	44.5	1.6	28.8
Amreli	46.7	25.8	1.1	26.5	44.9	29	1.5	24.6
Valsad	48.6	24.3	0.1	27	36.2	29.4	1.6	32.8
Gujarat	*46.1*	*30.7*	*1.4*	*21.8*	*41.6*	*26.3*	*1.7*	*30.5*

Note: Workers in Household Industries.

Source: Census of India.

The population census showed that in Gujarat there was a decline in the proportion of cultivators and agricultural labourers between 1991 and 2001 by around 9 per cent (from 46.1% to 41.6% and 30.7% to 26.3%, respectively). In the rural areas, agriculture is absorbing declining proportion of workforce. The reducing number of workers in agriculture indicates distinct rural occupational diversification. However, due to changes in the census category of workers, it cannot be stated conclusively whether the workforce has increased in the non-crop segment of agriculture or towards secondary and service activities. Household industries continued to account for 1.4–1.7 per cent of the workforce. The proportion of 'other workers' rose rapidly, this terminology is unfortunately a rather loose category. Rural employment analysis would gain in relevance if the 'other' category of workforce could be further disaggregated. The need for greater details is imperative in order to arrive at the location-specific issues.

For further evidence, we look at NSSO data to ascertain changes in industrial distribution of workers in Gujarat. This is based on the concept of 'persons usually employed by principal status' which comes close to the census definition of 'main workers'. Table 7 gives employment in Gujarat by location for 1983–1984 to 2007–2008. The census underestimates women participation ratios and hence suffers from inadequacies. The employment data generated by NSSO is largely free from such difficulties.

Table 7

Distribution of Usually Employed by Principal Status: Activity and Location, Gujarat, 1983 to 2007–08

	Rural				*Urban*			
	P	*S*	*T*	*Total*	*P*	*S*	*T*	*Total*
1983	83.64	8.28	8.08	100	14.80	36.48	48.72	100
1993–1994	77.12	13.37	9.51	100	6.09	42.20	51.67	100
1999–2000	78.40	10.70	10.90	100	9	33.60	57.40	100
2004–2005	75.58	11.91	12.51	100	6.89	43.46	49.75	100
2007–2008	73.50	13.90	12.60	100	4.80	44.90	50.30	100

Note: Per cent of each sector to total workforce. P: Primary, S: Secondary, T: Tertiary

Source: For 1983 and 1994 from Kashyap and Mehta (2005). For remaining years derived from NSSO, Employment–Unemployment Surveys.

The composition of the workforce is changing in both rural and urban areas and primary sector share has declined continuously in the rural areas, indicating a significant occupational diversification. During the 1990s, the workforce stagnated in rural areas. After 1999–2000, evidence suggests a gradual decline in the agriculture in rural areas and this slow pace of rural workforce diversification was shared equally by the secondary and tertiary sectors. Tertiary sector employment has halted at 12.6 per cent, while the secondary sector has risen from 11 per cent to 14 per cent. The primary sector however continues to be the dominant employment provider in rural Gujarat. As compared to 2004–2005 nearly 0.88 million workers shifted out of the primary sector by 2007–2008.

In urban areas, the secondary sector showed decline after 1993–1994, but since then has forged ahead. The tertiary sector has fluctuated in a narrow range, but there is an overall upward trend, and now half of the workforce in urban Gujarat is engaged in tertiary activities. We have refrained from including statistics for 1987–1988, as this was an abnormal year due to widespread drought.

To ascertain the regional picture, examining first the broad census worker categories for type 1 districts of Anand and Sabarkantha shows that rural agricultural workforce declined from 77.8 per cent to 67.4 per cent and 74.6 per cent to 66.5 per cent respectively (Table 6). In Category 2 districts of Surat and Valsad too, primary workers had declined to reach 69.6 per cent and 65.6 per cent respectively in 2001. Amreli is an exception, depicting increase in the agricultural workforce from 72.5 per cent to 74 per cent, largely due to the increasing proportion of agricultural labourers. The number of cultivators has fallen uniformly across the cross-section of the districts. The category of 'other workers' gained in all except Amreli. Household industry constituted a miniscule share of the rural workforce and did not report any variation across the districts. Except Amreli, all other districts reported rural occupation diversification in the 1990s.

Detailed sub-state information on sectoral break up of workers is not readily available either from the Population Census or NSSO. Hence to ascertain the changes in sectoral pattern of employment for the districts, we resort to information available from the Economic Census (EC) and compare changes in 2005 over 1998. EC as is well known, being enterprise based, under-enumerates the workers. Further, it does not provide information of employment in the crop sector, but only the allied agricultural sectors along with secondary and tertiary sector enterprises. However, the trends across districts can be easily discerned.

From EC data, it can be seen that in the year 2005 over 1998, employment in allied agricultural activities gained marginally from 21.2 per cent to 22.8 per cent in Gujarat. Roughly 1.27 million workers were added to these activities in the overall economy. This roughly constitutes 6.4 per cent of the total workforce in 2004–2005 (a decline from 10% ascertained for 1999–2000). In 1991, according to the Population Census, allied activities engaged 3.6 per cent of the main workforce. Despite differences in estimates from varied sources, the long-term trend strongly suggests significant changes within the diversification in the primary sector in rural Gujarat.

Table 8 provides changes in the industrial distribution of workers across the districts in the early part of the 2000s. Allied activities despite their falling numbers in employment continue to be prominent in Anand and Sabarkantha. In Anand, this may be due to the booming animal husbandry sector (milk and milk products). Anand is a progressive agricultural district with considerable specialized food crops but has very little employment in the secondary sector in rural areas. The backwardness of agriculture and the paucity of resources in Sabarkantha finds reflection in the underdeveloped nature of the macro economy. Secondary employment is declining in rural Sabarkantha and in 2005 comprised a minuscule share of 6.7 per cent of workers. Allied activities mainly livestock rearing and dairying also engage large segments of rural workers in Sabarkantha.

In rural Surat, the allied sector gained in prominence (from 38.7 to 43.3). Valsad also showed an increase in its share (22%). Secondary activities once dominant in rural areas have recorded a sharp decline in these developed districts. Even in Amreli, despite its proximity to the industrial clusters of Saurashtra showed a steep decline in secondary employment. Tertiary activities on the other hand have moved ahead in all regions; in Amreli and Valsad more than half of the rural

Table 8

Employment in All Enterprises (OAEs and Establishments), 1998 and 2005 (Percentage to Total Workers)

	Food grain-based agriculture				*Diversified agriculture*						*Gujarat*	
	Anand		*Sabarkantha*		*Surat*		*Amreli*		*Valsad*			
1998	Rural	Urban	Rural	Urban	Rural	Urban	Rural	Urban	Rural	Urban	Rural	Urban
Primary (exc. crop sector)	73.6	6.9	69.6	3.1	38.7	0.8	18.7	3.2	17.9	2.5	44.9	2.3
Secondary	9.5	26.1	8.3	9.3	33.3	56	29.4	43.5	40.1	59.8	21.6	34.7
Tertiary	17.2	66.9	21.2	87.4	27	42.9	50.6	53.3	41.9	37.7	32.7	62.9
2005												
Primary (exc. crop sector)	74.9	9.7	64.7	4.4	43.3	0.9	18.1	5.7	21.9	1.4	45.6	2.5
Secondary	5.5	26.3	6.7	15	25.9	58.2	22.9	44.1	27.4	50.1	16.5	36.9
Tertiary	19.6	63.9	28.6	80.6	30.8	40.9	59	50.2	50.7	48.4	37.9	60.7

Source: Economic Census, 1998, 2005 (GoG, 2000, 2010).

workers (excluding crop sector) were engaged in tertiary sector. It is apparent that in developed districts with vibrant industrial sector, rural areas share backward linkages with manufacturing, repairs, and service activities. Diversified and commercial agriculture further reinforces employment in the non-primary sector. Amreli, on the other hand, presents a situation where stagnancy in agriculture and secondary sectors forces people to move towards petty trading, traditional transport activities, and other tertiary activities for livelihoods. Possibly in Surat and Valsad, the pattern of rural employment diversification reflects an outflow of the urban growth. In these districts, significant agricultural prosperity and urban manufacturing are not necessarily mutually exclusive. Their effects cannot be isolated, yet urban influence, the surplus generated in the farming sector and access to infrastructure interact to explain growth-induced occupational diversification.

Recent experience of urban areas shows a somewhat contrasting picture. Secondary sector employment is rising nearly everywhere, except in Valsad where outside forces may be responsible for drop in employment in secondary activities. Services have shown a steep rise in Valsad. There has been a secular decline in the proportion of workers engaged in tertiary activities in other regions. These factors in any case largely comprise the non-productive government, community, and social sector jobs where access is highly restricted. This is especially true for the less developed district of Sabarkantha.

Examination of the sectoral distribution of workers in the districts underlines the fact that within the state, there exists a relationship between the nature of commodity production, levels of output, and the development of non-farm sectors. This has implications for employability of rural workers. In districts with dominant non-food-crop-based agriculture and higher overall output, the nature of employment pattern is oriented towards 'modern' sectors. Location factors and proximity to industrial units play a role in reinforcing backward and forward consumption linkages between sectors. Sabarkantha comprising a large section of tribal population and backward agriculture activities with dominance of less remunerative food crops has fewer opportunities for employment generation in the modern sectors. Allied activities do offer opportunities for supplementing rural incomes. Anand on the other hand has a productive and specialized agriculture which is linked to the processing sector and a vibrant livestock economy. The available evidence, though mixed, indicates that apparently the nature of resource base and endogenous growth impulses are shaping employment outcomes in rural Gujarat. Interventions are however required that would upgrade productivity levels and hence incomes from the dominant economic activities. This would also encourage local (possibly home-based) employment opportunities and arrest the growing marginalization in urban areas.

Inferences about Employability and Policy Directions

The discussions in the preceding sections reveal that in the state, the diversification in the cropping pattern is taking place at a rapid pace. The state has a highly commercialized agricultural economy, even though the nature of crops varies across regions depending on the availability of resources. These tendencies are gaining strength as can be seen from the cross-section analysis. Apart from crop diversification, evidence reveals a growth within primary sector diversification. Having said that for the state, as also for the districts examined, it is apparent that rural areas and agriculture sectors (despite revival) are not providing adequate job opportunities. Though employment diversification is occurring in varying degrees across the state, it could possibly be distress driven. Further, jobs in non-primary sectors may not always be remunerative and of good quality, given the rising informal sector in urban areas.

Secondly, the shift from rural to urban locations is visible and the developed districts with diversified/commercial agriculture (Amreli, Valsad, and Surat) offer far greater urban employment opportunities to the rural migrants. However, the gradual shift towards urban locations, particularly in tertiary activities, is again a reflection of being pushed out from the overburdened agriculture sector and hence has distress connotations. It is indicative of growing informalization of urban workforce that is increasingly engaged in less remunerative and 'residual' tertiary jobs. In this context, access is required to education and skill enhancement opportunities in rural areas. Renewed efforts in this direction would help better prepare urban job seekers and open windows for a wider range of livelihood options.

Recent years have seen declining marginalization of the rural workforce and possible improvements in quality aspects for rural workers who stay back. In developed districts, not only have the share of rural marginal workers declined but their absolute numbers too have shrunk. On the other hand, in the underdeveloped Sabarkantha region, this is not so, even the absolute numbers of marginal workers is rising. This calls for special interventions for education and skill development to improve individual capabilities and also create better infra-structure and efforts to improve the productivity of primary sector activities.

The relationship between output and employment outcomes may seem ambiguous across different categories of districts. Given our data it cannot be conclusively stated that increased rural occupational diversification along with declining marginalization in rural workforce is commensurate with enhancement of productivity in the rural sector. It is quite apparent that apart from endogenous growth impulses, exogenous factors, at least in some locations could be far more active in shaping the employment aspect in rural Gujarat. Global processes are infiltrating and the rural areas cannot stay impervious to such forces.

If we look at the employment situation from the broader context of growth in Gujarat, there are disparities in terms of employment and poverty among social groups. This is in addition to the regional disparities. This aspect unfortunately has not been examined in greater detail in the current paper. The hill districts where tribal populations reside have not experienced trickle down of growth benefits and very little employment or income growth has been witnessed here. Scheduled tribes comprise 15 per cent of the population in Gujarat, yet 43 per cent of the rural poor are concentrated in this group. Poverty in the state is unevenly distributed among social groups (Mehta, 2006). It is a reflection of poor resource endowments of productive assets, low education standards, and little access to any kind of regular employment. Self-cultivation engages such population in large numbers, but there are severe impediments for agricultural growth in the remote tribal areas, which need to be corrected through appropriate interventions.

This paper could be further enriched by the inclusion of human development aspects. Even at the sub-district levels the employment study could gain if looked from a human development perspective. A recent study on human development of the Sabarkantha district at SPIESR (2009) throws up interesting results. Multi-dimensional view by means of radars gives a magnificent view of the facets of human development. But it also stresses the need for differentiated strategy across talukas, given the strong regional disparities within the district that need special attention in development planning. The study has outlined the need for urgent spatial mapping of strategies and is thus of immense policy relevance.

The analysis in this paper has important implications for policy makers and planners. Attention needs to be focussed on school education as also vocational training. Education is the key to expanding personal endowments and builds individual capabilities so that physical and social barriers can be surmounted. Education, in addition to improving labour productivity, will enable rural workers to make use of economic opportunities created by the growth process.

The agriculture sector has been the backbone of employment generation in the state. Support to the farming population and those who cannot move outside the agriculture sector is of primary concern. The ultimate solution would be to reduce population pressures on land through long-term policy packages that raise labour productivity of rural non-farm sector too. To meet this objective and given the land constraint, productivity growth in agriculture is very important. Enhancing income levels of those engaged in farming is also important to sustain their interest in making investments and raising productivity in agriculture. The government needs to create an enabling environment to stimulate the growth of agriculture and rural non-farm activities. Low returns from agriculture, mainly in tribal and backward areas practising food grain cultivation, need to be tackled by targeted extension, timely credit, and information services, which are also the key to promoting productive non-farm avenues.

Industries in Gujarat are concentrated in pockets. In this context, it is necessary to activate and develop industrial clusters around rural areas which promote diversification away from agriculture but also reduce marginalization and attendant informalization in urban centres. Further, training of workers and technical assistance would crucially stimulate rural entrepreneurship by encouraging micro enterprises. Besides a policy focus on agrarian reforms, promoting organizing efforts aimed at poor workers, can also serve as powerful vehicles to resist social, political, and economic oppression for rural labourers and poor peasants. Such steps would also encourage entrepreneurship in non-traditional sectors (Mehta, 2009). Thus, in these areas, voluntary agencies and local governments would have an important role to perform. It needs to be reiterated that government policies have to focus on human capital to enhance productivity in traditional sectors and also promote entrepreneurship geared at non-farm activities.

References

Government of Gujarat (2000). *Report on Fourth Economic Census, 1998, Gujarat State*. Directorate of Economics & Statistics, Gandhinagar.

Government of Gujarat (2010). *Statistical Abstract of Gujarat State, 2009*. Directorate of Economics & Statistics, Gandhinagar.

Government of India, NSSO (2010). *Employment and Unemployment Situation in India, 2007–08, NSS 64th Round (July 2007–June 2008)*. Ministry of Planning & Programme Implementation, New Delhi.

Gulati, A., Shah, T., and Shreedhar, G. (2009). *Agriculture Performance in Gujarat since 2000 – Can it Be Divadandi for Other States?* [Mimeo]. International Water Management Institute & International Food Policy Research Institute.

Hashim, S.R., Kashyap, S.P., and Joshi, S.N. (2000). *Agriculture and Rural Development* [Mimeo]. Paper submitted for UNU/IAS Project

Review Meeting on India's Sustainable Framework, March, SPIESR, New Delhi.

Joshi, S.N. (1995). 'Yield gap analysis in agro-climatic sub-regions', *Agro-climatic Regional Planning in India, Vol II, Themes and Case Studies*, editors Basu, D.N., and Kashyap, S.P. New Delhi: Concept Publishing Company.

Kashyap, S.P., and Mehta, N. (2005). 'Rural non-farm sector in Gujarat: Growth and emerging nature', *Rural Transformation in India – The Role of Non-farm Sector*, editors Nayyar, R., and Sharma, A.N. Institute of Human Development. New Delhi: Manohar Publishers & Distributors.

Kashyap, S.P., and Mehta, N. (2007). 'Growth of a regional economy: Perspectives for human resource development', *Indian Journal of Public Audit & Accountability* 1(2), April–June.

Mehta, N. (2006). 'Imbalances in development between regions and social groups: Evidences from Gujarat', *Anvesak* 36(1), January–June.

Mehta, N. (2009). 'Some aspects of employment and wellbeing of farm labour households: Evidences from Gujarat', *Anvesak* 39(2), July–December.

Sardar Patel Institute of Economic & Social Research (SPIESR) (2009). *District Human Development Report-Sabarkantha (Gujarat)* [Mimeo].

Annexure 1

Workforce Estimation Procedure for 2007–2008

Workers for Gujarat and its districts for the year 2007–2008 are estimated as follows:

Step 1: At state-level, NSSO 64th Round work participation rates (WPR) for 2007–2008 (GoI, 2010) were applied to population projections of Gujarat state made by the Registrar General of India for the year 2007–2008. Census 'main workers' are equated to the usual principal status (UPS) workers and Census 'total workers' are equated with the usual status (principal + subsidiary status) (UPSS) workers. UPS and UPSS WPR (for males and females) were applied to the male and female population projections, separated by urban and rural areas, in order to arrive at state-level estimates for main and total workers for the year 2007–2008. The Census 'marginal workers' category is equated to the subsidiary workers of NSSO and was derived by substracting the estimated UPS (main) from UPSS (total) workers.

Step 2: Population at the district level for 2007–2008 was estimated by applying the districts' share of male and female population in 2001 (rural and urban separately) to the projected state population figures for 2007–2008. For all districts, the proportion of workers in each category (main, marginal, rural, and urban by sex) to the state-level aggregate in 2001 was worked out.

Step 3: The proportionate shares of workers to the state total in each district for 2001 were applied to the estimated (main, marginal, rural, and urban workers by sex) aggregate workers in 2007–2008. For the districts male, female main and marginal workers in rural and urban areas were separately computed for the year 2007–2008.

8

Globalization and Employment

A Case Study of Changing Structure of Employment in Gujarat

Shankar Jha and Sangeeta Jha

Employment generation is one of the main objectives of policy makers at both the Central and State Governments, particularly after liberalization from the 1990s. The liberalization policy has created a level playing field for the Indian and foreign companies. In such a case, creating new jobs is a challenge. Globalization has benefited many states in terms of investment, growth, and employment in India. In fact, Gujarat state has benefited much more than the other states due to the opening up of the Indian economy and since the 1990s, the structure of the state economy as well as the state of the manufacturing sector have changed significantly.

Many scholars have worked in the area of employment especially in the context of globalization. For instance, Kannan et al. (2009) and Ghose (2006) are of the opinion that following liberalization it is the economic growth, which should lead to the generation of more employment in the economy particularly in the organized manufacturing sector. Rao and Dasgupta (2009) asserted that due to high-income elasticity, there would be more employment in the food processing industries. Mukhopadhyay and Rajaraman (2007) concluded that between 1999–2000 and 2004–2005, rural unemployment in India across the states has increased. Sundaram (2007) found that there is a reduction in the poverty of the urban people because of more employment opportunities in the secondary and tertiary sectors, whereas in the rural areas, poverty did not decline. Sharma (2006) concluded that in the post-liberalization period, labour turnover is higher due to flexibility in the labour laws. Jha (2006) focused on disparity between rural–urban employment growth rate particularly in the non-farm sector, he found that the gap has widened. Hansda and Ray (2006) observed that in spite of 'jobless growth' in India during the 1990s poverty has reduced. Joshi (2004) emphasized the role of the tertiary sector in employment generation and poverty alleviation. Mitra (1998) studied the size and composition of employment in the informal sector. However, there is a dearth of research regarding the impact of globalization on employment in the state of Gujarat.

Gujarat has been dependent on the primary sector over the years for major employment. Nevertheless, there is a gradual shift from the primary sector to secondary and tertiary sectors where the per capita income is higher. The 2001 data reveal that out of a total employment, 56 per cent were in the primary sector, 19 per cent were in the secondary sector and 25 per cent were in the tertiary sector. This shows that though the agriculture sector employs the maximum number of people but its contribution towards net state domestic product (NSDP) is less than other sectors. This is due to low productivity. Whereas secondary and tertiary sectors employ less people but due to higher productivity, their contribution in NSDP is higher than the primary sector. Since Gujarat is one of the most industrialized states of India, where employment opportunities due to industrialization is higher, migration from other states and internal migration in search of employment from rural parts of Gujarat to the urban and industrially rich region is rising. Gujarat is the only state where the rate of net migration from outside state has gone up significantly during the 1980s, both in rural and in urban areas (Kundu, 2000); the same trend continues even today. In the fishing industry, many labourers from Kerala and Orissa have migrated to Gujarat, in the ship-breaking yard at Alang many labourers from states such as UP, Bihar, and Orissa can be found. Even the textile industry of

Surat has attracted many labourers from UP, Bihar, Orissa, Kerala, and Maharashtra to work on the looms.

It is in the context of the above situation that the main objective of this paper is presented particularly to assess changing employment trends in the industrial sector in the post-liberalization period of Gujarat. This paper is divided into four sections. The next section presents the structural change, while the third section looks into employment. The changing structure of employment is discussed in subsequent section and the last section concludes the paper.

Structural Changes in the State Economy

Typically, the process of economic development is marked by three distinct phases: an initial phase of dominance of agriculture, an intermediate phase dominated by industry, and a final phase dominated by services.

Table 1

Share of Three Sectors (in %)

Year	*Primary*	*Secondary*	*Tertiary*
1960–1961	48.8	22.7	28.4
1970–1971	53.4	20.6	26
1980–1981	44.1	24.8	31.1
1990–1991	31.3	31.7	37
2000–2001	17.5	37.7	44.7
2008–2009	17.76	41.05	41.19

Source: Socio-economic Review of Gujarat, various years.

The state of Gujarat follows the same path. This is noticeable in Table 1. At the time of the formation of the state in 1960–1961, the economy in the state was dominated by the primary sector and, thereafter, during the period from 1980 to 2000, the economy was dominated by the secondary sector, particularly the manufacturing sector. However, after the year 2000, the service sector dominated the economy. Seeing that there is a shift in the structure of the economy, income and employment also witness a change. Now, more employment opportunities are available in the secondary and tertiary sectors, which are clear in the above-mentioned data. The growth performance of Gujarat's economy since 1995 has been extraordinary. During 1995 to 2008, the per capita state domestic product (SDP) grew approximately by 8 per cent per annum. This phenomenal growth was driven by industrialization, especially in the manufacturing and infrastructural sectors. The share of manufacturing sector in SDP increased from 34 per cent to 41 per cent.

Compared to the entire economy, the manufacturing sector in Gujarat has grown at a faster pace. The manufacturing sector shows a 33.8 per cent growth in Gujarat, the NSDP is also higher at 27.7 per cent from the NSDP at all-India level. The state has also improved its relative rank from fourth in 1980–1981 to first in 1990–1991; it is number one in terms of contribution of manufacturing sector to NSDP among the states (Awasthi, 2000).

The recommendations of the Task Force on Employment opportunities focused on the four components of employment. These components of the employment strategy are as follows:

- Accelerating growth
- Encouraging labour-intensive sectors and inducing faster growth of such sectors
- Skill development of labours
- Modifications in the labour laws (Rangarajan, 2006).

Gujarat state has satisfied all these recommendations, registering high economic growth, flexible labour laws, encouraging the growth of small-scale-intensive industries, and educational institutions such as the IITs and through vocational training.

As far as the growth rate of the state is concerned, it is the highest in the country. It recorded a double-digit growth in the year 2008. It was observed that since 1995, the economy's growth rate is satisfactory. It is claimed that the high growth rate of the state is because of its secondary and tertiary sectors; however, researchers have found that globalization has positively affected the state of the economy of Gujarat, in terms of both growth and investment. Both in turn lead to higher employment generation. The manufacturing sector in Gujarat has shown a real impact of liberalization in the 1990s (Dholakia, 2000) and in the present decade too. Since 1991, the employment opportunities in the state have increased and that could be the reason behind the migration of people from other states to the state of Gujarat. Thus, it can be argued that the growth process has brought about significant changes in the structure of the state economy.

Employment Scenario in Gujarat at a Glance

India's labour force is growing at a rate of 2.5 per cent per annum, but the employment rate is growing at only 2.3 per cent per annum, whereas in the state of Gujarat it is higher than the national average. In Table 2, the district-wise employment growth has been depicted.

Table 2

Average Annual Growth in Employment 1991–2001 (in %)

District	*Rural*	*Urban*	*Total*
Ahmedabad	1.27	3.65	2.98
Amreli	1.49	0.65	1.34
Anand	1.14	3.43	1.59
Banaskantha	3.38	4.01	3.43
Bharuch	1.70	2.59	1.87
Bhavnagar	1.18	3.24	1.78
Dahod	2.94	3.77	2.99
Gandhinagar	2.31	4.95	2.93
Jamnagar	2.13	3.31	2.52
Junagarh	2.04	2.41	2.12
Kachchh	2.89	2.66	2.83
Kheda	1.89	2.03	1.91
Mehsana	1.39	2.56	1.57
Narmada	1.64	2.59	1.70
Navsari	1.20	1.49	1.26
Panchmahal	2.17	2.73	2.21
Patan	2.04	2.48	2.11
Porbandar	1.92	2.98	2.31
Rajkot	2.29	4.05	2.99
Sabarkantha	1.91	2.90	1.98
Surat	1.57	7.00	4.05
Surendranagar	3.20	1.50	2.84
The Dangs	3.20	–100	2.47
Vadodara	1.81	2.83	2.15
Valsad	1.52	6.68	2.44

Source: Bhandari and Kale (2007).

These statistics show that in each district, there is a growth in employment; in districts which are backward, the growth of employment is lower than the national average but developed districts such as Ahmedabad, Vadodara, Surat, Rajkot, Valsad, and Gandhinagar, where there is more concentration of industries, employment is in the manufacturing and service sectors is higher than the national average. Nevertheless, these districts also reveal a gloomy picture of the state, in the sense that employment is urban biased. In districts which are industrially backward, rural employment is higher than urban employment such as in Amreli and the Dangs, but in the other 23 districts, urban employment is higher than rural employment.

A comparative picture of non-farm sector in the rural sector vis-à-vis the urban sector shows significant disparity in terms of size and growth. The lopsided nature of growth of the non-farm sector is causing a problem of rural–urban migration (Jha, 2006).

The State Government, in their various plans to reduce poverty through employment generation, has given top priority to industrial development, for the benefit of rural and urban people. In the industrial sector too, top priority is given for the creation of maximum employment in agro-based rural industries for rural employment and for urban employment; the government offers many subsidies and concessions to entrepreneurs to start their own business. To generate self-employment and to encourage small entrepreneurs, some technical and vocational training is also imparted through the ITIs.

Changing Structure of Employment in Industries

For any state, industrial development is a pre-requisite for economic development. If industrial development is rapid, economic growth of the state is high. Consequently, employment and per capita income are high. The industrial sector gives the hope that it will create more employment opportunities due to strong backward and forward linkages.

Gujarat state has always led the country's industrial development scenario and continues to attract the largest quantum of investments, both domestic and foreign. Since 1991 until

August 2007, the state has received acknowledgements from 8501 Industrial Entrepreneurs Memorandum (IEM) with an estimated investment of ₹ 431,890 crores.

During the Vibrant Gujarat Global Investors Summit in 2009, 8,690 MoUs were signed with proposed employment opportunities of 2,682,737. Out of these MoUs, 543 were implemented with total investments of ₹ 9,901.46 crores and 1,238 projects are under implementation with investments of ₹ 259,220.63 crores.

Until 1960, the industrial economy of Gujarat rested primarily on the textile and engineering industries including ancillary units to textile industries. However, at present, the industrial activities are diversified to chemical, petrochemical, plastic, pharmaceuticals, and so on. Consequently, its rank among the states has steadily risen from eighth in 1960 to second at present.

Table 3

Workers Employed by Industry Group

Industry Group	*1960*	*1970*	*1980*	*1990*	*2000*	*2005 (provisional)*
Textiles	237,853	235,782	290,111	241,984	170,642	167,575
Food, beverages, tobacco and tobacco products	28,206	41,032	64,759	72,325	89,328	96,054
Wood, wood product, furniture and fixtures	3952	4559	6847	7659	10,946	43,326
Paper and paper products, printing, publishing, and allied industries	5670	9786	15,582	21,217	23,879	26,142
Leather and leather products	435	641	513	811	2289	1951
Rubber, plastics and petroleum, coal products	5663	7547	16,714	43,355	52,983	58,728
Chemical and chemical products	11,146	24,298	58,557	100,859	153,583	158,987

Cont'd...

...Cont'd

Non-metallic minerals products	19,451	29,953	40,295	54,848	63,731	70,255
Basic minerals industries	2475	9042	18,456	33,659	51,960	57,080
Metal products	2659	8775	26,135	32,866	43,488	54,672
Machinery except electrical machinery	12,148	32,965	44,833	55,958	59,306	65,087
Electrical machinery, apparatus applies and supplies	287	7745	13,945	26,674	27,577	28,356
Transport equipment and pass	12,338	16,157	8815	15,138	21,074	18,309
Others	479	9272	30,122	40,216	95,934	131,735
Total	346,462	437,554	635,684	747,569	866,720	978,257

Source: Socio-economic Review of Gujarat, various years.

Gujarat is one of the leading industrial states in India and the textile industry in particular has contributed immensely to industrialization in the state. The textile industries have been one of the oldest and most important sectors of the state economy. In fact, developments of many other industries such as dyestuff, chemicals, engineering, foundry, and cotton farming are dependent on this sector. From Table 3, it is clear that textile industries are the second largest employment provider in the state next to agriculture. The structure and nature of employment in the registered SSI has been analysed from data published by the Commissioner of Industries, Gujarat State. In 1960, out of the total non-farm employment, this sector alone contributed 64 per cent of employment. On the other hand, over a period of time, the relative significance of this sector in employment generation has receded. In 2005, out of the total non-farm employment, it accounts for only 17 per cent. On the contrary, over a period of time, the relative importance of other groups of industries has increased. Industrial structure shifted in the 1980s in favour of chemical and its by-products. Chemical and pharmaceuticals accounted for only 3 per cent of the total employment in 1960 has increased to 16 per cent of the total employment in 2005.

After globalization, these traditional groups of industries are now loosing their importance in terms of employment and new groups are now replacing them. These are the IT sector, retail sector, real estate sector, banking and insurance sector, and telecom sector that are generating more employment. These are the sectors where growth rate of employment is higher.

Where special economic zones are concerned, the Central Government has approved 60 such zones. Gujarat is considered far ahead in terms of land sanctioned for special economic zones, which is a sign of high future employment.

The state has experienced an affirmative impact of economic reforms on the economy and thereby on the overall employment growth. Since the 1960s, after the formation of the state, Gujarat has had strong policies to promote small-scale industrial sectors, which is labour intensive and in this way created more jobs. The total number of small-scale units in the state as on September 2006 were 312,782, giving employment to more than 10 lakh people. Employment has grown up in every group of industries except textiles in our study period from 1960 to 2005.

Industrial units having an investment of more than ₹ 10 crores in plant and machinery are classified as large industrial units. In Gujarat, there are 2059 medium- and large-scale industrial units, giving employment to about 4 lakh people. Again, among large- and medium-scale industries, textile has lost its position and chemical and chemical products have increased its position by generating more employment. In the post-liberalization period, investment in medium- and large-scale industries is growing faster. More and more MOUs have been signed for medium- and large-scale industries. Therefore, more employment is expected from these sectors.

The presumably less important sectors are now contributing significantly in generating more and better employment opportunities as compared to yesteryears. A large number of workers continue to work in the unorganized sector but outside the preview of statutory cover and earn wages below the subsistence level. The improved literacy rates and increasing job opportunities in the urban areas encourage migration of rural people leaving cultivation. In this state, the employment in unorganized sector is also rising. The overall status of employment in the unorganized sector of Gujarat reveals that quantitatively the share of self-employment is the highest because of the business skills of the people of Gujarat.

As per the reports of the NSSO's 61st round (2004–2005), 60.99 lakh people were employed in 24.26 lakhs establishment in different economic activities of the unorganized sector. In the non-farm sector, 22.73 lakh people were self-employed, while 38.26 lakh people were employed in the rural areas and 32.19 lakh people were employed in the urban areas. Like in the formal sector, in the informal sector too, employment was found to be higher in the urban areas. The major activity in the non-farm sector was retail trade with 46.23 per cent followed by manufacturing with 17.27 per cent and other community personal services with 9.49 per cent. Nevertheless, where employment is concerned, the informal sector was higher in the manufacturing sector (14.68 lakhs), followed by the retail trade sector (13.77 lakhs). In the informal sector too, trend in employment has been changing, more now-a-days people look for employment in the IT, real estate, and construction sectors.

In the rural areas of the state 10,180,000 jobs have been generated in the cottage and rural industries in the year 2009. The Khadi Gramudyog in the year 2006–2007 has given the employment to 44,689 people. Out of the total workforce in the state, 81.20 per cent works in the informal sector, against 92 per cent of Indian average.

Currently, the total employment in the formal sector is manufacturing sector (7.65 lakhs), closely followed by community services (6.27 lakhs), finance, insurance, real estate, and business services (1.67 lakhs), wholesale, retail trade, and restaurants (0.58 lakhs), electric trade, gas, and water (0.57 lakhs), construction (0.50 lakhs), agriculture, hunting, forestry, and fishing (0.24 lakhs), and, finally, mining and quarrying (0.16 lakhs).

Conclusion

Globalization has played an important role in the generating employment in Gujarat. Since the 1990s, the employment scenario in the state has significantly changed. The sectors, once considered less important, have now more employment in the state.

Thus, it can be said that globalization has made an affirmative impact on the employment growth of the state. It has not led to 'jobless growth' but has instead given an impetus to growth in the state. Future trends in employment would veer towards IT, home appliances, health care, automobiles, beauty care, etc., where income elasticity of demand for these is higher.

References

Awasthi, D. (2000). 'Recent changes in Gujarat industry: Issues and evidence', *Economic and Political Weekly* 35(35/36).

Bhandari, L., and Kale, S. (Eds.) (2007). *Indian States at a Glance 2006–07: Gujarat Performance, Facts and Figures*, A PHDCCI Initiative. New Delhi: Indicus Analysis Pvt. Ltd.

Dholakia, R. (2000). 'Liberalization in Gujarat: Review of recent experience', *Economic and Political Weekly* 35(35/36).

Ghose, A.K. (2006). 'Economic growth and employment in labour surplus economics', *Economic and Political Weekly* XLI(31).

Hansda, S.K., and Ray, P. (2006). 'Employment and poverty in India during the 1990s – Is there a diverging trend?', *Economic and Political Weekly* XLI(27/28).

Jha, B. (2006). *Rural Non-farm Employment in India: Macro Trend, Micro Evidences and Policy Action*, IEG Working Paper.

Joshi, S. (2004). 'Tertiary sector driven growth in India: Impact on employment and poverty', *Economic and Political Weekly* 39(37).

Kannan, K.P. and Ravindran G. (2009). "Growth Sans Employment: A Quarter Century of Jobless Growth in India's Organised Manufacturing" *EPW* March 7 vol. XLIV No. 10.

Kundu, A. (2000). 'Globalizing Gujarat: Urbanization, employment and poverty', *Economic and Political Weekly* 35(35/36).

Mitra, A. (1998). 'Employment in informal sector', *The Indian Journal Labour Economics* 41(3).

Mukhopadhyay, A., and Rajaraman, I. (2007). 'Rural unemployment 1999–2005: Who gained, who lost?', *Economic and Political Weekly* XLII(30).

Papola, T.S. (2008). *Employment Challenge and Strategies in India*, ILO Asia Pacific, Working Paper Series, January.

Rakesh, M. (1989). 'Industry and urban employment, 1961–81: A preliminary exploration', *Economic and Political Weekly* 24(44/45).

Rangarajan, C. (2006). *Employment and Growth* [Monograph]. Madras School of Economics.

Rao, N. Chandrasekhara and Dasgupta, Sukti (2009) "Nature of Employment in Food Processing Sector" *EPW* vol. 44 No. 17 April 25.

Sharma, A.N. (2006). 'Flexibility employment and labour market reforms in India', *Economic and Political Weekly* XLI(21).

Socio-economic Reviews of Gujarat–Various Issues. Gandhinagar: Government of Gujarat.

Sundaram, K. (2007) 'Employment and poverty in India, 2000–2005', *Economic and Political Weekly* XLII(30), pp. 3121 to 3131.

9

Options of Survival for Marginalized Labouring Poor in Deteriorating Employment Situation

Floating in Informal Fringe Sector

Kiran Desai

This paper attempts to narrate labour market scenario at the bottom rung of the urban economy with reference to a few pockets in Gujarat state in the present context of Globalization era. While making an attempt to arrive at a generalized statement pertaining to employment situations at the lowest rung of the labour market in an urban setting, it primarily depicts conditions and lives of workers seeking livelihoods in industrial and other activities of the informal sector with respect to mainly two prominent industrial centres of the south Gujarat region, namely, Surat and Vapi.

A good many scholars have critically and clinically analysed the impact of neo-liberalization on labour and quite candidly have established the nature and the magnitude of detrimental effects that the globalization project is having on the labouring poor. Papola (2005), for instance, has observed that along with an increase in the growth rate, employment in the organized sector has decreased and that of informal sector has increased. Citing NSSO data, he has observed that '... there occurred a significant deceleration in the growth of employment over the period following the initiation of major economic reforms towards globalisation in the early 1990's' (Papola, 2005: 4). He has particularly drawn attention towards the shift from regular wage paid jobs to casual work and feared that this shift '... is likely to continue with increasing pressure for greater labour flexibility to improve competitiveness of enterprises in the liberalized trade and globalising production system'. He has also mentioned another study conducted by a team of scholars which has clearly indicated that during the 1990s, after introduction of the new economic policy, the share of permanent workers had declined and those of non-permanent, casual workers as well as contract labour had increased in industrial firms[1] (Deshpande et al., 2004: 8). Thus, in other words, at the lower echelons of the economy labour has been encountering two-dimensional vulnerability and adversity; both inter-connected and their combined effect aggravating harshness and oppression in life situations and shrinking space for marginalized labour. On one hand, more and more workers are entering into the existing vast army of unorganized labour force as the door of organized sector has been shut for them and on the other hand, as a study revealed, 'the coverage of social security schemes has been largely against economically and socially vulnerable sections' (Sakthiwel and Joddar, 2006: 2113) and this includes casual and contract workers (even in the organized sector) as well as a vast mass of self-employed, the size of the last group been growing alarmingly in recent years. The Report of the National Commission for Enterprises in the Unorganized Sector (NCEUS) quite candidly concluded that '... the overarching problem ... is the lack of adequate and decent employment at a fair wage for the large segments of the workforce hovering around the bottom of the informal sector economy' (Breman, 2010: 42). The report has also clearly indicated that between the decadal period of 1993–1994 and 2004–2005 when the neo-liberal reforms were in full swing, the rate of employment growth had declined considerably. Not only that but whatever growth that took place was mainly within the informal economy. As Breman remarked, '... these years of high economic growth were not accompanied by a spurt in employment generation and a rise in average earnings of the workforce' (Breman, 2010: 43). The NCEUS reports also pointed out that in order to hang on to their work, more and more formal sector livelihood earners have no option but to put up with informalization with regard to security measures and provisions in working conditions. They too are forced to share the predicament of informal sector livelihood seekers in the form of '... absence of job security, income security and social security' (Breman, 2010: 43).

The present write-up is based on a continuum of empirical studies which have been undertaken, goaded and guided by an ongoing research interest on labour situations especially pertaining to industrial and informal sector of urban economy in the specific locational settings of the southern part of Gujarat state (Desai, 2000, 2001, 2002; Desai and Raj, 2001a, 2001b). The observations and findings of a recently concluded that collaborative research[2] has also been taken into consideration and it also incorporates preliminary observations of a very recently launched study.[3] This paper tries to capture empirical evidences of process and nature of informalization with reference to labour at the lower echelons of urban economy. More than quantitative information this description would endeavour to lay hold of qualitative details gathered through the life sketches of labour at the lower order of the economy. As has been sharply pointed out, most of the quantitative figures-based findings pertaining to impact of globalization on labour have been indicating significant gains in terms of employment generation and opportunities (Breman, 2003). However, in his recent work, he has clearly stated that in terms of quality of life, especially with regard to working and living conditions, one hardly finds any distinguishable improvement, on the contrary the conditions have deteriorated considerably for the labouring poor (Breman, 2007). The NCEUS reports too have confirmed this fact (Sengupta et al., 2006).

The main focus and intention in this description is to highlight how labour at the lower echelons sustain and survive against all odds in the globalization era. The present narration tries to capture the other side of neo-liberal regime in terms of effects and consequences in the form of severity of hardships and struggles the large masses, who are toiling and languishing at the bottom of the social and economic order, have to undergo and their ever deteriorating conditions. This paper deliberates on questions of struggles and survivals within the limited choices and spaces available with regard to livelihood options for these toiling masses. Enquiries pertaining to the kinds of spaces the poor have or have managed to obtain to keep themselves afloat have to be pondered on. The kinds of coping mechanisms and the ways and means of accessibility to these miserable people for survival against adversities have to be also deliberated on. The various groups of labouring poor which have been included in this narration are temporary, casual, and contract workers from industrial units, labour in construction activity, and those earning their livelihood by working in other secondary and tertiary sectors as well as organizations; also covered are the self-employed engaged in varied activities, visible again mainly at the lower rungs of the economy. Case studies from people across different sections (in terms of characteristics of activities and other socio-economic details) were gathered from Surat and Vapi. The general essence of information provided by them is narrated in the forthcoming sections. Attempts have been made to understand and analyse information gathered from the case studies in the backdrop of other studies done related to labour of the same region and touching similar aspects. Apart from concluding observations, this paper has three more sections. In the first section, profile of labour forces will be delineated, making an effort to deliberate on various aspects pertaining to migrant labour extensively. The working conditions will be the subject of second section and the third section will highlight various means available with workers as coping mechanisms. The intention is not to prove and provide evidences that even in this globalization era the labouring poor have opportunities and the scope to sustain as has been proclaimed by the advocates of this new economic regime, but to underline the wretched conditions they have been plunged into due to the absence of social- and work-related securities as well as non-implementation and infringement of human and labour rights enshrined in the Constitution of India. Though this paper does highlight the cover of social security mechanisms in forms of kinship, familial bonds, caste, village, and other primordial ties as kinds of coping mechanism, it does not intend and wish to abet stance of the World Bank and the other supporters of neo-liberal policy that an overall economic growth would eventually reach the labourers and that social ties are robust mechanisms that can take care of social security of these livelihood seekers in informal sector (World Bank, 1995). Breman has de-mystified the proclamations made by the proponents of the new economic regime about the informal sector with regard to its ostensible elasticity, absorption capacity as well as vast space provided in terms of livelihood to the large masses at the bottom rung of the economic ladder (Breman, 2009). The aim of this paper is not to glorify potential and capacity of fringe sector activities at the lowest bottom of the informal economy in terms of its capacity and potential for providing space for sustenance to the vast army of labour but on the contrary to depict the arduous struggles and the tremendous stress and hardships subjected on these vast masses in the urban economy.

Deciphering the Labour Force of Informal Sector

As the recent CSS study (Shah et al., 2007) has revealed the proportion of Gujarat's working population is around 42 per cent. Figures indicate that in the last two decades, the proportion of marginal workers has increased from 4.96 per cent in 1981 to 8.34 per cent in 2001, whereas the share of main workers remains the same during the period. The proportion of female main and marginal workers in rural areas has sharply increased from 27 per cent to 39 per cent during 1981–2001, which is not the case of male workers. Among the main workers, the proportion of cultivators has declined remarkably from 37.76 per cent in 1981 to 27.56 per cent in 2001. Though nearly 52 per cent of the workforce is engaged in the primary sector, employment opportunities in the farm sector have reduced in the last two decades, mainly due to the near stagnancy in agriculture production, changes in the cropping pattern and mechanization. In the industrial sector though employment in medium- and large-scale industries have increased manifold (from 141,000 in 1981 to 103,900 in 1990s), it has not matched up with the magnitude of investments on various 'development' projects. As a matter of fact even the Government of Gujarat's document admits that industrial employment has gone down between 1991 and 2002 and it has shown an erratic trend between 2002 and 2005. Absolute number of unemployed has not gone down. The number of the job seekers registered with the employment exchange has increased from 122 thousand in 1960 to 470 thousand in 1980 and 1067 thousand in the year 2000.

Though the state has registered growth in terms of overall employment, there is striking decline of employment in organized sector, the sector that provides some kind of security as well as various welfare benefits in jobs which are legally protected. Data suggest that the proportion of regular salary employed workers in both urban and rural areas has declined in between 1987 and 2000 and here it must be emphasized that all these 'regular' workers are not employed in the so-called 'organized' sector with statutory protection and social security. Similarly, all those who are employed in the organized sector are not protected with social security mechanism. Add to that, duration of their employment is not necessarily fixed and secured in all the cases. They can be fired at any time at the will of the employers. Most of them are not sure whether they would get work next day or week not to speak of the next month. Similarly, a woman employed in an unorganized sector say as a maidservant for domestic work and getting regular monthly remuneration of ₹ 300 is also treated as a 'regular' worker. In the same vein, other examples of regularly employed are factory, office, or apartment watchman, lift operator in multi-storeyed building, quarry worker, shop assistant or tea-stall attendant, and so on. A yawning gap exists between the monthly emoluments of varied 'regular' workers. It ranges from monthly salary of 1.5 lakh to 2.5 lakh with perks in the case of a CEO of the corporate sector establishment on the one hand to a lift operator of a multi-storeyed office building earning ₹ 2,000 per month. Data indicate that overall proportion of self-employed has increased in post-reform era, whereas that of casual labour has increased in urban areas but it has gone down in rural areas indicating dwindling scope of employment in agricultural sector. Similarly, the vast gamut of the self-employed includes legal and medical professional earning in six-digit figure which a roadside vendor earning less than ₹ 1,500 per month.

Profile of Workers

After having a glimpse of overall scenario pertaining to employment and work, the further narration in this section will dwell on characteristics of the labour and considering its significance addressing segment of migrant workforce in detail, with specific references of urban locations such as Surat and Vapi. As per one study (Desai, 2000), large majority of the industrial workers of Vapi hailed from socially and economically lower strata. Among the local workers of this bubbling industrial town, tribals formed majority and though social status of migrants was difficult to assess data on landholding and other possessions clearly indicated their weaker economic status. The data revealed that one-third of the Vapi's workforce was landless, whereas another large section of 64 per cent was small and marginal land holders. It can be deduced from the case materials of the latest investigation (Shah et al., 2007) too that most of the workers are landless and poor as well as belonging to socially backward groups. A study on workers of fringe sector of Surat (Desai, 2002) shows that eight out of every ten workers belonged to socially lowly placed groups. Although among the diamond workers of Surat members belonging to an intermediate caste of Patidar have significant presence, in terms of economic status and social hierarchy of Saurashtra region, the native land from where they have migrated, Patidars did not have a dominant status and as a matter of fact were harassed and oppressed by Darbar community once upon a time.[4] Moreover, taking into consideration an indicator of landholding as a criterion determining social and economic status in a predominantly rural agricultural socio-economic setting, the data of a study on diamond workers of Surat indicate that more than 70 per cent of diamond workers came from the families with small landholdings (less than 2.5 acres) or landless households (Desai and Raj, 2001a). The same study further revealed that even large landholdings did not indicate higher status as by and large agricultural yield was poor due to lack of irrigation facility and insufficient and sporadic rain in most part of Saurashtra region. Case materials of the same study too showed clearly that landholding of even 10 acres or more had not been good enough to sustain the family for the whole year. Add into that this region as a whole does not show either industrial development of much significance or presence of any other alternative means of livelihood.

A study conducted by South Gujarat University, Surat, indicates that vast majority of the textile workers came from the weaker sections of the society especially the socially and economically backward communities – SEBC (63%), scheduled castes – SCs (10%), and scheduled tribes – STs (9%) (SGU, 1984). In terms of economic status, the same study shows that more than 60 per cent of the textile workers did not own any property except small dwelling place and in terms of land holding 63 per cent were landless, whereas another 22 per cent had less than four acres of land.

It is difficult to estimate proportion of Muslim workers in industries of Vapi but in certain localities of the town such as Gitanagar and Dungari Falia, sizeable population of Muslim migrants belonging mainly to states of Bihar and Uttar Pradesh were found residing, most among them were working in industrial units. In Surat too, migrant Muslims from Bihar and Uttar Pradesh are found mainly working in processing houses. They too are staying in certain pockets such as Unn village, a village with predominantly Muslim population and slum areas mainly inhabited by Muslims. Both local and migrant Muslims can be spotted significantly in various activities related with informal sector, chiefly in self-employment sub-sector. For instance, a very large number of auto-rickshaw drivers are Muslims. Similarly, their presence can be seen among vendors selling various items by moving with their carts on the roads of Surat. In lucrative construction business of Surat, migrant Muslim workers are seen engaged in plumbing work and painting work. Similarly, the tribal migrants from Panchmahal and other predominantly tribal districts of bordering states such as Madhya Pradesh have been working as labourers in construction activity (see Patel, 2004).

With regard to educational background, as the case materials of Centre for Social Studies (CSS) study (Shah et al., 2007) revealed, only a handful of them have gone up to higher secondary level and getting into collage were rare cases. Another study indicated that in Vapi 35 per cent of the workers have studied till primary level of schooling, whereas another 50 per cent have reached up to eighth to tenth standard (Desai, 2000). A study on child workers of diamond industry of Surat clearly suggests that six out of every ten workers have studied in between fifth and seventh standard, whereas another 30 per cent have formal education up to primary level (Desai and Raj, 2001a). Even among those who were engaged in other industrial activities as well as self-employed livelihood options, education above secondary level of schooling was not reported. The SGU study (1984) of textile workers shows that 27 per cent of them were illiterate, whereas another 63 per cent had studied up to secondary level. The recent NCEUS reports also clearly indicate a very high proportion of illiterate workers in unorganized sector.

The study conducted by Anarde Foundation (2000) has estimated that the proportion of female workers is as low as 2.5 per cent among Vapi's industrial workforce. In general, tribal women belonging to villages located on the fringes of Vapi were found working. Another very interesting characteristic of the female workers of Vapi, as revealed by another study (Desai, 2000) was that 73 per cent of them hailed from nuclear families. A study (Desai, 1995) regarding workers of small-scale industries in various industrial places of Gujarat such as Rajkot and Mahesana has also indicated low proportion of female workers compared to male workers in these two places and most of them were belonging to socially lowly placed groups.

Same is the case of Surat which is clearly reflected in the gender ratio of the population of this industrial and economic capital of the state. SGU report indicates that proportion of female workers in textile industry of Surat was as low as 6 per cent in early 1980s (SGU, 1984). Breman (1996) has also estimated roughly the same percentage of female workers working in this major industry of Surat in the 1990s. Presence of females can be more prominently seen in *jari* industry (Punalekar, 1988; Soni, 1990) as well as in self-employment activities of petty nature such as selling vegetables, sea food, and other eatable items such as *vada pav* and omelette on the roadsides, also among domestic workers and home-based activities in Surat. A study (Desai, 2000) focusing on labour situation in informal sector of Surat city also clearly indicated significant presence of women in various activities of subsidiary or fringe sector. Case materials of later studies (Shah et al., 1997 and ongoing research on fringe sector, Desai) also showed that in recent times presence of females has become more prominent in fringe sector especially in self-employment activities. The closure of large textile mills that had rendered the main male livelihood earners of the families jobless should be considered as the major causal factor for female members to join workforce. Apart from Vapi, local women belonging to socially lowly placed groups such as Halpatis as well as girls belonging to other tribal groups from rural hinterland near this mega city are being found doing mainly bobbin work in power loom units (Desai and Raj, 2001b and case materials from above-mentioned studies). So far as city's other major industry of diamond work is concerned, conservative Patel community had not been allowing their womenfolk to work alongside male workers in diamond units till late. However, things have changed considerably in last five years and presence of daughters of Patels as well as female members of local social groups have increased mainly in office work of diamond ateliers; though entry of wives and daughter-in-laws of Saurashtra Patels into diamond workforce is still a far-fetched possibility. The level of education among young generation of Saurashtra Patels has gone up considerably in recent times and Patel girls are not lagging behind compared to boys and they are even seeking employment in other activities than diamond industry (Desai and Raj, 2001a and case materials from present study).

In terms of age group workers in the range of 17–37 years formed the largest group (of approximately 62%) in Vapi (Anarde Foundation, 2000). As another study has reported (Desai, 2000), nature of work in Vapi's industries has not been suitable either for too young (below 18 years) fellows or for too old (above 45 years) persons. SGU study has shown that a large majority of workers in the textile industry of Surat were in the age group of 14–25 years (55%) and another very large group of 34 per cent was of age group of 25–40 years (SGU, 1984). As Breman has noted, 'Only one in ten powerloom operators is older than forty. The labour process is so exhausting that very few are able to perform adequately after middle age' (Breman, 1996: 61). The case studies carried out in later studies too indicate scant presence of individuals above 50 years of age in various activities of fringe sector. The proponents of new economic regime who have been glorifying achievements of it in terms of employment opportunities in informal sector should take notice of this hard-hitting fact of shortening of working age of informal sector workers. Presence of child labour can be distinctly seen in both the premier industries of Surat (Desai and Raj, 2001a, 2001b).

The series of studies mentioned above have brought out clearly that most of the workers eking out their livelihoods in urban informal sector are migrants in character. At both the places, Surat and Vapi, large proportion of work-hands have come from other states. In Vapi, migrants have come from almost each and every nook and corner of the country. States such as Orissa, West Bengal, Tripura, and Bihar from eastern part; Maharashtra and Rajasthan from western India; Andhra Pradesh, Kerala, Karnataka, and Tamil Nadu of south zone; and Uttar Pradesh, Bihar, Punjab, Madhya Pradesh, and Himachal Pradesh from northern part; all these states are being represented in the industrial workforce of Vapi. From within Gujarat, migrants have come from districts of Banaskantha, Sabarkantha, Kutchch, and few districts of Saurashtra region which are considered as agriculturally poor and also neighbouring rural areas of Valsad district in which Vapi is located. A study conducted by a voluntary group has estimated that Vapi has as large as 86 per cent of migrant workers in its total labour force (Anarde Foundation, 2000). Another research put the figure in the vicinity of 80 per cent (Desai, 2000). The latter study further reveals that the proportion of the migrants from other states among them is around 60 per cent and tribals from neighbouring villages and talukas formed another large group among migrants of Vapi.

It is difficult to get similar figure with regard to Surat city but as per one guesstimate 50–60 percentage of the city's population is migrant in nature and very large portion of them are eking out their livelihood from industrial and other informal sector activities. For instance, as per one study, in diamond production activity, almost 93 out of every 100 workers are migrants and 71 per cent of them have come from Saurashtra region, mainly from three districts of Amreli, Junagadh, and Bhavnagar (Desai and Raj, 2001a). As another study indicates that among textile workers too migrants have formed the largest group with little less than 70 per cent and out of them slightly above 70 per cent are those from other states (SGU, 1984). As the same study has shown these migrants were mainly from Orissa (42%), Andhra Pradesh (12%), Maharashtra (8%) as well as small proportion from Uttar Pradesh and Bihar. Breman too has mentioned large influx of work seekers in booming urban economy of Surat (Breman, 1996).

Some Issues Pertaining to Migrant Workers

Scholars have conflicting sets of explanations to offer on factors which can be considered as causing migration. One school gives importance to individual factor, whereas the opponent theoretical model considers structural reasons more vital. Someone like Anthony Giddens is of the view that both set of factors have to be taken into account. He argues 'that an analysis has to take account of both sets of factors – of structures and of individuals'.[5] This theoretical deliberation requires detailed account.

Neo-classical school considers people as rational actors, who are striving for an economic optimum. This school believes that people are supposed to have a fair judgement with regard to the best option and move to the job or opportunity which gives them most gain. 'Push–pull' interpretation is one of this kind which says that 'Individuals choose between the various gains and losses which may result from migration' (see de Haan, 1994: 33).

Surplus model accepts the assumption of rationally choosing individual. But the scholars of this school do not accept the labour market as one homogeneous unit. This school does not accept to migrant's move from the subsistence rural sector straight into the modern urban economy. It is of the view that migrants do not find employment immediately upon arrival and they have to rely on informal or 'traditional' sector in between. It argues in nutshell that '(T)he migrant is supposed to weigh the difference between the expected earnings from formal sector urban employment, including a period of informal sector employment, and the expected earnings in the village' (see de Haan, 1994: 33). This model though has lost its vitality, as the globalization project has almost wiped out the formal sector.

The above two models are criticized for their total disregard of socio-economic and political context of the migrant livelihood seeker. Neo-classical model especially does not distinguish migrant labouring poor from the one who moves away on her/his will for better job prospect. This school ascribes each of the migrant worker characteristics of a single economic unit.

In the structuralist method of analysis, migration is seen as the only option of survival for the poor people who are not having any control over means of production in the socio-economic order. The structure does not allow any space of choices or selection as envisaged by neo-classical model for migrants belonging to weaker sections. Free labour market does not exist, it argues; it is always segmented and migrant work seeker has restricted entry and scope in it. The proponents of neo-liberal regime who have been glorifying informal sector have overlooked, either deliberately or unintentionally, this crucial factor.

Someone like Arjan de Haan who has studied migrant workers of Calcutta, while in agreement over segmentation of labour market, gives equal emphasis on social, religious, and ethnic factors apart from economic factor for the segmentation (see de Haan, 1994: 36). He also believes that structures and individuals cannot be described independently and along with structural factors, individual choices have also to be taken into account.

The present paper argues that for the weaker sections of the population, the root set of causes of the migration is the social and economic forces. It is true that an individual cannot be separated from his/her social existence. As case materials of our studies poignantly suggest that for people at the bottom of social-economic order who are most of the time occupied in the struggle of eking out livelihood, course of life mostly tread along social forces. And then an individual's choices are not shaped in vacuum. It is the very social milieu that shapes the preferences and choices of an individual. Thus, it is difficult to isolate an individual in terms of his/her choices from the social forces under which he/she lives. For a common social being, it is the set of larger social forces which determine his/her way of thinking. Importantly, the apparent set of choices for an individual has not been broad and open. The visible availability of various choices seems to be deceptive. People of lower social and economic echelons have extremely limited scope in terms of choices. What sort of choices do they in effect have? Are they really being considered as choices? Case materials of our studies have provided the answer categorically in negative.

With reference to general scenario prevailing in rural India, Papola (2005: 5) has observed that '... (A) poor employment performance of the growth during the 1990's can primarily be attributed to a virtual stagnation of employment in agriculture which accounted for 60 per cent of total workers'. Case materials of various studies reveal that in broader terms, most of the migrants have to leave their villages as they provided limited scope for all their population to sustain and survive, mainly in agriculture. Not all of them are landless and in fact, some of them have substantial size of land. But yet they had to migrate for one or the other reason, mainly related with lack of or poor quality of livelihood options. Albeit aspiration for betterment of life can also be considered as one factor causing migration for a small segment.

Patil (1987: 159), in his study on small town of Ichalkaranji of Maharashtra, has noted that 'the smaller industrial centres attract workers from the surrounding rural areas'. He further added that '(T)his process is different from that observed in big industrial centres like Bombay (now Mumbai) and Bangalore'. Patil's observations were intended to unearth a pattern of migration.

It is assumed that small industrial centres such as Vapi and Ichalkaranji, in general, induce labour migration from surrounding and nearby rural areas, whereas in big industrial centres, likewise Mumbai and Surat, in-migration takes place from far-off places, mainly from places outside state. This proposition, in other words, supports age-old theory of Ravenstein (1885) concerning migration. Ravenstein has given a pattern of migration wherein immigrants first go to nearby smaller places and then later on move to big cities, which become their final destination points in most cases (for detailed discussion on various theoretical premises regarding migration pattern, see Patel and Desai, 1992). The empirical evidences of some of the earlier studies too confirmed the above proposition. The metropolises such as Mumbai, Bangalore, Kolkata and other big industrial centres definitely have very large section of migrant workers from other states (see for instance a study on Calcutta migrant labour by de Haan, 1994). As the study of South Gujarat University (1984) clearly shows that in the textile industry of Surat, 71 per cent of the workforce had come from other states.

Similarly, in addition to the above pattern pertaining to destination places of migration, based on limited studies, a migrant job seeker's supposed flight and route concerning nature of livelihood were also generalized. The first destination of migrants would be informal sector activities of nearby urban or semi-urban location. After gaining experiences of working in non-agricultural informal sector at such places and also reaping confidence, they would then slowly continue journey by working at several places which ultimately ends up at final destination, i.e., large cities. Even in those places too, their voyage had mostly particularly carved out routes. Employment seeking migrants would accept whichever work is in the offing, mostly in the informal sector of the big city after arriving there. While working in the informal sector, they would look for permanent job opportunities in a formal sector. Their efforts were directed towards industrial sector mostly. Scholars used to describe workers of informal sector as reserve army for formal sector industries.

However, the age-old theory pertaining to route of migration and supposedly fix pattern concerning livelihood options needs to be scrutinized in the present context. As CSS recent studies with reference to industrial town of Vapi indicate, this relatively smaller industrial place too records an overwhelmingly large group of migrant workers from far off places of other states. Thus, the frame of explanation on the pattern of in-migration from far off places in terms of size of destination industrial centres needs reconsideration in the present context. On more concrete ground, at present, big or small cities provide employment opportunities mainly in informal sector only. Those seeking livelihoods are getting information regarding this changing scenario from their friends, relatives, and acquaintances working at different places. They prefer to move to the places where a group of persons from their own community or village have already been working and have established strong links, through which the new entrants can not only get work but also other support system required at a new place.

Advent of globalization has hastened the process which has already been underway since the late 1980s. First and foremost, the so-called formal sector has been shrinking and disappearing rapidly and secured and regular jobs available in large mills of big cities have been declining and recruitment at that level has almost been brought to a standstill (for detailed account see Desai, 2001; D'Monte, 2002; Breman, 2004). Even the giant corporate industrial houses such as Reliance, ESSAR

Steel, L&T at Surat employ most of the workforce on contract and casual basis. Thus, possibility of getting permanent and secured jobs in industries of the city centres is almost non-existent for newcomers to the urban locations in the present context. Hence, the entire formulation concerning pattern of journey of migrant workers and their absorption in city labour market migrants slowly climbing ladder from informal to formal sector and from insecurity to security has become irrelevant.

From the academic perspective, one major area of interest has been nature of linkages and interest of the migrants with the native places, not only in terms of emotional bonding with motherland but also with relation to primordial and social ties as well as live material interest. Often, process of nuclearization from erstwhile joint family is being associated with industrialization as work-seeking migrants move away from rural native places and in turn move out of joint family. But as studies have shown, this is too simplistic and linear formulation as the nature of relationship is rather complex and have shades of differentiation with reference to changing context of time and situation as well as to some extent different individuals. If we leave out the last variable in order to reach at a statement of more generalized nature, even earlier empirical evidences did not suggest any uniform pattern of association. On one hand, findings had indicated that migrant workers had kept their links and interest alive with their undivided families at native places. A very large majority had kept their wives and children at native places, and hence they had been visiting their villages every year regularly. Some of them also had to go in order to take care of their small piece of land and whatever meagre material interest they had over there (SGU, 1984; Desai, 1995). A study conducted by Anarde Foundation of Vapi town has shown that out of the total migrant workers, 96 per cent are having married status and of them 84 per cent have come alone, keeping their wives and children at their native places. A study on famous Bombay (now Mumbai) textile strike of 1982 (Van Wersch, 1992) inferred that one of the major responsible factor for relative success of that strike in terms of its prolonged duration was workers' alive interest in native places which allowed them to go back and sustain during the period of strike. Similarly, albeit migrant workers did not nurture any hope to get kind of work in their native places which was comparable in terms of remuneration and other added values with their work of informal sector in the city places, they could never be identified with destination places' socio-cultural milieu. Though they have been making efforts to reproduce their own socio-cultural setting at their livelihood places in order to overcome feelings of alienation and home sickness, visiting family and village has been vital for them to recharge and resuscitate them as alien and hostile city milieu and harsh working conditions have been taking their toll on them. However, at the same time, in the 1970s and 1980s and even early 1990s, another pattern could also be deduced as studies did suggest (Desai, 1995). The migrants who had come to place, such as Surat from far-off regions of Orissa, Uttar Pradesh, or Maharashtra, showed tendency to establish themselves at destination place wherein they expected a permanent foothold as workers with permanent status and package of security and benefits sooner or later and hence, as years passed frequencies of visits to the native places were getting less and later on wives and children were also brought. Both textile and diamond industries were growing steadily during that period and, hence, the milieu was of stability and security in terms of employment. The migrant workers were envisaging and planning their own and their children's career based on their employment in the city.

But the scenario has changed drastically in recent times mainly due to advent of neo-liberal policies. Getting secured and regular employment or work has become more and more difficult for the migrants in both the premier industries of Surat and this changed situation has made them realize their vulnerability as well as fragility with reference to employment situation in the city. Permanent and secured work conditions have become things of the past and everything related to work is unstable and temporary. Most of them are now opting to stay as long as possible at city centres without bringing their families and earn as much as possible as till their bodies allow and the situation permits them to. Now they do not view their destination as a permanent place to settle and have realization that in future at one point of time they have to go back to their native places. The detailed case studies conducted in CSS recent research endeavours (Shah et al., 2007; ongoing research concerning fringe sector) have clearly shown that workers have to depend extensively and heavily on familial and social ties for all sorts of support and assistance and in the process institution of joint or extended family as well as social ties and network have got strengthened. This point will further be discussed later on with reference to coping mechanism and its theoretical underpinning.

But strengthening of social ties should not be celebrated and projected in order to legitimize neo-liberal policy structure. Breman has rightly criticized a claim of proponents of new economic regime that migrant livelihood seekers in urban informal sector always have support system in their native rural areas in terms of not only social security but also economic opportunities in the form of employment to fall back upon if urban informal sector comes under crisis. Providing evidence from his own study, he has shown that there is hardly any sort of labour demand in agriculture or elsewhere in rural areas (Breman, 2009). It is too early to make any concluding remark but launching of National Rural Employment Guarantee Act (NREGA) has already started creating ripples in urban employment market. Newspaper reports and some informal discussion with power loom owners of Surat indicate that of late the units have been facing labour shortage and one major reason for this is implementation of NREGA as the workers who have been making their yearly routine visits to their native places have not been returning because they are getting employed in NREGA work that not only has been providing them wages of around ₹ 130 a day for a minimum period of 100 days but also warmth of familial milieu and most importantly freedom from harsh and oppressive working and living condition in Surat city. This trend is discerned despite the fact that in textile industry, the worker gets almost a double amount of wages compared to NREGA. But then it should also be taken into cognizance that at their native places along with them their other family members too are getting work in NREGA, thereby increasing the total family income and thus making the overall package of a good substantial family income, comparatively less living expenses and solace of family life much more robust and comforting compared to informal sector industrial working life in the city centres. As per one report, the textile industry has lost 25–30 per cent of its migrant workers – about 3 lakh out of the total of 10 lakh – from states such as Uttar Pradesh, Bihar, Orissa, and Andhra Pradesh during the last 3–4 years mainly due to NREGA. Either proponents of new economic regime or the industrialists would not consider this change, i.e., waning flow of migrant labour, quite positively. For both, cheap migrant labour is essential for margin of profit and to stay in the business amidst fierce competition while celebrating social ties of native places as that would unchain them from their responsibility concerning social security towards their workers. So it was not surprising that a chairperson of Federation of Indian Art Silk Weaving Industry (FIASWI) of Surat even has proposed to the Central government to affiliate NREGA with the industry so that the free flow of migrant labour from these states does not stop. The concerned associations of migrants of particular states such as Surat Odiya Welfare Association and Bihar Vikas Parishad too confirmed that due to the NREGA, flow of migration from these two states has certainly dwindled.[6] A systematic investigation is definitely needed to validate the said impact of NREGA on urban labour market such as observed in the case of Surat. Preliminary investigation does indicate paucity of workers in textile industry and embroidery industry of Surat. Apart from this apparent factor of NREGA, the other reasons, if any, for this reverse trend should be found out through further in-depth investigation. As per another report, industrial development induced and promoted by the state governments of Andhra Pradesh, Orissa, and Bihar through various policy measures too have worked as a deterrent factor as job seekers obviously prefer working nearer to their native places. Another moot point in this regard is over-emphatic importance given to NREGA. It seems the planners as well a group of scholars and intellectuals have been pinning hope that the NREGA would take care of all the ill-effects especially with reference to marginalized and weaker sections, such as widening disparities, poverty, unemployment, casualization in working condition, and fragmentation of working class, which are primarily generated by globalization project. But it seems that they are, consciously or unconsciously, overlooking social and political dynamics as well as debilitating effects caused by the administrative structure that would interact and intercept with any development programme or welfare measure and crippling them in terms of its desired and targeted objectives and effects. The past experiences with regard to ambitious and large-scale development programmes such as IRDP, DPAP, Jawahar Rojgar Yojana, and Mid-Day Meals Scheme are some of the glaring examples indicating failure in achieving stated objectives due to administrative malpractices and dominant social–political groups seizing control of the programmes for serving their own interests.

Before moving on to the section pertaining to working condition, the case of diamond industry of Surat needs specific mention. Patels of Saurashtra region had started migrating to Surat to work in the industry in the 1960s of last century and in four decades time they not only have made diamond industry of Surat famous worldwide but also have elevated their social and economic status through the industry. They too have become a political force due to it (see Engelshovan, 1999). They in fact have reproduced 'new Saurashtra', in an area called Varachha in Surat and have created, in turn, 'Other Surat', within Surat. However, on the other hand, as case materials of CSS recent studies mentioned above suggest that not only migration to Surat from Saurashtra has declined in last decade or so but also a large section of diamond workers are finding it difficult to sustain in industry and considering options of moving out of the city, back to native places or nearby places to their homeland. Recent crisis in the industry has laid off a very large number of diamond workers, almost 50 per cent of the total workforce, approximately 200,000 (Breman, 2010) and most of them are compelled to go back to their native places in Saurashtra. This trend has begun much earlier in premier industry of textile in Surat. We have come across a section of Telugu workers who had settled here with their families but had to leave Surat as employment situation deteriorated in mid-1990s. And now due to NREGA and other employment initiatives by state governments of Orissa and Andhra Pradesh, not only in-migration has declined but also workers are returning back to their homeland.

The narration so far has indicated how and under what sort of parameters a migrant seeking livelihood in urban centre has to take decisions. As our studies have revealed, the migrants are not in a position to have any long-term plan or goals considering their present situations. They are forced to have ad-hoc or short-term goal which is to get livelihood option that is better than what is available at their native places. The selection for destination is mainly based on support system available there. They know and understand quite well the limited space and sphere available to them and within it they have to make effort to survive, sustain, and uplift their standard of living in a limited sense. Situation is worsening day by day and harshness of life has intensified for them and their space is shrinking; this realization has struck them hard.

On Work

By and large, barring a few exceptions, migrants have come to urban centres of Surat and Vapi to get work mainly in industries. In case of former, the two premier industries of textile in Surat have been providing employment opportunities of gigantic proportion. It is impossible to get exact estimate of labour force earning their livelihood from these two industries, as most of the units employ work-hands on temporary and casual basis. As per Census 2001, out of total population of 2,702,247 of Surat city, total numbers of workers are 1,036,220 (38.35%) and out of that 1,014,153 are main workers, i.e., mainly industrial workers. Table 1 provides the estimation of proportion of working population industry wise.

Data of Table 1 are for year 1996. Considering Surat's decadal growth rate for 1991–2001 as 62 per cent (Census, 2001), it can be deduced that at present around 5.50 lakhs and

3.50 lakhs workers are earning their livelihoods from textile industry and diamond industry, respectively.

Table 1

Major Industrial Activities and Employment in Surat

Major industries	*Production (Rs in crores)*	*Export (Rs in crores)*	*Employment (in lakhs)*
Textile	7750 (44.79)*	175 (12.10)	4.50 (57.69)
Diamond	8000 (46.24)	8000 (86.38)	2.50 (32.05)
Colour chemical	1550 (08.95)	125 (01.50)	0.80 (10.25)
Totals	17300	8300	7.8

*Figures in bracket indicate percentage with reference to column figures.

Source: Reproduced from Ghosh and Ahmad (1996).

Table 2

Estimate of Industrial Employment in Vapi

Production units	*No. of workers*
Chemical units	45,000 (28.1)*
Paper mills	33,000 (20.6)
Engineering units	22,000 (13.7)
Plastic units	24,000 (15.0)
Others	36,000 (22.5)
Total no. of workers	160,000

*Figures in the bracket show percentage.

Source: Reproduced from Anarde Foundation Report, 2000.

In case of Vapi going by the estimation of Anarde Foundation study of 2000, at present juncture around 175,000 industrial workers are employed in various industries of Vapi. Table 2 shows their distribution over different kinds of industries.

Since industries provide a major pool of employment opportunities, general scenario prevailing in that sphere will first be dealt with. Work opportunities in various branches of industrial activities should not be considered as monolithic in terms of their nature. There is a casual work, which is available on daily basis. Then there is temporary job that provides some ray of hope for permanency, not in terms of security and other benefits protected by legal enactments, but as a regular employment, i.e., availability of work on regular basis. Gangs of contract labourers who have not been directly associated with the main management are widely utilized for many industrial operations. In small-scale industries, each unit has few permanent hands who are mainly holding senior technical positions or dealing with clerical and office-related work. But the rest of majorities are either casual daily workers or contract workers or temporary workers as mentioned above.

A study conducted on Vapi industries indicated that in a good number of large units, comparatively significant number of permanent positions were also in the offing (Desai, 2000). This category of workers had been enjoying legally protected package of benefits and security and any breach in this regard had been fiercely contested by labour unions, which had a very strong presence in Vapi during that period. But situation has undergone change since then and as observed by Sehgal (2005), labour is increasingly under assault from capital and processes of casualization, degradation and feminization of labour have accelerated. Sehgal (2005) has referred a good many studies pointing out that '(S)ignificantly, it is not one segment of the labour force that is being subjected such disciplining (means casualisation) but the entire labour force. This is evident even in the upper echelons of the work hierarchy, where highly paid, skilled in-house employees are being transformed into well-paid "independent contractors" without benefits, pensions or any other form of job security. The well-paid flexible worker is now celebrated a foot-loose "consultant" with no ties or company loyalties' (p. 2291). This phenomenon is evidently visible in present day Vapi.

As narrated earlier, previously it was observed that any new entrants to the town eyed their attention firstly for whatever nature of work they could get in any industrial unit, though their ultimate ambition was to climb the 'steep slope' of labour market to get entry in the 'citadel'[7] of industrial larger units. It has been envisaged that small-scale industries 'would act as an absorptive reservoir and a clearing house for the raw labour, undisciplined and untrained, coming from the countryside. After a period of adjustment, these migrant masses would qualify for employment in the gradually expanding formal sector of the economy' (see Breman, 1996: 2). Mark Holmstrom has described labour segmentation in following terms:

> ...The organised/unorganised boundary is not a wall but a steep slope. Indian society is like a mountain, with the very rich at the top, lush Alpine pastures where skilled workers in the biggest modern industries graze, a gradual slope down through smaller firms where pay and conditions are worse and the legal security of employment means less, a steep slope around the area where Factory Act ceases to apply ... a plateau where custom and the market give poorly paid unorganised sector workers some minimal, then a long slope down through casual migrant labour and petty services to destitution. There are well defined paths up and down these slopes, which are easier for certain kinds of people. (1985: 319)

This more than two decades old description of steep slope of labour segmentation needs a complete modification in the present context. Holmstrom and Breman as well as others have cherished some hope that those at the bottom, at least some of them, may climb the steep slope, albeit with difficulties and reach the pastures at top. But as situation has unfolded in last two decades and as a matter of fact, hastened in globalization era, the upper part of slope, the well-imagined Alpine pastures have become barren on one hand, and on the other hand, the steep slope has become insurmountable for those at the bottom. Case materials of our later studies (Shah et al., 1997; Desai, 2002 and ongoing research material) indicate that unprecedented nature of informalization and casualization has taken place all around industrial world. Permanent status with security was rare in Surat's textile and diamond industries even earlier. But clear signs of degradation in terms of workers status are sharply visible in Vapi. More and more industrial operations have been handed over to contract workers. Even a study done in 1990s mentioned that only one out of every ten workers was having permanent status. It denoted that around 60 per cent of the workforce was contract and non-permanent labour, whereas another 30 per cent were of casual nature (Desai, 2000). Another feature indicating deteriorating work conditions is that number of working days is reducing. So even if wage rate has increased, total monthly emolument has not swelled. It ranges from ₹ 3,000 to ₹ 7,000, with casual and contract workers with work experiences of 1–5 years are on lower side, whereas workers with more years of work and who have gained experience in one branch of industry and handling skilled operation get more emoluments.

At the same time, labour market in industrial sphere is highly fragmented. The argument that varied nature of industries provide plethora of employment opportunities in informal sector of urban economy is a myth[8] and needs scrutiny. It is argued that scope and possibilities do exist in terms of intra-industry and inter-industrial mobility, i.e., both at vertical and horizontal levels. In city centres such as Surat and Vapi, labour market segmentation has taken shape mainly on the lines of demographic characteristics of labour, viz., regional specificities. In textile industry of Surat, for instance, power loom operations are mainly manned by migrants from Orissa and Andhra Pradesh, whereas migrants from Uttar Pradesh and Bihar, a good number of them are Muslims, are employed mainly in dying and printing units. Similarly, migrants from Saurashtra, mainly Patels, are found working in diamond units. When diamond industry was under crisis and workers were laid off, it was almost impossible for them to get jobs in power loom units or dying-printing units as nature of works in both the industries are quite varied and entirely different from diamond industry. Even otherwise in a highly segmented labour market where a particular job or operation in one industrial activity has been mainly taken care of by a group with specific demographic characteristic crossover is extremely difficult.

Thus, in the sphere of industrial employment, workers' condition has been deteriorating immensely in recent time as casualization and degradation have become rampant. On the other hand, as has been pointed out by Breman (2010) informalization of production processes in unorganized sector affects labour detrimentally in terms of work and social security but it strengthens position of capital as they remain organized and not only their labour cost gets reduced but they get out of control net of state regulations, thereby inflating their profit margin exceedingly.

We will now move the focus on an important sub-sector of informal sector, in terms of not only its employment potential but also other implications pertaining to labour market scenario, which is termed as 'fringe sector'.

The Fringe Sector

Industrial development of enormous nature and presence of the large masses of industrial workers have created a large market of commodity buyers and service seekers which have resulted into emergence of 'parallel alternative' market and which in turn created plethora of livelihood activities at the bottom of the economy in urban centres such as Surat and Vapi. These activities can be described as fringe sector activities. This term is being adopted for set of activities through which large masses are eking out their livelihood at the bottom of the urban economy and which have not been properly taken note of either by planners or by academicians, especially as it should be, considering the great number of people who are depending on them, not only in terms of a large basket of livelihood opportunities but also in terms of availability of market of all kinds of items and services at affordable rates for people of lower echelons of socio-economic order. In terms of technical specificity, the livelihood activities which are covered under this rubric though are part and parcel of informal sector, they are 'non-industrial' in nature and, hence, need different treatment as well as nomenclature. Most of the industrial workers, working as casual, contract, or temporary workers, cannot afford to purchase household commodities and other articles for daily use and other purposes as well as spend on services available in 'mainstream' market as they are beyond their reach in terms of their financial bearing. So for their all requirements they rely on fringe sector which are much cheaper and affordable for them. Broad canvas of economic activities in this sector also gives scope to other family members of industrial workers to join as secondary earning members of the family and make life somewhat easier in expensive urban locations.[9] Even middle class and lower middle class too take advantage and benefit of fringe sector. Table 3 provides glimpse of various activities of fringe sector with reference to Surat. In Vapi too, evidences of fringe sector are widely seen as in most of the urban locations.

Table 3

Nature of Fringe Sector Activities and Income (per month)

Category	*Activities*	*Approximate average income per month (Rs)*
Self-employed		
Not-so poor	Waste depot, ice cream parlour, cutlery, tea stall, frame shop, lodge, etc.	6000–8000
Poor	Vegetables vendor, datan seller, water bottle seller, chana dana seller, pan stall, liquor seller, cold drinks and sarbat seller, food item seller, etc.	3000–4000
Destitute	Boot polish, embroidery, barber, watch repairer, bag maker, etc.	1500–2500
Casual labourers		
Poor	Centring, mason, rickshaw driver	5000–6000
Destitute	Waiter in hotel/lodge, tea-stall worker, domestic servant, construction worker, shop worker, watchman, newspaper worker, garage and small workshop worker, prostitute etc.	2000–3000

Source: Reproduced from Desai (2002).

The workers of the fringe sector may be divided into two categories: (1) self-employed, and (2) casual wage labourers. Self-employed constitutes larger part of 'fringe sector'. Seven out of ten fringe sector earners are self-employed (Desai, 2002). They sell some products and commodities or provide services through skills. They are providing all sorts of services and they have been selling items of all kinds such as water, *tadi* (fermented juice of palm tree), country liquor, ice cream, *sarbat* (soft drink), tea, *khaman* (eatable), fruits, vegetables, dana chana (dry grams and pop cone), eggs, omelette, fish, meat, newspapers, artefacts, cutlery, utensils, pans, and pirated CDs. Some of them are having technical skill for repairing gadgets such as stove, cooker, lock, beg, and shoes as well as vehicles. Ragpickers and waste collectors form the lowest bottom of fringe sector earners. The list is very long and can never be exhaustive.

Casual wage labourers are found working in activities and places such as construction and repairing of buildings and roads; small workshops for repairing equipments and vehicles; and as helpers to self-employed skilled artisans and sellers. They are also working as domestic servants as well as security guards at housing societies and industrial units, as shop assistants, hotel-restaurants' attendants-waiters, hospital attendants, and servants. Some of them stand at places known as *majdoor bazaar* or labour market every morning to sell their labour. Apart from manual labourers, they include skilled workers such as carpenters, masons, and others. They work all days in a week and 10–12 hours a day depending upon availability of work. It is not certain that all of them get work every day and workless day remains wageless day for them. Nevertheless, these activities do provide subsistence to a very large population. Among casual labourers of this sector, child labour constitutes a very significant section. They are mainly found working at shops, hotels, garages, tea stalls, industrial units, and as ragpickers.

In terms of income, the fringe workers are stratified lot. Nearly 70 per cent are at the bottom floating around poverty line (PL). In favourable situation, some of them move up the PL temporarily, for short duration, and again go below the line. Heavy monsoon or biting summer, flood, epidemic, riots, serious illness in family and marriage, or other social occasion disrupt their activities and adversely affect their monthly income. In such a situation, one who is not so poor may also be pushed below PL. Nearly 70 per cent people earn less than ₹ 3,000 per month. On an average, more than one-third of the fringe sector workers live below PL. They earn less than ₹ 1,500 per month. It should be remembered that this is not a per capita income. However, there is a small stratum, nearly 11 per cent claimed that they have improved their economic condition (Desai, 2002).

The fringe sector although provides some scope for floating and flexibility at the lowest bottom of informal sector in terms of availability of work as casual labour and self-employment, that space too is not that expansive and have a set of constraints such as fierce competition. Likewise, industrial sector, labour market segmentation has taken shape in fringe sector too. In Surat, for instance, in construction activity, manual labour work is being carried mainly by migrant tribals from central Gujarat as well as bordering states of Madhya Pradesh and Rajasthan, whereas plumbing work is monopoly of Muslim migrants of West Bengal. Similarly, migrants from Uttar Pradesh are found doing colouring job. In hotel industry, most of the attendants are migrants from West Bengal.

On Survival Strategies

The workers eking out their livelihoods from various informal sector activities, industrial as well as non-industrial work in 'fringe sector', are exposed to extremely adverse conditions. Their powerlessness and debility has been exploited by the owners and affluent section to gain maximum advantage. They are denied their legal rights. They are made to work in oppressive conditions and the wages they received cannot be called attractive, substantial, and remunerative in accordance with their labour. The self-employed are mostly self-exploiting themselves. While those who are eking out their livelihood through wage labour as casual and contract labourers constantly face uncertainty in terms of getting work and have to labour under oppressive and harsh working conditions, self-employed livelihood seekers have to face vagaries of weather and other circumstances as well as stiff inner competition. State machinery which is supposed to protect these vulnerable masses has acted hand in glove with dominant groups. For instance, in Surat, vendors and hawkers who are selling various items on the street corners and roadsides are being constantly targeted by vocal middle and elite classes mainly through media for creating nuisance and under their influence and also instruction of the state government which is keen for beautification of the city under its globalization project, this group of self-employed is being harassed severely by police and municipal authorities. The fringe sector earners have been facing adversities not only in the sphere of work but even with regard to their living conditions. Apparently, the policy under the Jawaharlal Nehru National Urban Renewal Mission (JNNURM) for relocation of slum dwellers has been formulated to upgrade the living conditions of slum dwellers. But the way and manner with which the policy is being implemented by Surat Municipal Corporation (SMC) clearly has indicated that under the garb of upgradation of living condition through JNNURM, the SMC's intention has been to make city clean and beautiful by removing slums from the middle of the city[10] and push them away in the name of relocation to far off places, in the outskirts of the city where they have been not provided proper facilities. Added to those miseries, they have been pushed away to distant places from their working locations.

How then this marginalized lot keep themselves afloat? Do they have any space to sustain and further their interests? How they cope up in adverse and hostile work milieu and unfavourable surroundings of city? Their responses and strategies can be delineated in brief as follows.

Labour and State

State's labour department under Labour Commissioner is supposed to protect the interest of labour and take care of their welfare. The labour department's urban and rural divisions and their functionaries' responsibility is to see that the labour laws get implemented and those who violate them are penalized. But the state of affairs has been rather pathetic as on one hand, the numerical strength of the staff of the department has more or less remained the same since 1970s, even though the number of industrial units and workers have increased several times and on the other hand, attitude of most of the functionaries is indifferent and callous towards the labour as they too have imbibed stereotypes against labour and their affinity is more with capital and there is no pro-labour political pressure. The factory inspectors, even earlier and at present too, are more interested in getting personal gain from the owners rather than to protect labour's rights. After liberalization, labour inspectors have become more indifferent with regard to implementation of the labour laws. The Industrial Policy 2003 promises labour reforms for 'conducive labour environment'. Labour department is 'already considering amendments (in labour laws) *suo moto* in many provisions'. It notes that 'the Labour department has already initiated an exercise of rationalizing all inspections carried out under its control'. The rules have been relaxed in the special economic zones (SEZ) created in 2005. All industrial units and other establishments in SEZ are declared as 'public utility service' under the provisions of Industrial Dispute Act. In this zone, the powers of the Labour Commissioner are delegated to the Development Commissioner. The labour officer is expected to function as Registration Officer, Conciliation Officer as well as Inspector under various Labour Laws to provide 'Single Window Service'. The industries and establishments are provided initiatives for 'self–certification' for fulfilment of labour and environmental laws. The judiciary is also seen tilting increasingly towards establishment against the interest of labour.

Accepting Reality and Getting a Patronizing Favour

Workers make all sorts of effort to be in good book of their employers, who may be unit owners or contractors. In diamond industry of Surat, practice of recruiting relatives, kith–kin, and acquaintances facilitates this tendency. Workers do not view their employers as their masters but someone who support them in need and crisis situation. In present context, at both places, Surat and Vapi, most of the industrial operations are being carried out through employing contract workers. Most of these mediating persons have brought relatives and acquaintances. Migrant workers have to depend on them not only for work-related aspects but also each and every matter concerning social security, from shelter to medical treatment.

On Vertical and Horizontal Mobility of Workers

Breman in his seminal work on informal sector workers (see Breman, 1996) mentions high turn over of workers in two major industries of Surat, i.e., diamond-processing and textile. The study on Vapi's industrial workforce also indicates high mobility among them (Desai, 2000). It shows that seven out of every ten workers had worked in more than one unit, i.e., they had changed workplaces, though mainly in one industry and in the same operation or nature of work within that industry. Breman too has mainly narrated horizontal mobility within one industrial activity. This sort of mobility gives them 'space' in a tight situation. However, as has been mentioned earlier, mobility from one industry to another is quite difficult, workers passage from industry to non-industrial activity, mainly in self-employment activities and vice versa can also be possible only in a limited way. In the present context, vertical mobility is mainly confined to increase in monthly emoluments by opting to skilled operations through self-learning but it is not associated with conferring technical status or grade. A small minority are also trying to venture into self-employment by investing their savings.

But this mobility should not be glorified with reference to informal sector as if all the shortcomings and lacunae concerning globalization project especially with regard to workforce would be taken care of due to flexibility of this nature of informal sector. First, as we have discussed earlier labour market of informal sector, both in industrial sub-sector and fringe sub-sector, is highly segmented, making inter-sub-sectoral mobility quite difficult. Second, though compared to industrial and quasi-industrial sub-sectors, flexibility and fluidity does exist in self-employment activities, it is not all that expansive and have too many constraints.

Finding Alternative Sources of Livelihood and Increasing Income

A segment among the industrial workers may look out for alternatives outside industry, in fringe sector, to get freedom from oppressive work conditions. Apart from that in order to increase their income amidst vagaries regarding getting work regularly, a group among them does other work simultaneously in spare time. Those eking out livelihood in fringe sector especially are found doing multiple activities. For instance, working as security guard at night hours and driving autorickshaw in daytime. Also, their families, more often than not, have more than one earning members. The increase in proportion of female workers in informal sector should be attributed to the vulnerability and fragility seen and experienced due to uncertainties of employment opportunities.

Creating a Safety Cell through Segmentation

The phenomenon of labour market segmentation as has been observed in industrial sphere as well as fringe sector has been extensively deliberated in the previous text. That mechanism can also be looked at as a safety device being employed by the labour. Though it might serve the interest of one ethnic group of workforce, the other groups suffer due and because of it.

Unions: Facing Extinction

A study on Vapi's workers conducted decade earlier had observed that

> ... However, without taking note of streak of protest and disgruntled voices, howsoever minor and limited they appear to be, the picture remains incomplete. A good number of workers are well aware about exploitative tactics of owners and about their rights, which are protected by laws. Though not all among this enlightened group of workers protest openly due to fear of consequences, some have guts to wage a battle. (Desai, 2000: 258)

Vapi has been known for vibrant and militant union activities. Around 10–12 unions have been making their presence felt. Both violent and peaceful means of protest and response were demonstrated by unions. Even Vapi Industrial Association (VIA) had to take weary note of these unions. Surat's textile industry too shows presence of a handful of unions. Its representative union though has become extremely feeble and ineffective. However, at present, on the whole, union activity is in decline. Widespread use of contract workers and casual labour covering most of the industrial operations has escalated this process further. Industry owners now do not have direct relationship with workers. Workers simply shy away from not only getting involved in union activity but even uttering a word about unions. The historical institution of labour union is fast becoming dysfunctional. The workers, as a group, have never been as fragmented and as atomized as of today.

Reproducing Innate Community

Migrants started their journey from far off rural areas to destinations of industrial places by banking on their social ties. They have to recreate their innate community at these industrial places in order to survive in alien and unfavourable milieu. In both the places, Surat and Vapi, migrants from the same region or sub-region are residing in the same neighbourhood. For instance, in Gitanagar locality of Vapi migrants from some pockets of Bihar and Uttar Pradesh are living together and significant proportion of them are Muslims. Similarly, in Umaraonagar slums of Surat, migrant textile workers of Ganjam district of Orissa are residing side by side. In hours of crisis, whether related to work or a health problem or a quarrel with local group, people from own village or community come to their rescue or help. As mentioned above, employers too have been one agency to lean on at the time of financial needs or health problem. This support system is still relevant in Surat's textile and diamond industries but scenario of Vapi has undergone change considerably. Employers' accountability towards their workers has been shifted to contractors who are more or less part of their social network. Thus, in the present context, the primordial ties have become the only mainstay for informal sector workers in terms of social security and support as unions are facing extinction and casualization and disciplining of labour have become more rampant. This development certainly raises theoretical issue of relationship between industrial and urban social order vis-à-vis primordial social institutions. It is envisaged that with the evolution and advent of industrial urban social order, traditional and primordial social ties and bonding would get weakened and that pertaining to work-related interest would get strengthened. But this relationship is determined more by the nature of industrialization and urbanization than by their mere evolution and existence. In the case of many of the European societies, decline of age-old social institutions was witnessed and caused due to an advent of robust nature of industrialization that had marked advancements of individual freedom and organizations based on achieved status. But this formulation concerning relationship between urban and industrial social order and traditional social setting certainly needs in-depth deliberations and analysis.

In Lieu of Concluding Remarks

In the end, the relationship of labour and globalized capitalism or globalization has to be viewed from the prism of reproduction of labour.[11] Rakhi Sehgal has put it aptly as follows:

> It is conceivable that the devaluation of formal protective safeguards that contemporary processes of globalization favour, encourages capital to seek out precisely those pools of labour that are least proletarianised and to a large degree remain assimilated in communities predicated on customary social bonds. ... (c)apital may be attracted to communities that are based primarily on the logic of reciprocity and therefore most likely to assume the burdens of social reproduction of the labour force as part of their cultural practice. (2005: 228)

Globalized capital does not want any accountability or responsibility. In addition, it wants the state also to steer clear of their role with relation to reproduction of labour. The state has been performing it through industrial policies, labour market regulation, social policies and redistribution programmes (Sehgal, 2005). In present restructuring programme, state has become ineffectual and that too with design. Globalization is like a two-edged sword. On one hand, it encourages labour to seek alternative sources of support and on the other side, it destroys these support systems. At present juncture, informal economy is the only place of solace and support for poor labour but that space has also been under threat as the capital has set their eyes on fringe sector too if we go by recent development of multinational corporations taking keen interest in retail markets.

The NSEUS report, which is prepared by pro-poor and pro-labour intellectuals and experts, has recommended expansion of employment opportunities and decent working conditions for informal sector workers (Breman, 2010) that include the set of minimum requirements such as 8-hour working day with a recess, one-paid-day break, piece rate to be at par with time rate wage, women's wage to be remunerated at par, and right to organize. Human right organizations and labour unions have been raising voices and protesting over the same set of demands for informal sector labour since last several decades without much success. Perhaps, the pro-labour intellectuals and human rights activists who have prepared those excellent reports too know this fact but at the same time they have stark realization that they do not have a reach beyond raising this set of demands again and again. As Breman has mentioned, the concerned reports of NSEUS have been received by stony silence by the Central Government, especially the Prime Minister Office (PMO) which should not surprise anyone considering our economist Prime Minister's great fondness for neo-liberal ideology that makes people believe that the marginalized labour eking out their livelihood at the bottom of the economy are resilient enough to sustain and take care of themselves mainly through their primordial ties such caste, kinship, and familial bonds. This is evidently reflected in the approach of the World Bank, the chief architect and proponent of the new economic regime. In the mid-1970s, this premier international financial institution had emphasized that economic progress was only possible through the development of the 'modern' and formal sector of the economy, because of its high level of productivity and quality of employment and it had admitted too that the informal sector, on the other hand, was characterized by low productivity, less job security, and extremely low earnings for the workers and those who were working over there should be treated as 'reserve pool' who would surely be upgraded in formal sector over a period of time. Today, however, the World Bank as well as leading finance and trade-related organizations and bodies all over the world and that include India's government are strongly in favour of supporting the informal sector as part of its globalization and liberalization strategy. Job insecurity is now viewed as flexibility of work, while the fact that workers are forced to fall back on kinship, family, and community (caste) ties for survival has now been 'discovered' to be a social security arrangement (World Bank Report, 1995) and hence are glorified.

The Marxian ideological framework is obviously critical with the above formulation on the ground that due to fragmentation of labour in informal or fringe sector, class solidarity and organization based on class identity and affinity as well as common work experience that in final analysis would lead to working class emancipation from exploitation and oppression that have been associated with the system or structure is being jeopardized. This paper does not intend to support or vouch for proponents of globalization project in terms of glorifying informal sector with regard to celebrating primordial and social ties for providing social security in the present systemic compulsion, whereby state is withdrawing gradually from its earlier avatar of *welfare state* in terms of extending social security to weaker sections. But on the other hand, as a social observer it has to be taken into account that for hapless livelihood seekers at the bottom of the economy, these social ties are the only means and rescue devises of survival at hand, especially in hours of crisis.

Lastly, it is difficult not to reflect on the observation of eminent sociologist Jan Breman who has done pioneering work on labouring poor of western India, especially Gujarat. He is of the view (Breman, 2009, 2010) that compared to Indian capital, their European counterparts had vision for sustainable development of capitalism and hence, they had seen to it that the labour got leeway and space in the form of welfare measures so that labour could be reproduced in order to sustain and endure capitalism longer. This paper begs to differ with this view on the ground that this formulation does not have universal sustainability, in a sense that it has to be examined and assessed with reference to changing context. In 19th and 20th centuries when those European colonial countries were having over-abundance of wealth due to their plundering of third world countries and exorbitant extent of profit as the capital of those countries had no competition in international market, the capitalist state of those countries were in a position to be benevolent for their labour. Of course, evolution of enlightenment and other progressive philosophical and ideological schools too had played their part. But again without wealth and associated comfortable lifestyle production of those ideas would not have been possible. The same European states and their capitalists allies that are governing most of the international financial organizations today such as World Bank and International Monetary Fund (IMF) have been chiefly responsible for present adversities and miseries of informal sector labour in Third World country such as India as they are under crisis in the changed context and have to resort to compel Third World countries such as India to adopt neo-liberal policy which is anti-labour and anti-human to the core.

Notes

1. This study has covered 1300 firms, spread over 10 states and 9 major product groups.
2. The study, which was supported by National Foundation of India (NFI), Delhi, investigated effect of globalization on various sectors with reference to Gujarat state, with a title, 'Globalization, Gujarat state and Welfare for Poor'. The study team comprises Ghanshyam Shah, Hemant Shah, and Kiran Desai. The author of this paper has focused his investigation on component of labour.
3. The study, which is funded by ICSSR, New Delhi, mainly covers livelihood earners at the lowest bottom of the informal sector, termed as fringe sector, mainly consisting of self-employed and casual as well as contractual labourers with reference to Surat city.
4. For detailed account of Patidars' rise from oppressed community in Saurashtra region to politically strong group in Gujarat mainstream politics see Engelshovan (1999).

5. For detailed discussion of Giddens argument see Arjan de Haan (1994).
6. Based on a report from *The Times of India* (Surat city edition), 17 December 2009.
7. These two terms: 'steep slope' and 'citadel' were invented by Holmstrom (1985) with reference to industrial workers.
8. Breman (2009) has dealt with this point.
9. Kiran Desai has done case study research on fringe sector livelihood earners of Surat (see Desai, 2002) and based on that research, he is carrying out more extensive study on the same theme at present.
10. As has been pointed out by some observers, the influential and powerful builder lobby has been eyeing greedily the land plots on which slums are located in the heart and middle parts of the city and have played instrumental role in removing slums.
11. Entire discussion is based on elaborate treatment on this subject by Sehgal (2005).

References

Anarde Foundation (2000). *Need Assessment Study of Industrial Workers of Vapi* (Unpublished report). Vapi: Anarde Foundation.

Breman, J. (1996). *Footloose Labour – Working in India's Informal Economy*, Cambridge: Cambridge University Press.

Breman, J. (2003). 'Urban poverty in the early 21st century', *The Labouring Poor in India*. New Delhi: Oxford University Press.

Breman, J. (2004) *The making and Unmaking of an Industrial Working Class*. New Delhi: Oxford University Press.

Breman, J. (2007). *The Poverty Regime in Village India*. New Delhi: Oxford University Press.

Breman, J. (2009). 'Myths of global safety net', *New Left Review* 59, September–October.

Breman, J. (2010). 'India's social question in a state of denial', *Economic and Political Weekly* June 5–11.

de Haan, A. (1994). *Unsettled Settlers: Migrant Workers and Industrial Capitalism in Calcutta*. Rotterdam: Faculty of History and Art Studies.

Desai, K. (1995). *Nature and Conditions of Workers in Small Scale Industrial Units of Gujarat* (Unpublished report). Surat: Centre for Social Studies.

Desai, K. (2000). *Profile and Conditions of Industrial Workers – A Case Study of Vapi* (Unpublished PhD thesis). Surat: South Gujarat University.

Desai, K. (2001). 'Workers of closed textile mills: A case of south Gujarat' (Unpublished paper), Paper presented at the seminar on 'Collective Care Arrangement among Workers and Non-workers in Informal sector', Centre for Economic and Social Studies, Hyderabad, 1–2 March.

Desai, K. (2002). 'Searching for space: Workers in the fringe sector of Surat', *Development and Deprivation in Gujarat – In Honour of Jan Breman*, editors Shah, G., et al. New Delhi: Sage Publications, pp. 150–172.

Desai, K., and Raj, N. (2001a). *Child Labour in Diamond Industry of Surat*. Noida: V.V. Giri National Labour Institute.

Desai, K., and Raj, N. (2001b). *Child Labour in Textile Industry of Surat* (Unpublished report). Surat and Noida: Centre for Social Studies and V.V. Giri National Labour Institute.

Deshpande, L.K., Sharma, A.N., Anup, K., and Sarkar, S. (2004). *Liberalisation and Labour: Labour Flexibility in Indian Manufacturing*. New Delhi: Institute of Human Development. [As referred in Papola, T.S. (2005)].

D'Monte, D. (2002). *Ripping the Fabric: The decline of Mumbai and Its Mills*. New Delhi: Oxford University Press.

Engelshovan, M. (1999). "Diamond and Patels: A report on the diamond industry of Surat', *Contribution to Indian Sociology* 33(1/2), January–August.

Ghosh, A., and Ahmad, S.S. (1996). *Plague in Surat – Crisis in Urban Governance*. New Delhi: Concept Publishing House.

Holmstrom, M. (1985). *Industry and Inequality: The Social Anthropology of Indian Labour*. Cambridge: Cambridge University Press.

Industrial Policy (2003). Government of Gujarat document, Downloaded from the website: http://Indiaholic.blogspot.com.

Papola, T.S. (2005). 'Workers in a globalising world: Some perspectives from India', Paper presented at the conference on 'Globalisation and Labour Mobility in India and China', Asian Business and economic Research Unit, at Monash University, Melbourne, Australia, 29–30 September, Google.co.in.isid.org.in/pdf/ workglobal/world.pdf

Patel, A. (2004). 'Pattern of development and tribal migration: A case of tribals from Dangs and Panchamahal in Gujarat', *Tribal Issues in India*, editors Sah, D.C., and Sisoda, Y.S. Jaipur: Rawat Publications, pp. 175–194.

Patel, A. and Desai, R. (1992). *Gramin Gujaratma Sharm-Sthalantar* (in Gujarati). Surat: Centre for Social Studies.

Patil, R. (1987). 'Migration and industrial workers in Ichalkaranji', *Migrant Labour and Related Issues*, editor Vidyut Joshi. New Delhi: Oxford & IBH Publishing Co. Pvt. Ltd. pp. 153–164.

Punalekar, S.P. (1988). *Informalization and Dependency: A Study of Jari and Embroidery Workers in South Gujarat* (Mimeographed report). Surat: Centre for Social Studies.

Ravenstein, E. (1885). 'The Laws of Migration', *Journal of the Statistical Society* 48.

Sakthiwel, S. and Joddar, P. (2006) 'Unorganised sector workforce in India – Trends, patterns and social security coverage', *Economic and Political Weekly* 27 May–3 June.

Sehgal, R. (2005). 'Social reproduction of third world labour in the era of globalisation – State, market and the household', *Economic and Political Weekly* 28 May–4 June.

Shah, G., Shah, H., and Desai, K. (2007). *Globalization, Gujarat State and Welfare for Poor* (Unpublished report). New Delhi: National Foundation for India.

Sengupta, A. et al. (2006) Social Security for Unorganised Workers – Report, New Delhi: National Commission for Enterprises in the Unorganised Sector.

Soni, J. (1990) *Jari Industry and Women Workers* (Unpublished paper). Paper presented at the seminar on 'Women and Work', Centre for Social Studies, Surat.

South Gujarat University (SGU) (1984). *Working and Living Conditions of the Surat Textile Workers: A Survey*. Surat: South Gujarat University.

Van Wersch, H. (1992). *The Bombay Textile Strike: 1982–83*. Bombay: Oxford University Press.

World Bank (1995). *World Bank Development Report*. New Delhi: Oxford University Press.

10

Implementing NREGS in Gujarat

Evidence from the Initial Phase

Amita Shah

The National Rural Employment Guarantee Scheme (NREGS) is an important landmark for promoting inclusive growth in India. The scheme, based an a rights-based approach, not only provides guaranteed employment but also empowers rural communities to demand work as part of their basic entitlements that are essential for participating in the larger process of development in the country. Besides these, NREGS like most other employment generation schemes could potentially play an important role in boosting the overall economic growth by way of enhancing wage income through the creation of productive assets, especially in an otherwise under-invested and stagnant rural economy (Patanaik, 2006). The strategy may work marvels in an economy such as India, where the agriculture sector continues to play a crucial role in sustaining the momentum of overall economic growth besides reducing poverty (Bhaduri, 2005; Shah, 2009; Ambasta et al., 2008).

Implementation of the NREGS, however, throws up significant challenges, given the multiple objectives on the one hand and breaking through the micro-level dynamics – political as well administrative – on the other hand. In fact, the most important initial hurdles seem to emanate from the demand-driven nature of the scheme. This, among other things, essentially calls for revitalization of local communities and institutions of decentralized governance such as (Gram Sabhas and Panchayats) at the village level. This is difficult, given a scenario where those who need to demand guaranteed work under the scheme and those who are actually vested with power to accord formal approval and also take that forward with the administrative machinery beyond the village level, often turn out to be from different segments of society whose interests may have little in common and at times are at logger heads within the local dynamics in a micro setting.

There are difficulties in planning for the creation of productive assets and generation of awareness among the community (Ambasta et al., 2008). Further there are issues about the method of assessing the quantum of work performed and the associated rates (i.e., schedule of rates – SOR) prescribed for different types of work. This, at times, leads to ambiguity about the total amount of wages being paid as there is no prescribed wage rate per day. Administrative delays in starting the work, continuity, and more importantly predictability, seasonality, and transparency in payments, all remain major teething problems at least during the initial phase of implementation of a demand-driven scheme such as this.

Besides, some of the well-known problems of supply side management observed during most of the employment generation/guarantee programmes including the Maharashtra Employment Guarantee Scheme (MEGS) seem to loom large in this early phase of NREGS (Shah and Mehta, 2008).

Last but not the least is the issue of the perceived need or urgency for extending administrative support for implementation, which is often shaped by the political economy influencing policies at the state level. Apparently, states with a high incidence of rural poverty, or those with a rich history of mass-based organizations/movements, or those tilted towards political ideology of the then ruling alliance of the left parties, happen to have made significant achievements in implementing NREGS, especially during the initial phase. At a macro level, Gujarat state does not confirm any of these parameters leading to better implementation of the scheme. As a result, the progress of NREGS was fairly dismal till the end of 2008. It has, however, started picking up in the last few months apparently due to a number of factors, viz., growing sense of lagging behind in a competitive scenario across states, economic melt down, and onset of the general election, 2009.

Against this backdrop, this paper tries to examine the experiences of the initial phase of the NREGS with special focus on certain important aspects of project implementation that may have crucial bearings on larger goals for promoting rural economy, democratic decentralization, and poverty reduction besides enhancing wage income among the rural workforce.

Objectives and Methodology

Objectives

The objectives are two-fold:

(i) To undertake concurrent monitoring of the extent, processes, and outcomes of NREGS, and

(ii) To examine practices with regard to project design, implementation, monitoring, and evaluation systems.

The specific objectives are to:

(a) Assess the coverage, intensity, and composition of works and workers engaged in the NREGS

(b) Understand the processes of implementation at various levels by focusing on important aspects such as awareness, creation of the demand for work and obtaining job cards, participation in planning and implementation, efficacy and transparency in financial transactions, and social auditing.

(c) Ascertain the impact on wage income, asset creation, and equity across caste, class, and gender.

The study is based on primary as well as secondary data collected from a sample of households from selected districts, talukas, and villages in the state. The selection is based on a common methodology developed by the collaborative team. Accordingly, four districts were selected from the list of six districts where implementation had taken place during the first phase of the NREGS in Gujarat. The districts have been selected in a manner that may cover diverse socio-economic, geographic, and agro-climatic scenarios in the state.

Selection of Study Areas

The four districts selected for the study in Gujarat are Banaskantha, Sabarkantha, Narmada, and Valsad. Since the area selected for implementation in the initial phase of the NREGS had a built-in bias towards relatively more backward; hence, tribal-dominated districts in the state, the four districts selected for the study, represent these scenarios. The other two districts were Dahod and the Dangs. Initially, the Dangs was selected from the southern part of Gujarat as the district is almost entirely dominated by tribal population and is very remote. However, it had to be dropped as the district consists of only one taluka. The next step was to select two talukas – one having relatively higher concentration of project activity and another with low levels of activity. Table 1 presents a brief profile of the district and talukas selected for the study.

Table 1

Profile and District and Talukas Covered by the Study

District/Taluka	*No. of HHs (2001)*	*Spatial and agro-climatic features*	*% of BPL HHs*	*% of SC+ ST population*	*% of literacy*	*% of irrigational area*	*% of worker non-agriculture*	*Backwardness rank*
1. Banaskantha		North and Arid						
1.1 Dantiwada (H)	15,664		50.78	15.23	47.25	53.7	40.97	111
1.2 Vadagam (I.)	40,735		36.07	19.01	68.78	61.0	48.3	139
2. Sabarkantha		North and Dry Region						
2.1 Khedbrahma (H)	32,903		53.29	72.5	42.33	23.0	26.6	49
2.2 Idar (L)	42,255		18.12	21.04	72.06	46.5	47.5	210
3. Narmada		Central and Sub-Humid						
3.1 Dediapada (H)	28,232		76.14	96.19	48.55	1.2	12.92	12
3.2 Tilakwada (L)	11,267		50.19	57.09	64.44	18.0	19.42	39
4. Valasad		South and Humid						
4.1 Kaprada (H)	35,674		82.97	94.09	33.98	10.6	10.25	3
4.2 Dharampur (L)	30,310		48.18	92.34	48.54	11.2	25.2	58

Note: H – High Concentration; L – Low Concentration of NREGS activities.

Source: Census of India, 2001; BPL ratios are obtained from the socio-economic survey (2004), Department of Rural Development, Government of Gujarat.

It may be noted that the talukas selected for the study are characterized by fairly high proportion of households below poverty line (BPL). An exception to the case is Idar. Accordingly, these talukas also represent very high levels of relative backwardness among the 225 talukas in the state. For example, Kaparda in Valsad district is the third most backward taluka in the state. Similarly Dediapada, Tilakwada, Khedbrahma, and Dharampur have ranked lower than 60 (in a descending order) in terms of relative backwardness.

An important feature emerging from Table 1 is that the talukas with high concentration of project activities are more backward as compared to talukas in the category of low levels of project work. This confirms positive bias (or discrimination) in favour of relatively more backward areas to be undertaken for the project.

Two villages from each taluka were selected for the study. In all, 16 villages spread over four districts have been covered for the field study, which was conducted during 2008.

Selection of Households

A quota sample of 35 households was selected from each village. This consisted of 20 beneficiaries (BN) and 15 non-beneficiary (NB) households. The selection within each of the two categories of households was based on prior information pertaining to the socio-economic status cf the households. A random sample was drawn from three categories of households, viz., landless and artisans, marginal farmers, and medium farmers or those with small business, etc. In all 560 households were covered under the survey – 320 BN and 240 NB.

Survey Tools

The data collection was based on various instruments for different categories of respondents, viz., taluka-level officials, functionaries of the village/Gram Panchayat, and households (BN and NB). In addition to these, group meetings were conducted and physical verification on the work sites was also documented (along with photographs). Secondary data were collected from the records of the local authorities as well as from the Census Handbook.

Implementation of the NREGS: Performance and Institutional Arrangements

Performance of the NREGS

Driven mainly by industrial urban growth and mediated by intra-state migration, the NREGS in Gujarat was perceived to be of lower priority among policy makers in the state. The main reasons for this being that the work under the NREGS is mainly of manual type; such work is often available on large-scale infrastructural projects going on in various parts of the state. Another reason could be that the time period for launching the NREGS coincided with an unusual spell of good rainfall since 2004. Together with the initial perception that people in Gujarat may not need state assistance as they were not willing to undertake manual work under this scheme. The perception is likely to have strengthened further by political considerations at the time of election in the state where the economic development of Gujarat was highlighted as the central thrust by the ruling party; NREGS being promoted by a coalition of other political parties at the Centre may not have been viewed this as an important agenda, at least at that point in time.

A combined result of various factors such as these seems to have led to a very slow start in terms of implementation of this scheme, which was initially confined to only six districts in the state (Table 2).

Table 2

Performance of the NREGA in Gujarat

Year	*No. of districts*	*Total expenditure (Rs Crores)*	*Total person-days (in lakhs)*	*Per district*		
				Expenditure (Rs Crores)	*Employment person-days (in lakh)*	*Cost per person-day (Rs)*
2006–2007	6	85.85	100.48	14.31	16.75	85.44
2007–2008	9	81.84	90.06	9.09	10.01	90.87
2008–2009 (up to December)	26	100.73	118.8	3.87	4.57	84.79
2009–2010 (up to February)	26	569.13	252.3	21.88	9.7	255.57

Source: Website of the Government of Gujarat (http:/ruraldev.gujarat.gov.in/nrega.html).

In 2006–2007, Gujarat was one of the states that lagged behind, ranking 23rd out of the 27th states in terms of expenditure under the NREGS in the country. The scenario has rapidly changed in the last two years as shown in Table 3.

Table 3

Summary of Progress of the NREGS in Gujarat

Indicators	*December 2008 (in lakh)*	*February 2010*
Households registered	25.58	34.80
Job cards issued	25.58	34.80
Demand for employment (households)	5.15	14.80
Employment provided (households)	5.15	14.80
Person-days generated	105.87 (118.8 as per Table 9)	498.26
Fund available	18,827.32	74,627.12
Total expenditure	10,077.34	56,913.29
Cost per person-day Rs/day	95.18 (84.8 as per Table 9)	255.57
Works completed (No.)	23,275	252,298
Works in progress (No.)	12,895	34,022

Source: As in Table 2.

By the end of 2008, about ₹ 183 crores were made available for the project implementation in Gujarat. This increased substantially from about 163 crores till October 2008. Utilization of the fund is limited; it was 55 per cent during December 2008, which increased marginally from about 52 per cent till October 2008. The districts with relatively higher level of fund utilization obviously include those started in the initial phase.

What is in fact noteworthy is that the districts of Dahod and the Panchmahal have the largest quantum of funds allocated and utilized followed by Banaskantha. In fact, these two districts are known to have a high incidence of 'out-migration', conversely these districts have the lowest proportion of 'in-migration'. It may be recalled that Sabarkantha and Banaskantha districts covered in this study also have a lower proportion of 'in-migration'.

Table 4

Implementation of the NREGS across Districts in Gujarat (February 2010)

Districts	% of SC/ST in HHs with job cards		Person-days worked per HHs (No.)		% of women in HHs with job cards		Expenditure per HHs (Rs)		Wages per HHs	
	2008–2009	2009–2010	2008–2009	2009–2010	2008–2009	2009–2010	2008–2009	2009–2010	2008–2009	2009–2010
Banaskantha	46.76	46.97	20.93	23.76	37.46	31.60	1958.58	2583.97	1387.13	2076.21
Dang	99.59	98.86	18.42	44.99	46.04	49.04	2675.84	7650.55	1694.63	5038.01
Dahod	80.01	69.17	35.97	36.19	51.35	49.99	3055.56	6699.77	2413.14	4922.21
Narmada	90.09	89.33	16.09	43.42	45.76	41.54	2057.68	4937.95	1345.12	3279.27
Panchmahal	39.16	38.26	52.78	48.21	41.42	44.83	4546.81	5309.96	3157.48	3513.44
Sabarkantha	46.03	43.60	34.25	47.05	55.20	60.00	2252.65	4373.89	2049.17	3814.35
Bharuch	77.33	80.31	22.96	23.08	36.50	29.26	2467.09	3274.54	1382.64	1984.82
Navsari	93.44	85.60	23.99	31.70	31.38	40.37	3243.65	4587	2256.06	3184.83
Valsad	92.25	91.24	24.38	31.68	41.50	35.10	3393.20	4376.04	2066.17	3111.26
Ahmedabad	41.47	38.25	7.35	22.14	33.33	33.30	923.27	2462.96	727.61	1563.63
Amreli	32.99	49.86	26.13	49.79	26.35	30.17	1922.04	4507.47	1550.81	3433.78
Anand	21.55	21.96	9.51	24.09	34.09	35.60	946.05	3136.37	617.52	2176.60
Bhavnagar	10.86	14.14	14.83	36.52	41.68	50.00	1258.66	2980.37	1012.81	2617.59

Cont'd...

...Cont'd

Gandhinagar	22.48	8.14	6.68	37.08	29.41	38.12	1402.87	8951.20	615.99	3934.35
Jamnagar	18.04	32.33	24.45	43.50	64.29	33.01	2505.90	5192.91	1648.91	3808.45
Junagadh	38.96	45.32	73.44	45.75	38.27	44.33	5759.46	6876.50	5454.87	5300.81
Kachchh	27.15	29.16	17.29	51.62	43.27	36.42	1484.25	7037.50	1292.83	4486.53
Kheda	9.81	9.52	15.10	30.77	27.41	30.08	903.89	4402.11	659.61	2626.53
Mahesana	21.01	20.86	10.07	53.32	52.86	25.17	1364.02	7472.50	889.11	4737.26
Patan	23.81	13.80	34.53	40.95	28.80	46.02	2575.11	4206.55	1876.42	2981.93
Porbandar	31.69	26.65	60.82	67.76	37.24	32.99	5971.48	8946.67	4487.42	5627
Rajkot	25	30.40	8.70	59.51	34.01	65.23	1131.78	15486.47	754.66	11983.03
Surat	96.11	91.46	19.13	34.78	36.28	32.43	2700.61	5199.76	1614.45	3324.23
S. Nagar	10	22.56	31.75	33.99	40.25	3.07	1240.68	3873.68	991.12	2940.27
Tapi	99.05	94.85	10.92	33.33	36.73	52.20	1108	4892.74	762.73	3079.24
Vadodara	67.78	77.09	8.33	16.32	30.62	100	905.90	2303.17	561.77	1535.81
All	50.21	49.44	25.04	36.29	42.82	46.60	2304.09	4588.79	1697.13	3242.80

Note: Districts 1 through 6 were covered during I phase; 7 through 9 during phase II; 10 through 26 during phase III.

The situation has started improving as one observes the difference over a 3-month period between October and December. The trend seems to have continued and perhaps accelerated since then. This is reflected in the fact that the state Government is pro-actively inviting people to come forward and undertake work through the NREGS. Awareness is generated through TV and other media, hiring para professionals at the taluka level and inviting suggestions from civil society organization (CSOs). This in fact is a major turn around from the earlier approach where formal submission of demand for the NREGS was generally discouraged (Hirway, 2007) and the work to be undertaken was made subject to the priorities set by the individual departments such as irrigation, public works, watershed, and rural development. This is why the number of households demanding work and that provided with employment matches perfectly.

Among several reasons, the recent recession, especially affecting almost five lakh diamond workers in Surat city and other parts of the state, may have provided a special fillip to the scheme. Despite this, Gujarat continues to lag behind the other states which may also not work favourably at the time when the general elections are underway. The state thus looks forward to a more pro-active intervention with regard to the NREGS in Gujarat. Table 4 presents a district-wise scenario by the beginning of 2010.

Coverage and Activities in the Study Areas – Talukas

This section provides information about the status of work undertaken, expenditure incurred, and procedures followed along with the type of activities chosen for asset creation at the taluka and village levels.

Tables 5 and 6 provide information about the extent of work done and expenditure incurred in four talukas covered under the study. The following observations emerge from this study:

(a) Number of employment demanded varies significantly from 408 in Valsad to 2811 in Narmada district; the numbers, as expected, are higher in the talukas – in the category of high (h) levels of activities as compared to that in the category of low (l). Number of work completed is substantially lower than that proposed in three districts except Banaskantha.

(b) The average expenditure per number of work completed is inversely related to the total number of work; it varies from ₹ 41,000 in Sabarkantha to ₹ 3.34 lakhs in Banaskantha. However, we do not have information about the number of ongoing works.

(c) Wages account for 60–88 per cent of the total fund utilized. This may be subject to modifications as some payments (for wages as well as material) are likely to be pending.

(d) Number of proposed and sanctioned work is more or less the same except in Sabarkantha. At the same time, payment of unemployment allowances is nil in all the four districts. This, in fact, may substantiate the observation made earlier about a perfect match between the demand and supply, where the former is generally not encouraged or pro-actively mobilized.

We also looked into some of the important features of the processes undertaken at the taluka level. It was observed that the project offices at the taluka level have used a variety of devices for creating awareness and mobilizing demand from the communities. The catch, however, is that the demand was converted into a formal submission only when it was sanctioned through the line departments, which actually execute the work.

Another important feature is that most of the taluka-level offices do keep the requisite registers and a helpline in the common channel for grievance-redressal mechanisms. It is, however, not clear as to how often this facility has been actually utilized. The issue came up frequently during our visits when the village communities were wondering how and to whom they should approach for sorting out issues pertaining to work sites, assessment of work, use of machinery, delays in payment, amenities at work sites, etc., it was evident that most of them have already raised these issues with the work assistant, who in turn has made oral representations at the Taluka level. It is not quite clear as to how often these issues have been represented and whether there were written submissions.

Table 5

Details of Expenditure at Taluka Level: Banaskantha and Sabarkantha Districts (November 2008)

Indicators	*Banaskantha*		*Total*	*Sabarkantha*		*Total*
	Taluka – Danti-wada (H)	*Taluka – Vada-gam (L)*		*Taluka – Khedb-rahma (H)*	*Taluka – Idar (L)*	
No. of work Proposals received	85	90	175	1211	705	1916
No of works Sanctioned	73	90	163	1076	635	1711
No of works Completed	0	90	90	800	489	1289
Total fund receive (in lakh)	104.84	318.84	423.68	475	168.01	643.01
Total fund released (in lakh)	85.32	217.56	302.88	391.1	148.11	539.21
Total fund utilization (in lakh)	83.57	217.56	301.13 [3.34]*	391.1	150.11	541.21 [0.41]
Wage (in lakh)	50.57	152.39	202.96 [67.4%]**	389.8	90.91	480.71 [88.8%]
Material (in lakh)	0	19.24	19.24	1.3	00	1.3
Contingency (in lakh)	33	45.91	78.91	69.83	59.2	129.03
Unemployment Allowance	0	0	0	0	0	0

Table 6

Details of Expenditure by Talukas: Narmada and Valsad Districts (November 2008)

Indicators	*Narmada*		*Total*	*Valasad*		*Total*
	Taluka – Dediapada (High)	*Taluka – Tilakwada (Low)*		*Taluka – Kaprada (High)*	*Taluka – Dharam-pur (Low)*	
No. of work Proposals received	2365	446	2811	303	105	408
No. of works Sanctioned	2365	446	2811	303	105	408
No. of works Completed	582	290	872	25	58	83

Cont'd...

...Cont'd

Total fund receive (in lakh)	788.2	380.56	1168.76	115	50.15	165.15
Total fund released(in lakh)	723.71	336.91	1060.62	93.36	32.88	126.24
Total fund utilization (in lakh)	754.72	301.41	1056.13 [0.82]*	93.36	36.1	129.46 [1.5]
Wage (in lakh)	529.66	193.87	723.53 [68.5%] **	45.5	32.88	78.38 [60.5]
Material (in lakh)	144.95	76.07	221.02	42.09	0	42.09
Contingency (in lakh)	80.11	31.47	111.58	5.77	3.22	8.99
Unemployment Allowance	0	0	0	0	0	0

*Fund utilized per completed work; **Wages as % to fund utilized.

Village Level

Table 7 presents a profile of the activities undertaken in the study villages. These include wide ranging activities, though the most important among these are tank deepening (12), desiltation of water harvesting structures (6), farm ponds (5), plantation, group wells (5), land levelling (13), and roads (8).

Table 7

Village (Gram Panchayat) Level Activities

District/ village	*March 2007*	*2007–2008*	*2008–2009*	*Remarks*
Dhota	GV, PT, TD	Road		Limited demand due to social status and also access to work in diamond and marble processing
Timbachudi	FP	FP, PT	FP, GV, LL, PT	Plantation is also undertaken on private land at times of the better-off farmer; overall emphasis on private benefits
Dantiwada		TD, FP PT	BB, Clean	Limited availability of workers due to access to work on irrigation dam and the Agricultural University Campus in the village

Cont'd...

...Cont'd

Satsan	TD	FP, PT		Remote village on the boarder of Rajasthan; Relatively more demand for work; quality of work is good
Hingatiya	PT, FP, Road	Road	Road	Good quality of work, but mainly road; some objection due to loss of land for road construction, but likely to be sorted out; good demand as tribal workers are used to undertake such hard manual work; seen as better option for migration; also get better wage rates due to rocky/hard soil; an enlightened tribal woman as SP
Sembaliya	TD, Road	Road, PT, FP,TD BB	TD. Desilt, Road	Similar scenario as in Hingatiya; demand for more and assured work after monsoon
Ratanpur	TD	Desilt, BB PT	Desilt. TD	Workers not used to hard manual work hence get less payment, only shift during morning
Fichod	BB	PT	Road	Road in the undulating terrain made it difficult in absence of machinery
Nighat	TD	Road, Wall TD	Road, TD	Good work for road construction; about ₹ 120 of wages per day; no amenities; and delayed payment for over 40 days.
Bogaj	GW Desilt, TD, Wall	PT, Desilt, TD, Road	Road	Group well is an important activity, but the geological situation is not conducive as there is hard rock at the depth of 3.5 feet, hence requires blasting operation involving machinery
Tilakwada	Wall, VP, Drain, Road	Road, Wall	GW, LL, TD	More emphasis on work on private land especially benefiting some of the resourceful persons
Alava	TD, Desilt, Wall, Road, Pt	PT, Road, TD	Road, PT	Good quality of work and beneficial, but not predictability and continuity of work resulting in continued migration
Pendhardevi		PT	TD	Work is not continued at present; payment is not cleared since last year; plantation worth ₹ 12.5 lakhs seems to have completely failed
Kaprada	TD	TD, GW	GW	Good work on Group wells, which once again requires use of machinery for blasting hence increases the cost of construction

Cont'd...

...Cont'd

Kakadkuwa	PT	Desilt, GW	Presently no workers are available; partly due to proximity of industrial employment in Vapi at ₹ 125–150/75 per day to female and men workers respectively
Fulwadi	PT	TD, GW	Large number of workers (about 150) but delayed payment remains an issue

Activity Codes: Gram Vatika – (GV); Plantation – (PT); Tank Deepening – (TD); Farm Pond – (FP); Road–Road; Bori Bund – (BB); Gram Safai – (Clean); Land Levelling – (LL); Group Well – (GW); Check Dam and Canal Desilting – (Desilt); Protection Wall – (Wall); Drainage – (Drain); Vermi Compost – (VP).

According to the available data, about 1.06 lakh job cards have been issued to 2.37 lakh households in the eight talukas covered under the study. This accounts for about 45 per cent of the total number of households in these talukas. The number of job cards issued in the eight talukas is fairly large, given the fact that by December 2008, only 25.8 lakhs job cards were issued in the entire state. The relatively larger number of job cards issued in the study talukas is due to the fact that several of these were prepared just before the survey commenced in these areas.

The number of job cards issued in the 16 villages (GPs) is 6,738. This constitutes nearly 44 per cent of the total households in the GPs. Since we do not have the latest information about the number of households presently inhabiting in these GPs, it is likely that the proportion could be slightly lower than 44 per cent, given the increase in the number of households during this decade.

Implementation of the NREGS: Evidence from the Sample Households

This section presents the main features of implementation of the NREGS and the perceptions of the respondents from the sample households. The sample, as noted in chapter 1, consists of 560 households – 320 BN and 240 NB. A brief profile of the households selected for the primary survey has been presented below.

Sample Households: Selected Features

As large as 57 per cent of the households belong to scheduled castes (SCs). The proportion varies from almost 100 per cent in

Dediapada, Dharampur, and Kaparda talukas to 5 per cent in Vadgam taluka in Banaskantha district. It may be noted that the distribution is more or less the same among BN and NB households. Another 23 per cent of the sample households belong to scheduled castes (SCs), and 17 per cent belong to other backward communities (OBCs). Only 2.4 per cent of the samples belong to other communities, consisting of higher castes.

One-third of the sample households do not own any land. The proportion, once again, is more or less among the BN and NB households. However, proportion of households owning more than five acres of land is higher (11.2) among NB as compared to that in BN (7.5%).Ownership of livestock is relatively better among NB as compared to the BN households. For instance, the average number of cows owned by NB is 1.71 as compared to 1.44 among BN. A similar pattern is also observed in the case of ownership of buffalo, bullock, and goats.

Awareness among Households

What is the extent of awareness among the sample households regarding the various provisions for implementation? Findings from the sample households with regard to 31 provisions under the NREGS highlighted the following important observations:

1. Nearly 94 per cent of the sample households were given job cards. The average number of days worked under the NREGS was 27.
2. The extent of awareness was found to be relatively high (i.e., covering more than 25% of the sample households) in the case of 12 out of the 31 provisions under the NREGS. Some of these include time for providing work; entitlement for minimum wage rate, the wage rate to be paid; timely payment of wages; provisions for first aid and shade; period of rest; ban on use of machinery; approval by Gram Sabha, etc. However, only four of these provisions were known to more than 50 per cent of the sample households.
3. In most cases, the awareness was found to be higher among BN as compared to NB households. There is, however, no clear pattern in terms of awareness across social groups and other categorization of households.

Correlates: Awareness Score

We tried to examine some of the important correlates of the extent of awareness about the NREGS provisions among the sample households. This has been examined by working out distribution of households across different levels of awareness. The levels of awareness are captured in terms of the number of the NREGS provisions about which a particular respondent household is aware. (This has been grouped into three categories, viz., < 10 (low); 10–20 (medium), and > 20 (high).)

The main observations are as follows:

1. Most of the households have a low level of awareness as the awareness score is <10 in the case of a majority of households across most categories. On the other hand, none of the sample household scored higher than 20.
2. The households having medium level of awareness have been confined mainly to BN rather than NB households.
3. Among those with relatively larger proportion of households in the medium level of awareness are SCs (as compared to STs and OBCs); self-employed and regular employees; small farmers (as compared to other); and those with relatively higher income.
4. Variables such as type of ration cards, type of dwellings, type of household, marital status, number of female workers, and sex of the worker do not seem to exert any influence on the level of awareness across households.

Implementation Processes

Implementation of the NREGS involved a number of important steps. The question was to what extent the actual implementation was in tune with the stipulated processes. This issue has been examined in the light of the responses from the sample households. It may, once again, be reiterated that the processes captured in the survey pertained to the early stage of project implementation, which in the case of Gujarat state was at a fairly low key during that period. Major observations emerging from these tables are as follows:

1. All the BN had job cards, whereas 210 out of the 240 NB had job cards at the time of the survey.
2. Whereas all the BN reported the reason for getting job card as 'getting employment'; only 4 out of the 210 NB reported this as the reason; the rest of the NB did not specify the reasons.
3. On an average 2.86 persons were listed on the job card: 1.47 male and 1.55 female.
4. Only one-third of the BN (107) had all (38) or some (69) members listed on the job card had individual accounts. The remaining 213 beneficiary households did not have a postal account; the issue that has already been noted earlier.
5. None of the households (except 6) reported having paid money for getting the card. Of the sample households 257 (46%) had paid money for the photographs at an average of ₹ 27.
6. According to the information on the job cards, the average number of days worked were about 10–11. This was more or less same as the actual. The total number thus works out to be 28–31 days. This discrepancy could be because of the fact that job cards in many cases were given a few days before the survey and that there were delays in payment of wages.
7. The average wages paid per households is ₹ 600. This works out to be about ₹ 60 per day. The information about wage payment is also truncated. This is revealed from the fact that in most cases, information about the payment is linked to the last site of work. The average number of hours worked is about 7 per day.
8. While 140 respondents (44%) said that payment was received as per the rules, there is little clarity on the rules regarding the payment schedule among several of the beneficiary households as already noted.
9. While a minority of the respondents (40%) reported that the entries were incomplete, in reality this was the picture in most of the cases as observed during actual checking of the job cards. Similarly, the signature column was found to

be blank in 94 out of the 320 BN households. Notwithstanding these, only a few of the BN households reported fake entries (21) or over-writing of the entries (4).

The overall observations emerging from the field survey is that the responses from several of the BN households were not frank; and that the job card management was not in good order at least till the time of the survey. This is evident from both the informal discussion with the village communities and the inconsistent/incomplete information provided by most of the BN on several of the questions related to job cards.

These observations find support from the fact that hardly anyone reported having signed the muster roll, and most of the respondents were silent on the question whether all the workers were paid together or separately. Also most of the BN reported that no one had entered payment in the job card. Similarly, 189 BN reported that the payment was made in the Panchayat Bhawan and 66 reported that it was done in someone's residence. Whereas 144 respondents reported that the payment was read aloud, 167 households denied this.

Some of the other important features emerging from the survey are: (i) almost 50 per cent of the respondents preferred cash payment, whereas three-fourth of them preferred time based as against piece rate work; (ii) most of the respondents worked within the limit of the Gram Panchayat; and (iii) almost no one was paid any allowance for the repair of tools.

On the various aspects, pertaining to planning the scenario is found to be quite dismal. For instance, as many as 530 out of the sample of 560 households reported a Gram Sabha was held in the Panchayat, only about one-third of the respondents reported having attended that. Interestingly, the proportion was found to be higher among NB as compared to BN who in fact belong to socio-politically weaker segment of the community. Of those who attended the meeting, 62 per cent said that they had spoken up during the discussion.

While a majority of respondents said that selection of work under the NREGS was discussed during the Gram Sabhas, only 62 per cent of the sample households reported that the NREGS was discussed during any of the Gram Sabhas. This once again suggests that the discussion about selection of work may not have actually taken place in these meetings; they may have been informed about the decisions taken at the level of the project office in the block. None of the sample households responded to the question on exclusive Gram Sabhas being organized for NREGS.

Impact on BN Households: Initial Findings

The observations in the foregoing analyses are based on the initial phase of the implementation of the project. This obviously is somewhat premature for capturing the impact on workers and their households. Nevertheless, information on some of the important parameters such as extent of employment obtained, gender composition of workers, wages received, contribution to household income, changes in livelihood base, and perception about future participation may provide broad indications about the actual benefits received by the workers. This section presents evidence on the selected parameters of initial impacts at three levels: household, intra household, and village.

Household Level

The NREGS could directly contribute towards enhancing employment and income of the households. We tried to gauge the extent of contribution made by the NREGS towards these two parameters.

Earlier we had noted that average employment under the NREGS was about 10–11 days per worker, which worked out to be around 28–31 days per household. This information pertains to all the days that workers in the sample households worked under the NREGS till the time of the survey. When enquiries were made about the reference year, the number of days per male worker turned out to be only 7.9 per worker (Tables 8 and 9). This is because the reference year was the first year of the implementation of the NREGS in the state. Given this caveat, the survey findings indicate that the scheme, at least in the initial year, did not contribute much to the employment scenario in the households. This is evident as on an average, the

Table 8

Employment and Unemployment among the NREGS Participant and Non-participant Household (Mean) by Districts (Male)

Particulars	*Beneficiary (Male)*					*Non-beneficiary (Male)*					*Total*
	Sabar-kantha	*Banas-kantha*	*Narmada*	*Valsad*	*Total*	*Sabar-kantha*	*Banas-kantha*	*Narmada*	*Valsad*	*Total*	*All*
Employment and Unemployment during 2007–2008 (1 + 2 + 3)											
Working days under NREGS (a/h × 100)	6.5 (83)	9.8 (65)	8.9 (63)	7.1 (81)	7.9 (292)	NA	NA	NA	NA	NA	NA
Working days under non-NREGS (b/h × 100)	52 (133)	80.7 (105)	71.4 (134)	57.5 (107)	65 (479)	51.9 (82)	75.5 (65)	64.6 (71)	64.4 (58)	63.4 (276)	64.4 (755)
Self-employment days (c/h × 100)	55.8 (117)	63.2 (55)	55.4 (95)	57.2 (111)	57.2 (378)	71.9 (77)	73.2 (64)	73.2 (82)	70.6 (83)	72.2 (306)	63.9 (684)
Unemployment days (d/h × 100)	78.6 (128)	113.9 (99)	93.1 (142)	84.5 (113)	91.5 (482)	100.7 (84)	93.4 (74)	83.9 (86)	65.6 (73)	86.4 (317)	89.5 (799)
Total days available for work	229.9 (140)	223.4 (126)	221.1 (154)	247.8 (131)	230.2 (551)	222.9 (98)	239.3 (96)	242.6 (106)	257.7 (96)	240.6 (396)	234.5 (947)

Table 9

Employment and Unemployment among the NREGS Participant and Non-Participant Household (Mean) by Districts (Female)

Particulars	*Beneficiary (Female)*					*Non-beneficiary (Female)*					*Total*
	Sabar-kantha	*Banas-kantha*	*Narmada*	*Valsad*	*Total*	*Sabar-kantha*	*Banas-kantha*	*Narmada*	*Valsad*	*Total*	*All*
Employment and Unemployment during 2007–2008 (1 + 2 + 3)											
Working days under NREGS (a/h × 100)	8 (83)	16.2 (76)	7.3 (64)	7 (89)	9.5 (312)	NA	NA	NA	NA	NA	NA
Working days under Non-NREGS (b/h × 100)	47.6 (111)	71.6 (104)	69.6 (107)	54.6 (104)	60.7 (426)	51.1 (67)	68.4 (49)	65.7 (64)	61.9 (39)	61.2 (219)	42.2 (645)
Self employment days (c/h × 100)	63.4 (100)	61.3 (54)	61.1 (78)	59.1 (108)	61.2 (340)	77.8 (69)	82.3 (54)	74.5 (67)	81.2 (81)	78.9 (271)	69.0 (611)
Un-employment days (d/h × 100)	149 (101)	248.9 (108)	121.2 (119)	96.2 (115)	152.2 (443)	134.9 (76)	133.9 (61)	104.4 (84)	110.4 (66)	120.1 (287)	139.6 (730)
Total days available for work	224.7 (123)	182.5 (120)	190.6 (127)	211.2 (127)	202.3 (497)	202.5 (88)	214.2 (78)	206.3 (92)	232.6 (90)	213.9 (348)	207.1 (845)

workers in the sample households reported that they were available for work for about 234 days during a year. In fact, the reported availability is some what higher among NB as compared to the BN households in Banaskantha and Valsad, though not in Sabarkantha district.

Part of the reason for this otherwise unexpected pattern is relatively larger number of days reported to be in self-employment categories among the NB as compared to the BN households; it is likely that actual work (in terms of intensity) in this category of employment may not be high, thereby suggesting higher incidence of under employment in this category. This is fairly clear from the evidence that the number of days of unemployment is only 86 as compared to the days for which the workers are available for work, perhaps for additional work.

Compared to men workers, women had worked for 9.5 person-days in the NREGS during the reference year. Conversely, the number of unemployed days is higher, i.e.,120 as compared to 86 among male workers.

Similarly, the average number of days under the NREGS were found to be higher among OBC households (as against SC and ST), and also among the landless and those with lower income groups. It may be noted that the OBCs have relatively lower income as compared to SCs and STs. This confirms the relatively better targeting in terms of workers obtaining work under the NREGS.

We now turn to the evidence on the income aspect. Since we did not get responses on the season-wise wage income earned during the reference year, the assessment of the contribution of the NREGS to household's income has been based on the information sought through source-wise income of the households. Table 10 presents estimates of total income and contribution of the NREGS across different categories of households.

The following observations are found to be important:

1. Whereas the total income of BN households is about 37,000 per year, that among the NB households is about 42,000.
2. NREGS contributed ₹ 1,622 per household, which works out to be 4.3 per cent of the total income. The NREGS

income works out to be ₹ 58 per average of 28 days worked by the BN households.

3. The contribution of the NREGS income is higher in Banaskantha (5.2%) and Valsad (5%) districts; among the landless (5.8%); and among the OBC (5.6%).

Overall, the results are fairly consistent, though do not indicate substantial contribution made by the NREGS at least in the initial phase.

Table 10

Wage Income from the NREGS of the Total Wage Income of the Participant and Non-participant Households in the NREGS during the Agriculture Year 2007–08 by Districts

District	*Beneficiary*		*Non-beneficiary*		*Total*	
	Total income	*NREGS income*	*Total income*	*NREGS income*	*Total income*	*NREGS income*
Sabarkantha	29,454.1 (80)	1100.3 (74) (3.7%)	28,923.3 (60)	NA	29,226.6 (140)	1100.3 (74)
Banaskantha	32,591.3 (80)	1689.4 (77) (5.2%)	53,048.3 (60)	NA	41,358.6 (140)	1689.4 (77)
Narmada	39,934.5 (80)	1385.4 (71) (3.5%)	61,454.1 (60)	NA	49,157.3 (140)	1385.4 (71)
Valsad	47,169.5 (80)	2362.4 (68) (5%)	54,157.5 (60)	NA	50,164.4 (140)	2362.4 (68)
Total	37,287.4 (320)	1622.5 (290) (4.3%)	49,395.8 (240)	NA	42,476.7 (560)	1622.5 (290)

Has this income exerted any impact on the household's level of living? This question has been explored at length. As many as 92 per cent of the BN households reported that the NREGS holds significance for the present level of living. What is more important is that 87 per cent of the BN households reported that the NREGS is important because it gives work at the door step. However, 11 per cent of the respondents indicated that the NREGS is important because it provides better wages.

These findings, as noted earlier, are not unexpected partly because of the initial impact and partly because of the scattered nature of works undertake. The next phase would address issues pertaining to planning and continuity of work under the NREGS on an urgent basis.

The above observations are further substantiated by the perceived impact of the NREGS on a household's well-being. Whereas an overwhelming majority of the people noted that the NREGS is very much or somewhat important, and it makes significant impact, the NREGS income does not seem to have helped redressing any specific distress such as hunger, migration, or promoting education for the children. Nevertheless, the scheme seems to have made contributions towards health treatment and redress from undertaking the non-preferred type of work. The positive perceptions are found to be relatively more prevalent among participants as compared to the non-participants.

Intra-household Level

Some of the findings noted earlier have already indicated that women have relatively better presence in the NREGS as compared to men; the average number of female workers was found to be higher (nearly 9.5) as compared to male workers (7.1). This observation is further substantiated by several other findings that may reflect positively on women's participation in the scheme.

As per the survey data, female workers constituted a majority (57.6%) of the total workforce among the BN households. Conversely, their share in the non-NREGS work was about 47 per cent. Among NB households, the proportion of female to total workers is about 51 per cent; this is because there were no workers in the NREGS among these households.

While we do not have data on wage income from the NREGS earned by season and gender, we have tried to examine the wage income earned by female workers in the NB households. It is observed that the average amount of wage income earned by female workers is ₹ 10,754 per year which is more or less the same across the districts. However, the average wage income among female workers was found to be higher among the general social groups and the lowest among the OBCs. This reconfirms the observation about relatively lower economic status among OBCs as compared to SCs and STs.

Do women have control over their wage income and how do they use the income? These questions could be examined in the light of the information presented in all 259 out of the 320 BN households who had reported the details about 'who keeps the wage income?' As per the information obtained from these households, about 72 per cent of the 259 households reported that women had control over the wage income. The households in which women kept the income constituted 73 per cent of the total female workers in the NREGS. The remaining 27 per cent of the female workers in the NREGS belonged to households where they do not keep the income.

Table 11

Utilization of Wage Income from the NREGS among Participant Households by Districts (Participant Households)

Particulars	*Sabar-kantha*	*Banas-kantha*	*Narmada*	*Valsad*	*Total*
Proportion of households reported that they have used for human development (1,6)	37.5	42.5	11.2	6.2	24.4
Proportion of households reported that they have used for food (4)	93.8	88.8	95	85	90.6
Proportion of households reported that they have used for accessibility of assets (2,5)	3.8	17.5	20	21.2	15.6
Proportion of households reported that they have used for repayment (8)	3.8	7.5	3.8	3.8	4.7
Proportion of households reported that they have used for working capital (3)	—	—	—	—	—
Proportion of households reported that they have used for savings	—	—	—	—	—
Proportion of households reported that they have used for health care during 2007–2008	37.5	42.5	11.2	6.2	24.4
Proportion of households reported	100	100	100	100	100

A relatively smaller proportion (66.9%) of those households with women having control over their income reported that they used the income for personal use as compared to those where women did not keep the income with them (75%). A similar pattern is found in the case of using the income for food. Only a smaller proportion of the households reported women using income for health/education or livelihood improvement. Strangely, relatively lower proportion (39.4%) of households where women kept their earnings had reported that where women received 'high respect' as compared to those households (57.7%) where women did not keep their wages (Table 11).

The above observations indicate a somewhat complex reality in which gender empowerment takes place where attainment of higher work participation and/or control over income per se has no direct relation to the notion of 'women's status', which is often constructed and perceived in the light of the existing socio-cultural milieu; economic contribution may constitute only a part of this reality.

It was, however, difficult to ascertain the use of the NREGS income among the BN households. This is mainly because of the fact that the details regarding wages were not found in most of the job cards; in any case, the NREGS income constitutes an insignificant proportion of the total income of the households as already noted. Similarly, very few households could respond to questions on coping with disturbing effects. We have therefore skipped this information from the analysis.

Village Level

We have also tried to capture perceptions regarding overall impact at village level. The important observations are twofold:

First as large as 98 per cent of the BN and 73 per cent of the NB reported that the NREGS could create useful assets at the village level; and about 59–65 per cent reported that the scheme has resulted in rural wages.

The second and somewhat discouraging observation is that only a very small segment of the sample households felt that the scheme could enhance agricultural productivity; and about 18–23 per cent of the households reported that the scheme has resulted in scarcity of labour during peak agricultural seasons in the area. These issues need special attention.

Additionally, we have analysed some details on the expenditure under the NREGS and stipulated income that may have flowed into the villages. The information on expenditure available from the Village Panchayat does not provide a clear indication of the wages being paid and the number of worker days of work generated in the GP. Alternatively, we could look at the information on total expenditure available for the 16 villages (GPs) covered under the study. This could be used for deriving the amount of wages being paid to the workers by applying a factor of 60 per cent. Table 12 presents the estimated amount of wage payment for the study villages. According to these estimates the wage income works out to be ₹ 145.95 lakhs till March 2009.

Assuming that the average earning per day is ₹ 60, the total wage bill amounts to 2.43 lakh person-days in the study villages (GPs).

Table 12

Estimated Wage Bill and Person-days among Study Villages (GPs)

(Rs Lakh)

Districts	*Expenditure up to March 2009*	*Wages @ 60%*	*Person-day @ Rs 60/day*
Banaskantha	19.14	11.48	19,133
Sabarkantha	83.86	50.31	83,850
Narmada	103.65	62.19	1,03.650
Valsad	36.63	21.97	36,616
Total	243.28	145.95	2,41,666

Note: Estimate of expenditure is obtained from Table 8.

Summary of Main Findings

The prior analysis presents a snap shot of the various features of the implementation of the NREGS in the initial phase in Gujarat. As noted earlier, the scheme had a somewhat slow start in the state, which apparently seems to have picked up in the past few months. In this sense, the findings from the analysis may not be fully representative of the present scenario. With this forewarning, we highlight some of the important findings from the study.

1. *Initial low start due to perceived lack of demand for manual work in the state:* By December 2008, 25.6 lakh households were registered under the NREGS; 5.15 lakh households were provided with employment for about 106 lakh person-days; with an average wage of ₹ 60 per day, and a total expenditure of ₹ 10,077 lakhs.
2. *Predominance of Tribal Areas:* Given the concentration of poverty in the tribal dominated areas, the NREGS has concentrated mainly in the districts and talukas with relatively higher proportion of scheduled tribe and SC households.
3. *Self-selection:* Nearly 80 per cent of the sample of 560 households belonged to STs (57%) and SCs (23%); and one-third of the sample households were landless. Although BN households were marginally better than the NB in terms of ownership of type of house, livestock, etc., most of the households faced problems of poverty and underemployment.
4. About 44 per cent of the households in the 16 study villages (GPs) were issued job cards. From the sample of BN, an average of two workers had undertaken work under the NREGS, with an average number of 27 days per person. About 51 per cent of the workers were female. The average wage rate worked out to be about ₹ 58 per day.
5. *Types of work undertaken:* The major activities include deepening of the existing tanks or water harvesting structures; land levelling, farm ponds, and road construction. While these areas are important assets for enhancing the productivity of rural economies, technical suitability/quality of work needs careful attention.
6. Awareness about most of the provisions of the NREGS is selective and limited. The extent of awareness was found to be relatively higher (i.e., covering more than 25% of the sample households) in the case of 12 out of the 31

provisions under the NREGS. Only four of these provisions were known to more than 50 per cent of the sample households.

7. The work so far is mainly supply driven rather than demand driven; this is how the estimates of demand for and supply of work under the NREGS is stated to be identical. Creation of demand requires both administrative support and social mobilization. At present, the state machinery at the taluka level is fairly under-staffed. There is not much involvement of the Community-based organization (CBOs) and social audits are seldom undertaken, although official records may not reveal this.
8. A large number of workers tend to opt for such work but on a continuous and predictable basis. This requires simultaneous reforms in planning processes within the line departments.
9. While women constitute a substantial proportion of the total workforce in the NREGS, it is difficult to ascertain the impact on their empowerment. About 72 per cent of the 259 households reported that women had control over their wages. Only a smaller proportion of households reported women using their income for health/education or livelihood improvement.
10. The NREGS contributed ₹ 1,622 per household, which works out to be 4.3 per cent of the total income. Nevertheless, 92 per cent of the BN households reported that the NREGS holds particular significance for the present level of living. What is more important is that 87 per cent of the BN households reported that the NREGS is important because it provides work at the door step. Only 11 per cent of the respondents indicated that the NREGS is important because it provides better wages.
11. As large as 98 per cent of the BN and 73 per cent of the NB reported that the NREGS could create useful assets at the village level; and about 65 per cent and 59 per cent reported that the scheme resulted in a hike in rural wages. However, a somewhat discouraging observation is that only a very small minority of the sample households felt

that the scheme could enhance agricultural productivity, and about 18–23 per cent of the households reported that the scheme resulted in scarcity of labour during peak agricultural seasons in the area.

12. Finally, the issue of sustainability of assets and drudgery also needs rethinking in terms of how to dovetail state funds for using the requisite amount of material and machines so as to ensure quality and reduce avoidable drudgery. On-farm activities thus may deserve better attention in this context.

Way Forward

In the context of the above developments, there is an urgent need to discuss the promotion of the NREGA in the right direction and in the right manner. Some of the areas of action that could be discussed in the proposed consultation could be as follows:

1. *Designing a macro approach for the NREGS*: The NREGS could be linked with one or a few of the major areas of concerns in the state. These could be drinking water, sanitation, fuel wood (plantation), etc.; NRM; agricultural growth; basic infrastructure and human development, etc. The proposed consultation could debate on the requirements, needs, and implementation.
2. *Strengthening planning component and capacity building*: Planning for the NREGS needs urgent strengthening. This calls for (1) developing long-term perspectives in planning for works, (2) systematic and effective convergence of the NREGS works with other developments, (3) multi-level planning as and when necessary, and (4) overall a strong planning element in designing the NREGS works.
   This also calls for focused efforts on recruitment to fill in all posts and capacity building. Systematic efforts are needed to develop planning capacity as well as in motivation achievement and goal orientation.
3. *NREGA: A rights-based approach*: The NREGA is a rights-based approach, and in this sense it is different from the rest of the programmes. There is a need to focus on the

following areas in the coming years: (1) enforcement of guarantee and generation of continuous employment, (2) enforcement of other entitlements including new minimum wages, opening bank accounts, etc., (3) ensuring transparency and creating good monitoring structures, and (4) ensuring effective social audit. Appointing of members on all committees right from the state council to village committees and ensuring technical manpower to villages, etc., are also important here.

References

Ambasta, P., et al. (2008). 'Two years of NREGA: The road ahead', *Economic and Political Weekly* 43(8), 41–50.

Bhaduri, A. (2005). 'Guarantee employment and right to information', *Economic and Political Weekly* 41(3), 267–269.

Bhattarai, M., et al. (2002). *Irrigation Impact on Income Inequality and Poverty Alleviation: Policy Issues and Options for Improved Management of Irrigation System*. Colombo, Sri Lanka: International Water Management Institute.

Datye, K.R. (1997). *Banking on Biomass, Centre for Environment Education*. Ahmedabad: Environment and Development series.

Ghosh, S.T., et al. (2008). 'National rural employment guarantee scheme', Chapter 15, *Alternative Economic Survey, India – 2007–08*. New Delhi: Daanish Books.

Government of India (2006). *National Employment Guarantee Act*. New Delhi: Administration Reforms Commission.

Hirway, I. (2007). NREGA: A Component of Full Employment Strategy for India – An Assessment (unpublished paper), Centre for Development Alternatives, Ahmedabad.

Hirway, I., and Terhal, P. (1994). *Towards Employment Guarantee in India: Indian and International experience in Rural Works Programmes*. New Delhi: Sage Publications.

Joshi, P.K., et al. (2008). *Impact of Watershed Programme and Conditions of Success: A Meta Analysis Approach* (Draft paper). Prepared for the Comprehensive Assessment of Watershed Projects in India, ICRISAT, Patancheru.

Joy, K.J., and Paranjape, S. (2004). *Watershed Development Review: Issues and Prospects* (Technical report). Bangalore: Centre for Interdisciplinary Studies in Environment and Development (CISED).

Kapur, D., et al. (2008). 'The case for direct cash transfers to the poor', *Economic and Political weekly* 36(15), 37–40.

Kerr, J. (2002). 'Watershed development, environmental services, and poverty alleviation in India', *World Development* 30(8), 1387–1400.

Kubaoub, F. (2007). *Employment Guarantee Programmes: A Survey of Theories and Policy Experiences*, Working Paper No. 498, the Levy Economic Institute, New York.

Mahapatra, R. et al. (2008). *The National Employment Guarantee Act (NREGA): Opportunities and Challenges*. New Delhi: Centre for Science and Environment.

Majumdar, N.A. (2006). 'Centrality of agriculture to India's economic development', *Economic Developments in India*, Vol. 98. New Delhi: Academic Foundation, 51–61.

Merhotra, S. (2008). 'NREG two years on: Where do we go from here?', *Economic and Political Weekly* 43(31), 27–35.

Panda, M. (2003). *Role of Agriculture in the Poverty Reduction Process in India* (Unpublished). Mumbai: Indira Gandhi institute of Development Research.

Pankaj, A. (2008). *The National Rural Employment Guarantee Act: Guaranteeing the Right to Livelihood* (Draft). New Delhi: Institute of Human Development.

Papola, T.S. (2005). 'A universal programme is feasible', *Economic and Political Weekly* 41(5), 594–599.

Patanaik, P. (2005). 'On the need for providing employment guarantee', *Economic and Political Weekly* 41(2), 203–207.

Patel, S. (2006). 'Empowerment, co-option, and domination: Politics of Maharashtra's employment guarantee scheme', *Economic and Political Weekly* 41(50), 5126–5132.

Planning Commission (2007). *Sub Group – IV, 2006, Working Group on Natural Resource Management for the Eleventh Five Year Plan (2007–2012)*. New Delhi: Ministry of Agriculture, Government of India.

Shah, A. (1998). 'Watershed development programmes in India: Emerging issues for environment development perspective', *Economic and Political Weekly* 32(26), A66–A79.

Shah, A. (2001). *Who Benefits from Participatory Watershed Development? Lessons from Gujarat, India*, IIED Gatekeeper Series No. 97. London: International Institute for Environment and Development.

Shah, A. (2004). *Benchmark Survey for Impact Assessment of Participatory Watershed Development Projects in India* (Mimeo). Ahmedabad: Gujarat Institute of Development Research.

Shah, A. (2005). 'Economic rationale, subsidy and cost sharing in watershed projects', *Economic and Political Weekly* 40(26), 2663–2672.

Shah, A. (2009). 'Natural Resources and Chronic Poverty in India: A Review of Evidence and Issues', CPRC Working Paper No. 152, Overseas Development Institute, London.

Shah, A., et al. (2008). *Revisiting Watershed Development in Madhya Pradesh: Evidence from a Large Survey* (Unpublished). Ahmedabad: Gujarat Institute of Development Research.

Shah, A., and Mehta, A.K. (2008). 'Experience of the Maharashtra employment guarantee scheme: Are there lessons for NREGS?', *Indian Journal of Labour Economics* 51(2), 191–206.

11

Social Income

Community, State and Private Support Mechanisms for Inclusive Growth in Gujarat[1]

Jeemol Unni, Guy Standing, Renana Jhabvala and Uma Rani

Gujarat has undoubtedly experienced rapid economic growth in recent years, at least until the global financial crisis hit the State at the end of 2008. In the decade leading up to 2008, the state's economic growth rate exceeded that of India as a whole, and at nearly 10 per cent per annum in the early part of the 21st century it was growing much faster than most of the world economy.

The issue that we will investigate in this paper is whether the poorer sections of society experienced the benefits of this rapid growth? Has the growth in the state been inclusive? We will also explore a concept termed 'social income'. We argue that besides the incomes earned by individual members, households also gain from the support given by institutions such as the community, state and private initiatives, or investments. To what extent do these support mechanisms help households in Gujarat to improve their economic situation? Another form of support comes from enterprises, organizations, or households where the employee works, but such workers and the benefits accruing to them are on the decline.

Gujarat's Rapid Growth

For some time now, the rate of growth of income in Gujarat has been higher than the average for India. The rate of growth in

Gujarat rose from 6.8 per cent a year between 1993 and 2000 to 7.7 per cent between 2000 and 2005, while the growth rate in India slowed from 6.3 per cent to 5.6 per cent during that period. From the 1990s onwards, Gujarat grew faster than all other rapidly developing regions such as the southern states of Karnataka, Andhra Pradesh, Tamil Nadu, and Maharashtra (Morris, 2006a). Although Gujarat did have a minor recession between 1997 and 2002, it grew exceptionally fast after that.

A slowdown at the all-India level at the turn of the century was partly due to the poor performance of agriculture. Gujarat also had a poor agricultural year in 1999–2000, although there was a sharp rebound after that, leading to exceptionally high agricultural growth. Incomes in the secondary sector also grew rapidly, mainly in manufacturing, which has been the engine of growth in Gujarat for many decades. It continued to be so after the reforms of the early 1990s, outstripping growth in other peer states. But thereafter it changed in character. From the late 1990s, although registered manufacturing enterprises continued to grow fast, it was unregistered informal manufacturing that really took off (Morris, 2006a). This brought the famed entrepreneurship of the Gujarati to the fore.

The tertiary sector did less well and the pace of growth slowed during the two periods, as it did in the whole country. According to Morris (2006a), the other sectors that grew as fast as in peer states were transport, storage, and communication. Perhaps surprisingly, the construction sector also did not do so well after 2000. But, although the growth of banking, real estate, and business services were also less spectacular than in some other states, the most puzzling fact is that electronics and information technology has not taken root in Gujarat.

Gujarat's Employment Growth: Less Spectacular

In overall terms, employment growth in Gujarat has not been as great as in the rest of the country, where the growth rate rose from under 1 per cent to over 3 per cent in the period after 1999 (Table 1). Growth of employment in Gujarat remained steady, growing slightly from 2.2 per cent to 2.8 per cent during the periods before and after 1999–2000. But what is striking is that

Gujarat experienced a major sectoral shift in output and employment over the two periods that was different from what occurred in India overall. There was a huge jump in employment growth in manufacturing and related industries, coupled with a decline in the growth rates of employment in both primary and tertiary sectors. By contrast, although secondary employment in India still recorded the largest increase, employment growth also accelerated in primary and tertiary sectors. Underlying the relative performance of secondary employment was a sectoral shift, with manufacturing sharply growing in Gujarat while construction employment stagnated, whereas in India overall construction was booming.

Another feature of the Indian labour market that has been growing is labour flexibility, measured in part by a shift from regular, protected employment to casual, precarious labour and various forms of nominally self-employment. Since this is important for understanding the changing structure of social income, it is worth dwelling on what the aggregate data seem to tell us.

First of all, the pattern of labour force growth in Gujarat seems to have differed from what was happening in India overall. While in all parts, informal types of labour relationship have continued to predominate, there did seem to be some formalization in the early years of the 21st century, when recorded regular employment increased (Unni and Raveendran, 2007). The growth of regular labour accelerated in Gujarat to a much greater extent than in India overall. Meanwhile, in both Gujarat and India overall, casual labour scarcely grew at all (Table 1).

The other puzzle is that 'own-account work' grew fastest of all in India, and its growth was much faster after 1999 than beforehand. Much of this might be really sub-contracted work, and effectively casual labour. Interpretations have varied.[2] We know that as of 2000, 'home workers' – those working at home for paid income as outworkers – comprised about 12 per cent of all the nominally self-employed in India, and 13 per cent in Gujarat (GoI, 2007, Table A4.6, p. 266). But it is debatable whether many of them should be called 'self-employed'. Many are part of sub-contracting chains controlled by middlemen and petty producers. Ideally, it would be sensible to differentiate between those in that type of status and those who are properly independent producers or vendors of goods or services. The term 'self-employment' is incorrect as a general description of the many millions across India and in Gujarat who are encompassed by the official statistics. As recognized by the National Commission for Enterprises in the Unorganised Sector (NCEUS), the 'employment status' of the self-employed 'can be considered to be along a continuum of dependence' (GoI, 2007: 58) with practically no autonomy.

Table 1

Growth Rate of Employment by Activity Status in Gujarat and India

Status	*Employment*	
	1993–1994 to 1999–2000	*1999–2000 to 2004–2005*
Gujarat		
Self-employed	3.4	2.6
Regular	0.3	8.3
Casual	1.4	0.3
Total	2.2	2.8
All India		
Self-employed	0.3	4.6
Regular	2.4	3.6
Casual	1.4	0.3
Total	1	3.1

Source: NSSO (1997, 2001a, 2001b, 2006a, 2006b).

What is undeniable is that even though growth rates might suggest some relative growth of regular labour, still most Indian workers face a precarious labour status. Bear in mind that those outside 'regular' formal employment tend to have only a tenuous link to the government and enterprise benefits and protection that are expected to come with development. For example, in Ahmedabad in 2004–2005, only 12 per cent of the non-agricultural workers were in the formal sector by the definition of working in registered/pubic enterprises. And even among them about 9 per cent were informal workers without formal contracts and social security benefits (Table 2). The percentage of women informal workers in formal units was double (nearly 15%) compared to men (7%).

Table 2

Distribution of Wage Employees in Non-agriculture by Formal and Informal Employment, Ahmedabad, 2004–05

Informal sector		*Informal employment*					
By enterprise		*All*		*Men*		*Women*	
Activity/ production unit		*Formal*	*Informal*	*Formal*	*Informal*	*Formal*	*Informal*
Formal enterprises	12	91	9	92.7	7.3	85.3	14.7
Informal enterprises	84.8	26.7	73.3	29.5	70.5	12.8	87.2
Domestic workers	2.2	0	100	0	100	0	100
Other	0.9	38.1	61.9	38.3	61.7	—	—
Total	100	38.1	61.9	40.5	59.5	27.8	72.2

Source: Computed from NSSO 61st Round, unit level records.

Micro Evidence from a Survey: Income, Employment and Days of Work

National statistics do not collect crucial information on incomes, days of work, multiple activities that are necessary to judge the levels of inclusion or exclusion of the population from the growth process as it has occurred in Gujarat. In the early 2008, following pilot testing, the Gujarat Social Income and Security Survey (GSIS) was launched.[3] While considerable economic growth had occurred in Gujarat between 2000 and 2008, there was widespread anecdotal and secondary evidence that many people living in the villages and urban slums were not benefiting as much as would have been hoped or expected. There were reports of some optimism – a feature examined in the survey as well – but the pilot fieldwork left us feeling that the mechanisms for ensuring a widespread distribution of the gains of economic growth were not functioning well.

To obtain reasonable incomes, work must be both remunerative and sufficient. To study incomes, we must look at daily earnings and the number of days worked. And, while work may be available on most days, it might be only for a few hours a day, so that the person remains underemployed and has low daily earnings. So, the crucial variables are daily earnings, days, and hours of work.[4]

All respondents were asked the number of days they had worked for income earning, and more detailed data were collected for piece-rate workers. The resultant figures on the number of days of work should be treated with due caution, since some may have worked for a few hours only, whereas others would have worked long working days. Information was collected on the work they did for the major part of the year (main activity) and the secondary activities they may have undertaken.

On an average, over the past year, those in urban areas did more days of income-earning work (272) than those in rural areas (240). Typically, men did over 270 days in their main work, compared with women's 234 days. By and large, casual workers had only half a year of work as the main activity in rural areas, while salaried workers had full employment, which was more than 300 days.

To explore this, we disaggregated the average days by gender and location. In their main activity, generally, urban men worked the longest period, nearly 300 days. Rural men averaged 260 days, while the statistics for urban women followed with 250 days. Rural women had the least, only 220 days as their main activity, using a liberal definition of at least one hour a day. Among all the groups, women employed as casual labourers in rural areas had the least number of days (175), followed by rural male casual labourers (199) and piece-rated women workers in urban areas (233).

While the average number of days provided a picture of the amount of work available to different groups, insight into the intensity of under-employment is obtained by analysing the distribution of work days.[5] Those doing less than six months (180 days) of work can be considered as underemployed. Those having more than 270 days were more or less fully employed, though the number of hours per day is an issue, particularly among the self-employed. For example, women looking after cattle may have been spending just two hours a day feeding and cleaning. If not engaged in any other activity, they could be depicted as underemployed, but would appear as being fully employed. Gross over-employment is also possible for such women if they were actually undertaking several activities.

On the positive side, about 58 per cent obtained near full employment from their main activity, more than 270 days, while on the negative side nearly 23 per cent had less than six months of work. Workers in urban areas were better off, with nearly 70 per cent having full employment, while 30 per cent of rural workers had less than six months in their main activity (Table 3). Workers outside agriculture were most likely to be fully employed, nearly 70 per cent, while only about 40 per cent of agricultural workers achieved that (Table 3). The seasonal nature of agricultural labour ensured that nearly 37 per cent were grossly underemployed in their main activity. Workers in rural areas undertook more multiple activities due to the nature of work.

Table 3

Distribution of Days of Work by Work Status and Sector

Status	*Days in main activity*		
	<180	*181–270*	*271–365*
Urban	13.7	16.6	69.7
Rural	30.3	20.6	49.1
Agriculture	36.5	24	39.5
Non-agriculture	14.4	15.6	70.0
Total	22.8	18.8	58.4

Winners and Losers

Rapid economic growth and the development of public infrastructure should translate into more employment and higher incomes. However, there are always some groups who gain and some who lose. Any process of rapid change affects some groups positively and leaves others at a grave disadvantage. Development is not a victimless process, and never has been.

The most glaring reality is that those in salaried employment were gaining in absolute terms and relative to those in other paid labour statuses. They have been a privileged minority. Almost all had more than 270 days in their main income-earning work. In terms of income-earning opportunities, it appears that casual labourers were the most disadvantaged, with more than two out of every five having less than six months of labour. The biggest variability in work days was among piece-rated home-based workers, with less than 40 per cent having full employment and about 30 per cent having less than 6 months.

Risk of poverty can be measured by looking at the proportion of workers falling below a minimum wage norm. The statutory minimum wage was about ₹ 135 for non-agricultural workers and ₹ 100 for agricultural workers. In 2004, a 'Floor-level Notional Minimum Wage' of ₹ 65 was proposed by the Ministry of Labour and Employment (GoI, 2007). Using these three norms as dividers, we disaggregated workers into five groups by level of daily earnings: under ₹ 65, 65–100, 100–135, 135–200, and over ₹ 200.

Table 4

Daily Earnings in Main Activity by Location, Gender and Sector

Rupees	*Daily earnings (₹) in main work*				
	<65	*65–100*	*100–135*	*135–200*	*>200*
Urban	38.1	21.9	6	13.7	20.2
Rural	47.2	16.7	10.1	10.8	15.2
Male	27.5	22.5	10	14.5	25.4
Female	59	15.6	6.4	9.6	9.3
Agriculture	51.9	17.2	12	11	8
Non-agriculture	37.7	20.2	6	12.8	23.3
Total	43.1	19.1	8.3	12.1	17.5

Nearly half the rural workers, compared to 38 per cent of urban, received daily earnings of less than ₹ 65 from their main activity. Women were much more likely to be receiving less than ₹ 65 (Table 4). Agricultural workers were worst off, with over half obtaining daily earnings of less than ₹ 65, compared to 38 per cent of non-agricultural workers.

The critical point – perhaps not surprising to most informed observers – is that a very large number of wage earners were being paid under the notional floor of ₹ 65 per day, which is below any acceptable norm (Table 5). Another one in every five obtained daily earnings less than ₹ 100, which put them below the agricultural minimum wage. A further 8 per cent received between 100 and 135, the norm for non-agricultural workers. So, less than a third of all earners received more than the minimum wage of ₹ 135, and about 18 per cent received more than ₹ 200.

Once again, work status made a big difference. The worst off were home-based workers being paid on a piece-rate basis, over half of whom were earning less than ₹ 65 per day, with another 15 per cent obtaining between ₹ 65 and 100. Nearly half of all casual workers obtained less than ₹ 65, with 27 per cent obtained between 65 and 100. By contrast, over a quarter of all salaried employees were receiving more than ₹ 200 per day. While a quarter of the self-employed were in a similar situation, about 37 of them obtained less than ₹ 65 per day. This highlighted a feature of self-employment that it is anything but a homogeneous category.

Table 5

Average Days and Earnings in Main Activity by Landholding in Agriculture

Landholding	*Average days in income-earning work in year*	*Average daily earnings (₹)*
No land	197	79.4
Marginal	222	72.6
Small	243	94.2
Medium	227	80.9
Large	295	119.4
Total	237	92.9

Note: Marginal: Up to 2.5 acres; Small = 2.5–5 acres; Medium = 5.01–7.5 acres; Large = Above 7.5 acres.

While asset endowment helped to raise household income, this was achieved in rural households by access to land and in self-employed non-agricultural households with business assets. Agricultural workers obtained more days of work and daily earning were positively correlated with size of landholding (Table 5). However, the winners were those with large holdings, more than 7.5 acres, with near full employment and daily earnings above the statutory agricultural minimum wage.

Self-employed non-agricultural workers were more fortunate. Most had 'full employment', irrespective of the size of investment in business, and their daily earnings rose with the value of business assets. Further, all size groups except those with business assets of less than ₹ 2,500 had daily earnings above the statutory minimum wage of ₹ 135 for non-agriculture (Table 6). As we have noted above, self-employed workers outside agriculture were winners, along with the salaried employees.

Table 6

Self-employed Outside Agriculture: Average Days and Money Earnings in Main Activity by Value of Assets

Value of assets (₹)	*Average days worked in year*	*Average earnings per day*
0–2500	287	120.2
2501–10,000	292	157.6
10,001–100,000	332	267.1
100,001–500,000	307	362.6
More than 500,000	288	541.1
Total	302	195.6

All in all, the principal gainers in terms of employment and incomes were men, urban, and salaried workers. Even more than casual labourers and agricultural workers, home-based women working for piece rates in urban areas were surely the most disadvantaged, and thus deserve more considered attention, if inclusive growth is the goal.

Social Income: Support from Community, State and Private

Community Support for Livelihoods

Community support was evident in society during times of crisis. Here we focus only on the support for livelihoods. The schooling level of most respondents was quite low. About 33 per cent reported that they were illiterate or uneducated and about 37 per cent had middle-level schooling. Such low levels could be due to their inability to afford schooling. This could lead to insecurity among workers as they lack marketable skills. Acquiring skills through assistance from the community is a very valuable asset as it makes the person employable or improves his employability without incurring any additional costs.

As formal vocational training is restricted to those having schooling of at least 10th grade, it deprives a majority of those entering the workforce or seeking work from having access to it. This would mean that only about a third of the respondents would be eligible for acquiring skills through formal training. For workers with low levels of education, acquiring skills from extended family and friends or on-the-job becomes the crucial way of learning.

The means for acquiring skills meant that those who did not have the necessary resources for several years of full-time formal courses could still acquire marketable skills. This is all the more important for young people who need to make some contribution to the family income and it helps to build economic security among workers. About 45 per cent of respondents reported that they acquired skills from someone in their extended family.

A much higher proportion of workers in rural areas reported having acquired skills through extended family compared to urban areas. This could be largely inter-generational transfer of skills, which is common in agriculture, salt farming, and other traditional rural occupations. It is possible that in urban areas with the changing nature of work, acquiring skills through extended family is reducing or declining, as a high proportion of respondents reported acquiring skills through on-the-job training or from older workers. It is largely those who are illiterate or have low levels of schooling who acquire skill from extended family compared to others (Table 7). In both rural and urban areas, a relatively high proportion of lower castes were acquiring skills from the extended family. This reflects an inability of the lower castes to invest in education compared to other castes. Women acquired skills more through extended family compared to men, especially in rural areas.

Table 7

Acquiring Skills from Extended Family by Schooling and Location

	Illiterate	*Primary school*	*Middle school*	*Secondary and higher secondary*	*Above higher secondary*	*All*
Rural	75.2	65.6	55.1	56.2	40	65.8
Urban	26.9	27.7	28.7	12.3	6.3	20.2
All	61.3	51.6	42.3	28.7	13.1	45.1

The widespread reliance on members of their extended family for acquiring skills reflected a lack of government training facilities and a lack of private sector training. However, nearly a quarter of all respondents' reported that they did want or need any training for their work. Of those who did wish to obtain training, only 13.4 per cent could do so and the remaining could not because the training was too expensive and they could not afford to lose their income while undergoing training.

For the self-employed, having access to credit is crucial for growth and survival. Borrowing money for business purposes has continued to be the biggest challenge, especially for those who did not have any collateral. In the absence of collateral, access to financial assistance is dependent on community support. Overall, about 37 per cent of the self-employed in rural areas and 17 per cent in urban areas said they had borrowed money for their business.

The support from local community to access capital was much lower compared to other sources, as only 14 per cent and 7 per cent of the self-employed borrowed from local community to undertake their business activities (Table 8). Dependence on extended family was much greater compared to other forms of community support to undertake their business activities, particularly in rural areas. Scheduled castes and scheduled tribes had less access to loans from extended family compared to upper castes in both rural and urban areas. This reflects these households' low-income base compared to their upper caste counterparts. Use of neighbourhood networks for loans for business was rare in both rural and urban areas, probably due to the risks involved. The proportion of self-employed borrowing money from economic organizations, such as self-help groups, was minimal in both rural and urban areas, while support from traditional identity organizations was almost non-existent.

Table 8

Financial Support for Business Activities from Local Community

	Scheduled caste/tribe	*Other backward*	*Upper caste*	*All*
Rural	12.1	13.4	19.9	14.1
Extended family	7.6	7.9	14.4	9.5
Neighbourhood network	1.5	2	3.3	2.2
Identity organization	—	0.5	—	0.3
Economic organization	3	3	2.2	2.8
Urban	6.8	3.1	16.2	7.4
Extended family	3.4	3.1	10.8	4.8
Neighbourhood network	3.4	—	2.7	2.1
Identity organization	—	—	—	—
Economic organization	—	—	2.7	0.5

State Benefits: In Search of Reality

State benefits are unlike other sources of income, generally speaking, in that they reflect a political decision-making arrangement. A person can lose a job, but cannot easily lose a 'state'. And a person who is led to believe he or she will receive something from the state could be expected to feel more secure than if told by an employer that if he performed work satisfactorily he would receive income and benefits. But other factors make for uncertainty, including a sense of powerlessness in the face of a bureaucratic process.

State benefits have traditionally had three main rationales – (i) to combat 'poverty' (or to provide a minimum level of support), (ii) to compensate for risks, hazards, and shocks, and (iii) to achieve income redistribution from the relatively rich to the income poor, the vulnerable, and those with some impairment.

Besides the ration card scheme, there are various other subsidies supposedly in operation in Gujarat. We asked those working in agriculture or belonging to rural households with an agricultural holding whether they were receiving various specified subsidies. Very few were receiving any – 1.9 per cent subsidized fertiliser, 2 per cent subsidized seeds, 1.1 per cent subsidized irrigation, and 0.9 per cent subsidized in any other respect.

The sole area where there was some evidence of subsidy reaching people was with respect to livestock. But the problem is that they only receive it when they purchase livestock, and very few people do that very often. Of those who did, the subsidy was significant. But those living in the most wretched conditions were slightly less likely to have received a subsidy. And upper caste households were more likely to receive this subsidy than those from scheduled castes or scheduled tribes, simply because they were more likely to purchase livestock. Those households reporting that they had insufficient income for food needs were less likely to receive a livestock subsidy than those who reported they had an income adequate for their food needs.

Awareness of and Application for State Benefits

There are obviously four stages in obtaining state benefits – awareness of their existence, self-identification of being in need of assistance, application for the benefit, and receipt of them.

We asked about awareness of the existence of ration cards and of government transfer schemes in general. As far as ration cards were concerned, nearly one in every five people was not aware of their existence. As far as awareness of targeted selective government schemes are concerned, a large number were mentioned – 38 in total. But detailed knowledge of what they entailed or whether or not they were entitled to them seemed rare.

Of those aware of the below poverty line (BPL) card, 81.7 per cent thought they might qualify for it, with more of those who had experienced a decline in their income over the past year. Given the actual number with a BPL card, that is obviously wishful thinking on the part of many people. However, it is notable that one in five respondents from scheduled castes thought they would not qualify, 7 per cent of scheduled tribe members and about 15 per cent of other backward castes thought they would not.

The fact that those whose incomes had declined in the past year were more likely to think they qualified for a BPL card also highlights one of the most critical failures of the ration card system. The procedures for obtaining entitlement are notoriously cumbersome and slow.

The survey identified various government schemes and asked if the household had applied for any of them. Just over one in five (21.5%) had done so. Again targeting shortcomings emerged. Although more people who had experienced a financial crisis had applied than those who had not (23.6% compared to 13.9%), it is clear that most who had a crisis were not applying, presumably because they did not think they were entitled to the type of help on offer or did not know whether they qualified or how to apply.

Of those who had applied, nearly a third had not received the benefit, and of those receiving it, nearly a quarter had had to wait more than six months before receiving it. Only about a quarter received it within a month. And of those who had received anything, 41.3 per cent believed the amount was inadequate. A further failing was revealed when we broke the figures down by caste. It appears that lower caste people have had to wait longer than upper caste applicants and were more likely not to have received the grants at all (Table 9).

Table 9

Time from Applying for Government Benefit and Receipt, by Caste

Time from applying to receipt	*Scheduled caste*	*Scheduled tribe*	*Other backward*	*Upper caste*
Under month	17.5	16.7	27.5	32.8
One to three months	17.5	0	16.7	27.6
Three to six months	10.3	0	8.7	1.7
More than six months	10.3	33.3	18.8	12.1
Not received	42.3	50	27.5	25.9

Moreover, the higher the income of the household, the shorter the period between application and receipt of a state benefit, and the lower the probability that the household did not receive the benefit. While not surprising that finding merely highlights the inequity of the design and implementation of state benefits.

We also asked about receipt of state benefits by those who were believed to qualify for them. About 60 per cent believed someone in the household qualified for a benefit who was not receiving it. Of these, 63.4 per cent had not received it because they did not know how to apply, 21.4 per cent had applied but had been refused, and 15.2 per cent were fearful of applying. This is a pattern of responses that is quite normal internationally.

There is one additional point that should be emphasized. Not surprisingly, the illiterate people were the most likely to have failed in their attempts to obtain benefits. This, of course, is ironic, given that they were almost certainly among the most deprived. A system claiming to be targeting the poor that requires or rewards literacy is a contradiction in terms. Of those households believing they had one or more members qualifying for a state benefit, the main reason they gave for non-receipt was that they did not know how to apply. However, that applied to three-quarters of those who were illiterate (Table 10).

Table 10

Reason for Non-receipt of State Benefit by Education Status

Reason	*Illiterate*	*Primary*	*Middle*	*Secondary*	*Higher*	*Tertiary*
Do not know how to apply	72.4	63.9	65.6	53.2	35.1	35.5
Applied but refused	17.3	22.2	20.4	26.6	32.4	29
Fearful of applying	10.3	13.9	14	20.2	32.4	35.5

Private Benefits

Private benefit (PB) income is a catchall for all sources of income derived from assets and investments, physical, and monetary. In a sense, it is rental income, gained from renting out assets such as land, buildings, or equipment, or from turning savings into interest-bearing investment. One can make a useful distinction between *traditional* PB income, notably land and money lending, and *modern* PB, in which savings are converted into income through financial intermediation, where intermediaries such as banks act as a conduit for turning savings into investment for economic growth.

Much of the savings made by households does not go into investment. This is commonly attributed to the narrowly based, or inadequately developed, banking system. But while this is surely an important factor, it is not the only one. Individuals and families save for one of three purposes – to defer consumption, to provide security, and to increase income. Usually, some combination of those motives is involved. But there is reason to believe that the security motive is high in India, for cultural and structural reasons.

Perversely, a high level of economic uncertainty and a high probability of shocks producing financial crises combine to encourage passive saving in which *risk avoidance* is the primary objective. To invest savings is to take a risk, and the willingness to take this step will depend on the cost of any possible loss as well as the probability of earning income. If there is a high probability of a sudden need for the money, through an illness or loss of a harvest, for example, then even the prospect of a high rate of return would not induce a rational person to turn the savings into a risky investment, particularly if the money would be tied up for months or years ahead.

This situation characterizes India today, and the market trends have almost certainly increased the tendency to keep savings in liquid, accessible form, *particularly for the income poor*. In a sense, the poor save to reduce the need to borrow, while the rich save in order to make money.

Another peculiar feature of PB is that *traditional* forms encompass both income accumulation and survival strategy. A landlord may make money from leasing out land, water, or a tractor, or do so by taking the proceeds from sharecropping. This has been the way of the powerful over the centuries. Similarly, a moneylender may just accumulate, living off the interest and debt bondage relationships he contrives to generate. By contrast, there are many much less powerful who resort to renting out assets as a *distress* survival strategy. Often such people may be descending poverty, but for a while they may gain sufficient income from renting out their remaining land or other assets to appear statistically to be 'above the poverty line'. For example, a widow with young children may not be able to earn from labour or be able to invest in financial assets, but for a while she would be less vulnerable if she owned land or had a room she could rent out. But this temporary security would be tenuous.

Dormant Savings as Security

As noted earlier, there are three uses derived from savings, as a source of income, as a source of deferred consumption, and as a means of economic security. In economically affluent and highly monetized societies, the first two motives usually predominate, but in less monetized ones one would expect that the security motive would be much stronger. There are several ways of testing whether or not this is applied here.

Table 11

Where Money is Saved by Household Income by Area of Residence

Household income	*Only in home*	*Only in financial institutions*	*In both places*
Rural			
Up to ₹ 20,000	61.3	29	9.7
20,001–40,000	60.7	33.9	5.4
40,001–60,000	56.2	28.1	15.7
60,001–80,000	54.2	34.7	11.1
80,001–1 lakh	51.1	33.3	15.6
Above 1 lakh	48.5	36	15.4
Total	55	32.9	12
Urban			
Up to ₹ 20,000	46.2	46.2	7.7
20,001–40,000	37.8	54.4	7.8
40,001–60,000	36.9	58.3	4.8
60,001–80,000	34.1	54.5	11.4
80,001–1 lakh	30.6	61.1	8.3
Above 1 lakh	21.6	58.3	20.1
Total	31.7	56.6	11.7

Nearly a third of households in both rural and urban areas said they had no savings, which is scarcely surprising, given the extensive poverty. But this meant that a majority (two-thirds) did save. The poor mostly kept their savings in their homes, or at least not in financial institutions. Over half of all rural households and nearly a third in urban areas said they kept *all* their savings at home (Table 11). However, over 60 per cent of the poorest rural families kept their no-doubt meagre savings at home, and nearly 10 per cent kept some of them there. The richer families were more likely to put money in financial institutions, even though a surprisingly high number kept savings in their homes.[6]

Private Investment

Once a person or family has started to save, and once the decision to use money as dormant or active savings has been made, the question obviously arises as to what form of active investment could be made. Savings could be invested in financial instruments, including insurance, savings accounts, and financial products, or in other non-financial assets, such as business or money lending.

In practice, in a typical Indian community, only the relatively affluent can afford to go through this process, unless they are aided by some community or social institution. In the absence of a countervailing body, the development of financial markets could be expected to increase income inequality, since it opens avenues to invest in financial products and gain more non-earned income. Some financial products, such as mutual funds, are also exempt from income tax, and the income earned enjoys tax benefits (Roy, 2005).[7] Without suggesting that this is the intention, the practice surely benefits the middle class and thereby increases income inequality.

In Gujarat, the main forms of private household investment were savings accounts and insurance, mainly life and accident insurance, and investment in these was mainly by high-income earners (Table 12). The type of insurance products is distinctive. In India in general, largely because it has been a feature of Indian society for over 50 years, promulgated via a vast network of offices, investment in life insurance has been a much more popular and better understood action than medical insurance, which has emerged only recently, largely since medical costs began to rise so alarmingly. There were no significant differences in saving and investment behaviour between rural and urban areas.

Table 12

Private Investment by Household Income by Location

	Under 20,000	*20,001– 40,000*	*40,001– 60,000*	*60,001– 80,000*	*80,001– 100,000*	*Above 100,000*	*Total*
Rural							
Insurance	5.9	9.2	16.8	21.9	21.3	25.4	16.3
Savings	11	12.4	19.1	30.2	23	36.7	22
Financial products	1.7	0.5	0	4.2	0	4.5	2
Non-financial assets	0	0	0.8	2.1	4.9	4.5	1.8
Urban							
Insurance	14.8	17	26.5	16.7	16.7	30.4	22.2
Savings	18.5	21.2	29.5	31.9	33.3	69.6	37.6
Financial products	1.9	1.2	2.3	4.2	4.2	25	8.3
Non-financial assets	0	0.6	1.5	1.4	4.2	3	1.7

Although Gujarat has had an active share market, only a small percentage invested in financial products, about 8 per cent in urban areas and merely 2 per cent in rural areas. While investment in financial products seemed largely an urban phenomenon, it was substantially higher (25%) in households with an annual income of above ₹ 100,000.

Evidently, investment by high-income earners in financial products has the potential to accentuate inequality, always depending on the non-earned incomes from such investment. It should be seen in the context of the considerable financial encouragement, in the form of tax subsidies, given by government to such use of savings. In effect, given that government policy is blatantly inegalitarian, since it favours the rich, it is this one group which is able to make extensive use of such products.

Investment in other non-financial assets, such as business or money-lending, was very limited in both rural and urban areas. Investment in these non-financial assets was also largely restricted among the high-income earners.

A traditional form of PBs is rental income, from land, house, assets, etc. In the absence of financial products in rural areas, rental income has remained an important source of PBs, mainly from land, whereas it was mainly a house that provided rent in urban areas.

A higher proportion of lower-income groups in rural areas compared to urban received rental income. This could be because low-income marginal farmers do not have the capacity to cultivate their land so they lease out their land, which is a form of distress renting. For such households, land was a source of security.

In India, a great many people own assets of some kind. A large proportion of the rural population owns at least some land, even though most have only marginal parcels. Land ownership ensures a minimal degree of security for the family, as land can obviously be used to generate income directly or by rent. In many areas, land is used to provide basic food security and income is earned from labour or other assets, although in Gujarat this practice has shrunk.

In general, families value these assets as their only form of security and rarely sell them even in a crisis, although land is sometimes mortgaged with the hope of recovering it in better times. In the GSIS, 9 per cent of households sold their assets at time of crisis, and 12 per cent mortgaged them. An important use of these assets is to earn an income from renting out land for sharecropping. In the GSIS, about 7 per cent of agricultural households rented out land. This practice was carried out not only by big landlords but also by those who do not have the means to farm their land, which is a form of distress renting.

Earlier we noted that rental income from physical assets was more prominent in rural areas compared to investment in financial products, while in urban areas financial products predominate. We also enquired through a question about the share of income obtained from investments and assets. A statistically significant higher proportion of rural households said they received some of their income from investments and assets, with nearly a quarter receiving more than half their income that way (Table 13). In contrast, less than one in ten urban households reported that part of their income came from assets. High-income earners were more likely to receive a share of their income from investments and assets in both rural and urban areas.

Table 13

Share of Income from Assets by Location

	Below 20,000	*20,001– 40,000*	*40,001– 60,000*	*60,001– 80,000*	*80,001– 100,000*	*Above 100,000*	*Total*
Rural							
More than half	18.6	11.4	19.8	30.2	37.7	40.7	25.1
Less than half	7.6	11.9	17.6	9.4	19.7	19.2	14.2
None	73.7	76.8	62.6	60.4	42.6	40.1	60.7
Urban							
More than half	3.7	1.2	1.5	2.8	8.3	6.5	3.6
Less than half	1.9	3.6	3	4.2	2.1	11.9	5.5
None	94.4	95.2	95.5	93.1	89.6	81.5	90.9

The main reason for the rural–urban difference is that many of the self-employed in agriculture obtain incomes from assets. Over 40 per cent of the rural self-employed said they received more than half their income that way. Of course, casual labourers scarcely received any income from investment or assets. Less than a quarter of salaried workers received non-earned income from investment and assets. As lower caste households tend to have a low asset base, their income from assets and incomes would also be low, which was true in both rural and urban areas. About half the rural upper caste households said they received more than half of their income from investment and assets, compared to 20 per cent among lower castes and other backward castes. As upper caste families were more likely to invest and receive a part of their income from it, compared to lower castes these incomes could be inequality enhancing.

Concluding Reflections

We demonstrate that though Gujarat is a high-growth state, employment generated is not sufficient to provide incomes to the households. The rapid growth in the state has distributed its benefits unequally across society so that while some groups are clear winners others are losers. The clear winners are on an average salaried workers; generally, these are men living in urban areas. Women in rural areas are the worst off in terms of employment and income, and being casual or piece-rate workers made them clear losers. Better endowed households with assets, land in rural areas, and business assets among self-employed in urban areas were among the winners.

Facilitating Communities

The households in Gujarat then relied on the community for help in times of stress. In fact with low levels of education and lack of formal training facilities, the households relied on the community to provide skill training to improve their income earning capacity. Basic skills for the trades were picked up either from parents or neighbours.

Old identity organizations, based on caste or religion, are weakening and no longer serve their traditional function of providing community benefits. As they wane, the main form of support structure has shrunk to 'the extended family', which in turn is shrinking little beyond the nuclear family. The community benefits from this source are also under strain as money incomes become so important in the lives of everybody. In urban areas, the notion of 'neighbourhood' is becoming more about a broader community of local residents that are more loosely linked together, as compared to caste and extended family. These neighbourhood networks could play an important role in slums, as a voice for making more 'inclusive cities', and as a means for maintaining the infrastructure. But to do so effectively, public action may be required to give them a legal status.

The state can play a stronger supportive role in this respect. Because of their positive externalities, in providing economic security and in potentially limiting sectionalism, there is an argument for providing subsidies and favourable regulations to strengthen genuinely multiple identity or *integrative communities* that promote social mobility across caste-based and other group-based communities, as well as social solidarity and a spirit of *civic friendship*, a willingness to give assistance, advice and encouragement to others in the community, not just in times of crisis but in normal times, as a matter of customary social cohesion.

The Sachar Committee (GoI, 2006) had suggested incentives based on a diversity index. Educational institutions, private sector, and housing societies could be awarded larger grants or tax concessions to promote composite living, study, and work places. This would help to encourage diversity and build up a sense of community outside the traditional caste/religious-based institutions.

Facilitating PBs

Over time as money incomes prove insufficient, private income benefits are likely to grow as a source of income. At present, traditional sources are limited and are inegalitarian – as in the case of rental income gained by landlords, for example, and interest on moneylenders' loans. Where some traditional private income has come to lower-income groups, it has commonly been a reflection of distress and possibly indicative of impoverishment, for instance, being obliged to rent out the small plot of land. It is likely that traditional sources of PB income will slowly fade, leaving a vacuum to be filled by modern commercialized sources. But as the earlier analysis indicated, these modern PBs are still inefficient, as well as accessible only to a minority of relatively affluent families.

In a developed economy with strong financial markets, a large proportion of people obtain an income from private investment. In a country such as India, where only 45 per cent of people have bank accounts, 40 per cent have some form of life insurance and merely 3 per cent have health insurance, there is much less reliance on financial investment in formal markets to supplement earnings from work.

This does not however mean that PBs are absent; rather they take a different form. Money which is not deposited in a formal financial institution is often used as a financial asset through money lending in the local area, or to friends and neighbours.

PBs are still mainly seen as providing a modicum of security against risks, shocks, and the hazards of life. Savings are widespread, mainly kept in the equivalent of 'under the bed' or in institutions such as the post office rather than in a financial intermediary. People want to keep them safe, available in case of unanticipated crisis. But a consequence is that savings are not used to generate income. It is a transition from savings-for-security to savings-for-income that is a feature of economic development. A reality is that in a world of high economic uncertainty, low-income groups on the margins of subsistence cannot afford to take risks with their savings, even though they do their utmost to have some savings, however modest.[8]

A further concern is that financial markets are mainly for the economically better off and hence operate to increase inequality. The Government of India has put a lot of effort in trying to increase financial access, especially in rural areas, and has granted concessions to commercial banks to encourage them to open branches as well as try out new outreach methods, such as the deployment of business correspondents. Although bank branches are accessible to villagers and to slum dwellers, the banks themselves obviously prefer richer customers, as they bring larger profits at less cost.

It is generally accepted that in India, insurance, particularly health insurance, is underdeveloped, along with private pensions. In the latter case, a basic problem has been the lack of a national regulatory framework. The experience of more developed countries has shown that, if left just to the market, both personal insurance and pension funds tend to be discriminatory strongly biased towards the rich. To ensure that lower socio-economic groups obtain more access, it is necessary to take a number of policy steps, which could include empowering community groups and organizations so that they could offer health insurance and pensions. It would also be necessary to require insurance companies and pension funds to devote a share of their portfolio for lower-income groups.

As far as health and old-age insurance is concerned, the reality is that, if these are left entirely to the market, high-risk groups will continue to face discriminatory barriers, being denied coverage or being forced to pay high premia or being offered only limited benefits. Unless a social solidarity principle is applied by some means, those high-risk groups will be penalized, precisely because they are in most need of insurance. In the end, government must both ban and penalize discrimination in insurance products or it must introduce a proper social insurance system in which non-discrimination principles would be effectively redundant because all risk-groups would be cross subsidized. The difficulty with social insurance in a country such as India is, of course, coverage and establishing a basis for contributions.

The major challenge is to ensure an equitable, efficient, and accountable financial intermediation is developed. The challenge is to find ways of combining security with a source of income.

Universalizing and Equalizing State Benefits

There is widespread realization that India's public social spending has been wasteful and ill-directed, supporting a large bureaucracy. There is no fiscal excuse for this and highlights the point that existing public resources could be redirected so as to do much more to overcome poverty and income insecurity. Government efforts to provide income security for the poor and disadvantaged in India have been quite ineffectual. They are poorly targeted, create perverse poverty traps, and are quite costly and inefficient.

At present, in India and across the world, there is an active debate on what 'line' to take with respect to state benefits – a 'commodity line' (provision of food, clothing, etc.), a 'labour line' (public works, such as NREGS) or a 'cash line'. The 'commodity' line has been pursued the most vigorously over the years, with the massive public distribution system and the identification of BPL and APL 'beneficiaries' under this system. With the passing of the National Rural Employment Guarantee Act in 2005, the 'labour line' has become more popular.

The cash line is gaining academic respectability, due in part to gathering evidence from around the world that cash transfer schemes can and do achieve considerable reductions in poverty and economic insecurity. In India, some recent advocates have assumed that they should be targeted by means tests (Kapur et al., 2008a).[9] The problem with this is that there is overwhelming evidence – further supported by our findings earlier – that means testing is both inefficient – not reaching many of those genuinely in need and reaching some who are not so in need – and inequitable, for the same reasons. Narrowly focused 'targeting' does not work, if the objective is to reduce poverty and income insecurity effectively and equitably.

In 2009, a new Indian government was elected on a platform of 'inclusive growth', a worthy slogan and a benchmark by which to judge all income-related policies. To be meaningful and laudable that should include a strategy to make incomes less unequal. A progressive redistribution of money income complemented by a reduction in the inequality of community, state, and PB income is a way to start.

Notes

1. This chapter is based on the main agreements in and contains extracts from Gey Stauding, Jeemol Unni, Renana Jhasvala and Uma Ravi, Social Income and Insecurity: A study in Gujarat, New Delhi, Routledge, 2010.
2. For a review of arguments, see Chandrasekhar and Ghosh (2006a, 2006b).
3. Due to budgetary constraints, the sample size was modest, the target being 1500 households, from which detailed household information was gathered along with personal work and earned income data from one randomly selected adult member who was identified as doing economic activity from 41 wards of Ahmedabad and 37 villages in three western *talukas* of Surendranagar. The sample was stratified randomly by activity status, gender and rural–urban location. The survey methodology is described in Appendix A in Standing et al. (2010). We cannot and do not claim that statistical averages relate to what Gujarat or Ahmedabad would be like.
4. The study is concerned with identifying the structure and levels of social income and has not been directly concerned with complex questions of labour supply. However, some information was collected on the amount of time used in income-earning activity. In that regard, one must be careful about interpreting a low amount of

time in such work as proof of 'underemployment', even though that may be the case.

5. The number of days worked in a year is divided into three groups: working for less than 180 days or 6 months, 180–270 days or 6–9 months and more than 270 days. Working for more than 270 days may be considered as full employment and working for less than 6 months as under-employment. This is, of course, a simplification, in that some of those working less than 6 months may have done so by choice.
6. These findings are very similar to those found in a nationwide survey carried by NCAER and Max New York Life, which revealed that most Indians prefer to keep 65 per cent of their savings in liquid assets such as bank or post office deposits and cash at home (Shukla, 2010).
7. The Indian mutual fund industry has grown mainly due to the tax incentives granted to it from time to time.
8. One perversity of a modern market economy is that commonly the middle class comprises the largest group of major indebtors, once they find ways of borrowing. Governments should be wary of extending that trend.
9. See also the critique by Shah, 2008, and the riposte by Kapur et al., 2008b. The critique did not deal with the points made in the above text.

References

Chandrasekhar, C.P., and Ghosh, J. (2006a). *Employment Growth: The Latest Trends*, Macroscan: An Alternative Economics Webcentre. www.macroscan.org (accessed November 2008).

Chandrasekhar, C.P., and Ghosh, J. (2006b). *Working More for Less*, Macroscan: An Alternative Economics Webcentre. www.macroscan.org (accessed November 2008).

Government of India (GoI) (2008). *Economic Survey*. New Delhi: Government of India.

GoI (2006). *Social, Economic and Educational Status of the Muslim Community of India*, Prime Minister's High Level Committee. New Delhi: Government of India.

GoI (2007). *Report on Conditions of Work and Promotion of Livelihoods in the Unorganised Sector*. New Delhi: National Commission for Enterprises in the Unorganised Sector (NCEUS), Government of India.

Kapur, D., Mukhopadhyay, P., and Subramanian, A. (2008a). 'The case for direct cash transfers to the poor', *Economic and Political Weekly* 43(15), 37–43.

Kapur, D., Mukhopadhyay, P., and Subramanian, A. (2008b). 'More on direct cash transfers', *Economic and Political Weekly* 43(47), 85–87.

Morris, S. (2006a). 'Economic performance of Gujarat in recent times', Chapter 2 prepared for the State Development Report, Planning Commission, Gujarat Institute of Development Research (Unpublished).

NSSO (National Sample Survey Organisation) (1997). Employment and Unemployment Situation in India 1993–94. NSS 50 Round (July 1993–June 1994), No.409. New Delhi: Ministry of Statistics and Programme Implementation, Government of India. (Raw data from this survey was used)

NSSO (2001a). *Employment and Unemployment Situation in India 1999–2000 (Part I)*, NSS 55 Round (July 1999–June 2000), No. 458 (55/10/2). New Delhi: Ministry of Statistics and Programme Implementation, Government of India. (Raw data from this survey was used)

NSSO (2001b). *Employment and Unemployment Situation in India 1999–2000 (Part II)*, NSS 55 Round (July 1999–June 2000), No. 458 (55/10/2). New Delhi: Ministry of Statistics and Programme Implementation, Government of India.

NSSO (2006a). *Employment and Unemployment Situation in India 2004–5(Part I)*, NSS 61 Round (July 2004–June 2005), No. 515 (61/10/1). New Delhi: Ministry of Statistics and Programme Implementation, Government of India. (Raw data from this survey was used)

NSSO (2006b). *Employment and Unemployment Situation in India 2004–5 (Part II)*, NSS 61 Round (July 2004–June 2005), No. 515 (61/10/1). New Delhi: Ministry of Statistics and Programme Implementation, Government of India. (Raw data from this survey was used)

Roy, M. (2005) 'Money market mutual funds: A macro perspective', *Economic and Political Weekly* 40(12), 1254–1262.

Shah, M. (2008). 'Direct cash transfers: No magic bullet', *Economic and Political Weekly* 43(34), 77–79.

Shukla, R. (2010). *How India Earns, Spends and Save: Unmasking the Real India*. New Delhi: Sage Publications.

Stauding, G., J. Unni, R. Jhasvala and U. Ravi (2010). Social Income and Insecurity: A Study in Gujarat, New Delhi: Routledge.

Unni, J., and Raveendran, G. (2007) 'Growth of employment (1993–94 to 2004–2005): Illusion of inclusiveness', *Economic and Political Weekly* 42(30), 196–202.

12

Fuelling the Retail Boom

Need for the Right Employment Policy for Gujarat

Arpita Mukherjee and Tanu M. Goyal

Retail is the largest private industry in India and the second largest employer after agriculture. This sector has witnessed significant transformation since 1995. Traditionally, the Indian retail sector was characterized by the presence of a large number of small family-owned stores, which were low-investment, low-profit outlets. These stores survived on family labour and had a high incidence of disguised unemployment. Due to the lack of mechanization, sometimes too many people worked in small retail outlets. The employees of such traditional outlets are generally clubbed under the 'unorganized sector' employment and the incidence of organized employment was low. In a family-run business in the unorganized sector, it is usually difficult to obtain data on employment.

With liberalization of the economy in the 1990s, modern retail formats started developing. After 1990, the restrictions on consumer goods industry were phased out, imports were liberalized and foreign investment was encouraged. This led to brand proliferation and the availability of a wide range of products/brands-enabled scale expansion in retailing. On the demand side, after the liberalization of the economy in the 1990s, income increased. The increase in income levels increased consumer spending. Growth in the service sectors, especially knowledge-based services such as information technology (IT) and business process outsourcing (BPO), led to greater employment generation. Penetration of credit cards, easier bank credits/personal loans, demographic changes such as nuclear families replacing joint families, and dual income with the entry of more women in the workforce are some of the other key factors that facilitated the growth of modern/corporate retail.

Retail, whether traditional or modern, is largely a labour-intensive sector. However, the impact of modernization on retail employment is highly debated. With increase in scale of operations, emergence of different formats, investments in retail infrastructure such as shopping malls and supply chain network, and employment in modern retail and allied sectors such as food processing industry and logistics have increased. Unlike traditional retailers, modern corporate retailers are covered under 'organized sector employment' and have to adhere to the labour laws and regulations. This gives employees job security and the quality of employment improves. In fact, globally, the retail sector provides opportunities for part time employment. It is also a major employer for women. On the other hand, the traditional retailers are now facing stiff competition, which can have negative impact on employment. By streamlining the supply chain, modern retailers have succeeded in reducing their dependence on intermediaries/middlemen in the supply chain. However, this may adversely affect employment opportunities.

Thus, the impact of modern retail on employment is complex. In fact, the Indian government is very cautious in allowing foreign direct investment (FDI) in the retail sector on the pretext that it can adversely affect employment in the traditional sector. This was the primary reason why the government imposed a ban on foreign retailer's entry in India in 1997 even when other sectors were being liberalized. However, in 2006, the single brand retail route was partially opened up for foreign investors, subject to some conditions.[1] To date, multi-brand retail is closed for foreign investment.

In reality, employment in retail has shown a significant increase since 2000. This is because both modern and traditional retail sectors are growing, with the modern retail sector growing at 30 per cent against 10 per cent in the traditional sector. The government acknowledges that modern retail is required for modernization and investment in the supply chain. Recently the Department of Industrial Policy & Promotion (DIPP) released a document titled *Discussion Paper on Foreign Direct Investment (FDI) in Multi-Brand Retail Trading* to facilitate discussions on whether FDI should be allowed in retail and if so what should be the conditions. One such condition proposed for discussion is reserving 50 per cent of retail jobs for the rural youth.

Given the fact that retail is growing, this paper examines what should be the right employment policy for Gujarat to sustain this boom. The paper is divided in four sections. The first section gives an overview of the retail sector in India, while the next section examines the retail sector in Gujarat. The subsequent section analyses retail employment in India and Gujarat, focusing on the employment policy in Gujarat. The advent of modern retailing has led to a shift in employment from 'unorganized' to 'organized' segments. Based on a primary survey, the next section summarizes the difference in employment in these two segments and highlights the issues and concerns that it brings up. The last section provides policy suggestions for Gujarat.

Retail Sector in India

Retail is one of the fastest growing sectors in India and its share in the gross domestic product (GDP) is rising. However, the National Accounts Statistics does not give the disaggregated data for retail. The Quick Estimates of National Income 2008–2009 (CSO) show that the contribution of trade (including wholesale and retail) to GDP at current prices is ₹ 7,914.7 billion ($172.09 billion).[2] It also shows that this sector has grown at an average annual rate of 16.2 per cent between 2004–2005 and 2008–2009. The share of trade to GDP is around 15 per cent, which has remained stable during this period. The share of retail trade in GDP is estimated to be 8.1 per cent and the share of private organized sector in total GDP from trade has been estimated at 23.2 per cent in 2008–2009.[3] The share of modern corporate retailers at present is around 5 per cent and modern retail has been growing at the rate of 30 per cent over the past decade. According to the Kearney report (2010) on the Global Retail Development Index, the Indian retail market is expected to grow up to $535 billion in 2013.

With over 15 million retail outlets, India has the highest retail density in the world. However, around 95 per cent of the sector consists of small 'mom-and-pop' stores which survive on cheap labour (often family members) resulting in high incidence of disguised unemployment/under-employment.

As per the latest National Sample Survey Organisation (NSSO) 64th Round, in 2007–2008, retail trade employed 7.2 per cent of the total workforce and provided job opportunities to 33.1 million persons.[4] The share of employment in the sector 'trade, hotels, and restaurants' in 2007–2008 was significantly higher compared to its share in 1993–1994 for both males and females, in rural as well as in urban areas.[5] More than two-third of the total employment in the category 'trade, hotels, and restaurants' is in the retail sector (see Table 1).

Table 1

Persons Working in Trade, Hotels and Restaurants (in %)

	Rural		*Urban*	
	Male	*Female*	*Male*	*Female*
2007–2008	7.6	2.3	27.8	12.8
Of which in Retail Trade	5.6	1.7	18.8	8.6
1999–2000	6.8	2	29.4	16.9
1993–1994	5.5	2.1	21.9	10

Source: Extracted from DIPP (2010b), Table C, p. 5.

The Indian economy is growing at a fast pace and both traditional and modern retailers are increasing. Existing survey-based studies have shown that since the traditional sector is also on the increase, there is no clear evidence of job losses in the traditional sector due to the advent of modern retail.[6] One estimate shows that modern retailing would generate over 2.5 million jobs by 2010 through backward and forward linkages.[7] There has been a sudden spurt in demand for retail-related skills in India. Modern retailers are facing skill shortages and are taking measures such as partnerships/tie-ups with management institutes and in-house training facilities to develop skills.

Retail Sector in Gujarat

Gujarat is one of the fastest growing states in India. In the year 2007–2008, the gross state domestic product (GSDP) grew at 12.79 per cent.[8] The per capita income at constant prices (1999–2000) in Gujarat is estimated to be higher than the national average for 2006–2007. Gujarat is also one of the most urbanized states of India with 38 per cent share of urban population as compared to 27.78 per cent share of urban population in the country on an average.[9] It is one of the pioneer states in initiating reforms, infrastructure development, and privatization (Hirway, 2000 and Bagchi et al., 2005). The key sectors in Gujarat include agro-processing and food industry, pharmaceuticals, chemicals and petrochemicals, textiles and apparel, and gems and jewellery (Menon, 2008).

Compared to other states in India, Gujarat has a conducive business environment for investors (KPMG, 2007). The World Bank *Doing Business Indicators* (2009) ranked Ahmedabad fifth among seventeen Indian cities in terms of 'ease of doing business' (World Bank, 2008). This state is ranked fourth among the Indian states in terms of FDI inflows but it receives only 5.83 per cent of the total FDI flows in the country as of March 2010.[10] Thus, Gujarat is still not the most favoured destination for FDI inflows, which is particularly true for the retail sector. But the government is continuously trying to attract FDI.

Gujarat is known for its trader communities and retail is one of the priority sectors in the state. The share of 'trade, hotels, and restaurants' in the GSDP was around 14.5 per cent in 2007–2008 valued at ₹ 311.48 billion ($7.37 billion).[11] The share of trade in GSDP is estimated to be around 13 per cent. As retail trade is more labour intensive than wholesale trade and the share of retail trade in total trade is higher, it can be assumed that the share of retail trade in GSDP is around 11–12 per cent.[12] The share of organized retail is 12 per cent of the total retail, which is higher than the national average of 5 per cent.[13]

As per the Indian Constitution, retail and agriculture are under the 'State Subject'. Hence, state governments play a major role in this sector. The focus of the Gujarat government is to link retail to agriculture by modernizing the supply chain. The Gujarat Agro Industrial Policy aims to achieve this. As a part of this policy, cold chain projects and retail outlets for perishables are entitled to incentives in areas under the jurisdiction of the Municipal Corporation (GAIC, 2008). Apart from this, policies are being initiated to promote competitiveness and efficiency; the government is taking steps to encourage standardization, grading and setting up of excellent facilities accredited by internationally acceptable agencies, especially in the agriculture sector.

Gujarat has also initiated other reforms, which facilitate the development of the modern retail sector. For instance, it is one of the few states to repeal the Land Ceiling and Regulation Act in 1999. Consequently, a vast amount of land was made available for commercial development activities (GUDC, 2008). Gujarat has an integrated township policy in order to give impetus to the new order economy; this is done by facilitating the creation of high-quality living/working environments with adequate infrastructure and services, in the form of sustainable integrated townships. Although retail is politically sensitive so far, retail modernization activities in Gujarat have not faced any anti-retail modernization movements.

Due to reforms and growth in industries, services, and agriculture, the per capita income in the state is rising and cities such as Ahmedabad, Surat, and Vadodara have become important retail destinations. Most of the large pan-India retailers have a presence in Gujarat. These include the Future's Group, Reebok India Company, Reliance Retail Limited, and ITC Wills Lifestyle Retail, among others. There are some regional retailers such as Rajya Khadi Gramudyog (handmade goods), Nilkamal Jewellers (jewellery), and Maspro Electronics (electronic equipments). Moreover, some large Indian conglomerates have started their operations in Gujarat and now have expanded their retail presence across the country. These include the Vimal Retail Group and Adani Retail Limited.[14]

Since the GDP of the state is growing and income is rising, there is further potential for the growth and penetration of modern retail outlets. The state government is undertaking steps to modernize the retail sector. In 2006–2007, the government disbursed ₹ 2.80 billion ($0.06 billion)[15] for the retail sector. Thus, the retail sector, especially the modern retail sector, is likely to be an important sector in terms of employment generation in the future.

Despite the favourable policies, there are some areas of concerns. Most global retailers have not chosen Gujarat as the first state to enter into the Indian market or for establishing major sourcing hubs.[16] Global retailers such as Wal-Mart Stores Inc., TESCO plc, and Metro AG entered India through states such as Punjab, Maharashtra, and Karnataka and have set up their sourcing base in the states. In addition, with the fast development of organized retail and proliferation of malls, proper urban planning is another area of concern for Gujarat.

Retail Employment and Policy

Globally, retail is one of the largest employers; it provides employment to around 11.7 per cent of the population in the United States and 11 per cent in the United Kingdom.[17] Comparatively, in India, the share of retail in the total employment is much lower (7.2%). This may be because of the high incidence of disguised unemployment in the traditional 'mom-and-pop' stores.

The traditional retail outlets were built on the model of entrepreneurship or sole proprietorship and hence they provide opportunities for self-employment. Hired labour was not common and skill requirements were low. With the growth of modern retail, the need for hired labour has increased and the skill requirements have changed.

Employment in the retail sector is divided into direct employment and indirect employment. Direct employment includes employment at the shop floor and store-level activities; indirect employment includes employment in allied activities such as logistics and supply chain, packaging, and retail inventory management. While the traditional retail outlets generate more intermediaries in the supply chain, the modern retail outlets generate employment in allied activities. Modern outlets also offer opportunities for contractual employment and part time employment. They often use employees on rotational basis to keep the stores open for long hours and this generates more employment as compared to the traditional sector where the same worker has to work for long hours. While the employees in the modern retail outlets consist of skilled labour, those in the traditional sector are mainly low-skilled employees with lower educational qualifications.

The retail sector faces multi-layered regulations by different departments of the central government, state governments, and local/municipal bodies. It is one of the few sectors where FDI is restricted; it is prohibited in multi-brand retail and only up to 51 per cent is allowed in single brand retail. Most multi-brand retailers enter India through the wholesale cash and carry route, by setting up distribution centres in the country. Apart from this, foreign retailers have entered India through exclusive licensing and distribution agreement, franchisee arrangements, and setting up wholly owned subsidiary through the manufacturing route, among others. All these modes have helped in creating employment opportunities. In fact, foreign retailers in India have employed the local population, as labour is cheap in India.

In India, there is a general perception that foreign retailers can have an adverse impact on employment in the traditional sector. However, this is not a foreign versus domestic issue but the problem is related to modernization in the retail sector and large retailers in general. Even domestic corporate retailers are facing backlashes in India on grounds that they may adversely affect employment in the traditional sector. The presence of foreign retailers in the country has increased sourcing from India, which has benefited the farmers and increased their earnings. Farmers supplying to Wal-Mart Stores Inc. have brought out the fact that it pays 5–7 per cent more than the local wholesale market.[18] Moreover, technology is percolating down from the global retailers to the farmers, which has improved the yield. Studies on small and medium enterprises (SMEs) and global retailers have shown that technologies such as tetra-packaging and bar coding are filtering down to SMEs through retailers such as Metro AG. Increased sourcing from India and in-house brands of retailers has generated employment in the manufacturing sector.

Unlike many states in India, where the agriculture sector is the largest employer, in Gujarat, the manufacturing segment provides the largest public and private sector employment. It has a share of 40 per cent in the total employment. The share of trade (wholesale and retail) and restaurants in the total public and private sector employment in 2007 is 2.83 per cent, which has increased from 1.5 per cent during 2000–2007. Retail employment in Gujarat almost doubled during the same period. However, studies have shown that due to the fast growth, modern retail is facing skill shortages.[19]

Gujarat has initiated reforms to improve the quality of employment to control the skill shortage. Gujarat is one of the few states in India[20] that has proposed labour reforms (Planning Commission, 2006). In a report to the Planning Commission, the state proposed to seek relaxation in some provisions of the central laws related to regulating the working hours, empowering the Development Commissioner to fix minimum wages, making provisions to allow women to work on night shifts, among others. If these changes are implemented, it will facilitate employment growth.[21]

Gujarat follows the Bombay Shops and Establishment Act of 1948. This Act has been proposed to be the model Shops and Establishment Act by the Retailers Association of India to the Planning Commission. This Act has been designed to provide good working conditions to the employees of the retail outlets (RAI, 2010). Gujarat has further amended this Act in 1980 to include social security benefits for employees. As per the 1980 Amendment, the employer has to provide for life insurance benefits to the employee engaged in the shops and commercial establishments.

The Employee Survey: Modern versus Traditional Retail

There are a few survey-based studies in India, which have assessed the impact of modern retail on retail employment.

Mukherjee and Patel (2005) compared the employment quality in organized and unorganized retail. Joseph and Soundararajan (2008) estimated the impact of organized retail on unorganized sector employment and found that the adverse affect (if any) of the existence of a modern retail outlet in the proximity of the traditional retail outlet wears off over time. The former was an employee survey, while the latter in 2008 was an employer survey. In 2009, ICRIER undertook a pilot survey of both the employees and employers to understand conditions such as wages, skill requirements, and training, in both traditional and modern retail sectors. The survey was conducted through semi-structured questionnaires. A total of around 200 retail employees were surveyed, which included 121 traditional sector employees and 79 modern retail sector employees. In addition, 254 small retailers and 78 large retailers filled the employer questionnaire. Separate questionnaires were designed for employers and employees and there were some common questions to cross check the findings.

The employee survey compared the working conditions in modern and traditional retail outlets. Specifically, it looked at employment density, hours of work, holiday entitlements, average remuneration across qualification and work experience, increments, incentives, and job prospects, among others.

Employment density refers to the average floor space (in square metres or square feet) per person in an occupied building. It is therefore a measure of how much space each person occupies within the workplace. In a retail shop, employment density helps measure disguised unemployment at the retail outlet and new employment opportunities created at the shop level by the modern retail outlets. The survey results indicate the presence of disguised unemployment for traditional outlets. For smaller shop sizes (see Table 2), the employment density measured in terms of square metres is less for traditional outlets when compared to modern retail outlets. As the shop size increases, more jobs are created at the modern retail outlets. These are in the form of security guards, lift operators, and more managers, among others.

Table 2

Employment Densities for Modern and Traditional Outlets

Shop size	*Modern retail outlets (in sqm.)*	*Small/traditional retail outlets (in sqm.)*
Less than 1000	111.4	94.8
1001–2000	221.86	183.19
2001–4000	129.12	218.71
Above 4001	503.88	666.66

Traditional retail outlets are mostly manned by family labour with a few employees. As the shop size increases, the average number of family workers declines and hired workers increases. However, the total number of hired workers is still lower in traditional outlets when compared to modern outlets. In modern retail outlets, there are permanent employees and contractual employees. As the shop size increases, both the number of permanent employees and contractual employees increases. In modern retail outlets with larger shop size, the average number of workers employed at each level is much higher than in small retail outlets (see Figures 1 and 2).

Figure 1

Average Number of Employees by Shop Size

Note: Key to chart: Less than 500 sqm. = Code 1, 501–1000 sqm. = Code 2, 1001–2000 sqm. = Code 3, 2001–4000 sqm. = Code 4, More than 4001 sqm. = Code 5.

As the shop size increases, more employees are hired in the modern retail outlets as compared to traditional or smaller retail outlets. Modern retail has been instrumental in opening new employment opportunities for the younger cohort of India. The average age of the employees in modern retail outlets is between 25 and 29 years, while that of the traditional retail outlets is between 30 and 39 years. In addition, the retail sector provides alternate job opportunities, especially to personnel with non-technical educational qualification.

Figure 2

Total Number of Employees in Modern and Small Retail Outlets

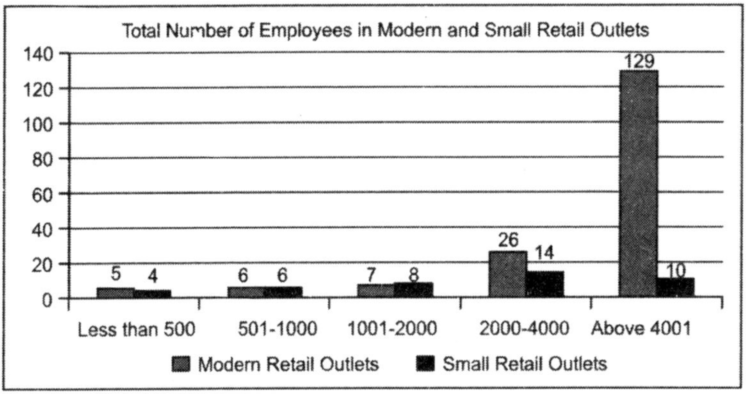

Note: Key to the chart: Less than 500 sqm. = Code 1, 501–1000 sqm. = Code 2, 1001–2000 sqm. = Code 3, 2001–4000 sqm. = Code 4, More than 4001 sqm. = Code 5.

The employees at the small retail outlets have lower educational qualifications. Moreover, they do not acquire any formal training at work. This is illustrated in Figure 3. As a result, they have limited alternate employment opportunities and growth prospects. Modern retail outlets employ skilled labour who have higher qualifications and provide greater opportunities for training and skill development. In fact, many foreign retailers selling luxury brands send their employees to their home country for product training and customer orientation. This helps in building employees confidence and it opens brighter prospects for the future.

Figure 3
Employee Qualification and Training and Skill Development

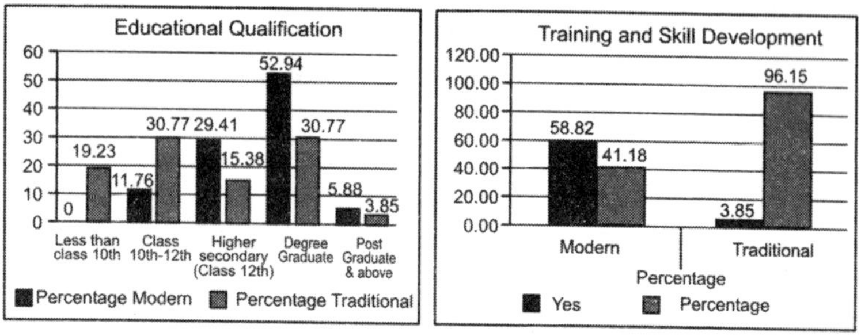

The employer survey results were similar to the employee survey results. The results, as illustrated in Figure 4, showed that while most traditional retailers do not impart any training to their employees, more than 90 per cent modern retailers provide formal training to the employees. According to the survey, all modern retailers who provide formal training are satisfied with the skill level of their employees, while the retailers who do not provide training are dissatisfied. In traditional retail outlets, most employees learn with experience, as managing and running the shop has been a family business in most cases. However, this kind of training is helpful at only the entrepreneurial level. Scientific training methods are more helpful for shop floor level employees as it helps them to

Figure 4
Training Provided by Retailers and Skill Level of Employees

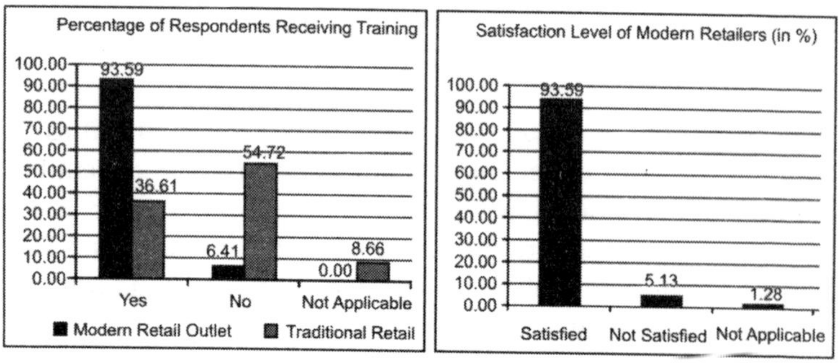

improve their future job prospects and make them employable in modern retail outlets.

Employee remuneration is determined by a number of factors. It is dependent on the person's qualifications, years of experience, designation, skill level, etc. While modern retail outlets have a larger number of employee gradation including managerial positions, junior managers, contractual employees (security guard, liftman, house keeping, etc.), such gradations are not there in small retail outlets.

It is difficult to compare salaries in modern and traditional outlets. Usually, the shop owners in traditional outlets double up as manager and have helpers to assist them. Comparing managerial salaries in modern outlets with the owner's salary in traditional does not reveal the true picture. This is because not only the nature of work is different, but also because the self-employed owners are hesitant to declare their earnings. Therefore, a comparison of the salaries of store help in traditional and modern retail sectors is presented in Figure 5. As the salaries vary depending upon the employee's qualification and years of experience, salaries of store help with similar qualifications and work experience were selected. Figure 5 shows that store help with similar qualifications and experience get higher salaries in modern retail outlets as compared to traditional retail outlets.

In addition to this, modern retail outlets offer higher opportunities to earn increments and incentives in comparison to traditional retail outlets. The salary difference between those employed in the modern and traditional sectors is as high as one-third from the total salary of an employee in the traditional sector. Increments in the modern retail outlets are linked to the performance of the employees, while in the traditional retail outlets they are linked to an employee's years of experience.

Modern retail outlets follow labour laws and employ personnel on rotational basis. They offer better quality of work life than traditional outlets in terms of hours of work and the number of holidays that an employee is entitled to take (see Figure 6). Modern retail outlets have a corporate set up; therefore, their management is more professional. Work guidelines and job responsibilities are clearly defined. As a result, the quality of life at modern outlets is considered to be better by the employees when compared to small retail outlets.

Figure 5

Average Salary Drawn across Different Designations and Increments and Incentives

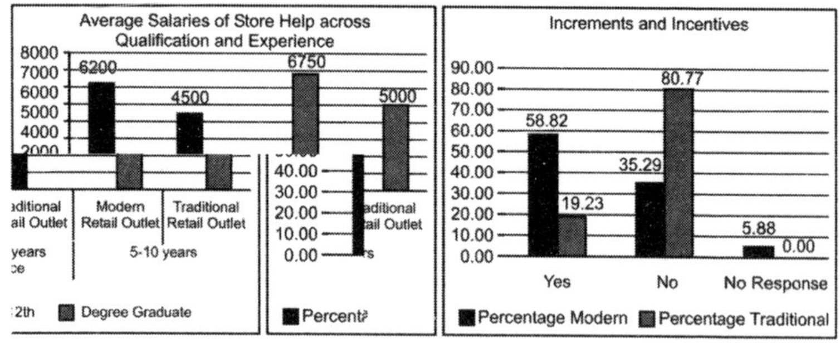

Figure 6

Hours of Work and Number of Holidays

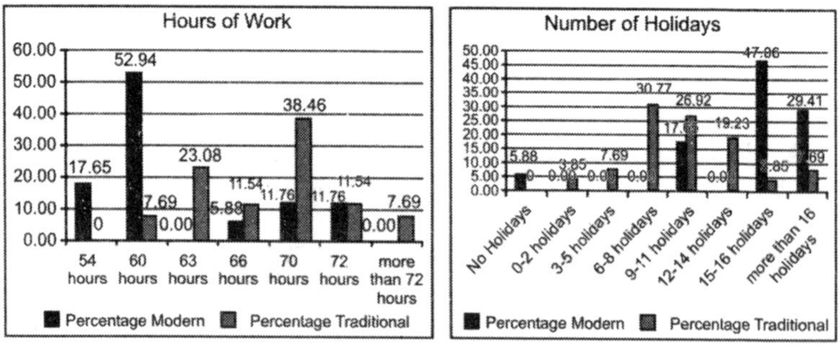

The survey results also indicate that short-term job prospects are good in the modern retail sector, while the job prospects in the small retail sector are considered moderate by most of the respondents (see Figure 7). However, most traditional retail sector employees found that the long-term employment prospects in the retail industry were good. This is because the retail sector is growing generating job opportunities in this sector. Most employees of the traditional retail outlets felt that they are not threatened by the growth of the modern outlets since they offer more job opportunities. In fact, 65 per cent of the traditional sector employees pointed out that they would like to work in modern retail outlets.

Figure 7

Short-term Job Prospects and Employment Prospects in the Industry

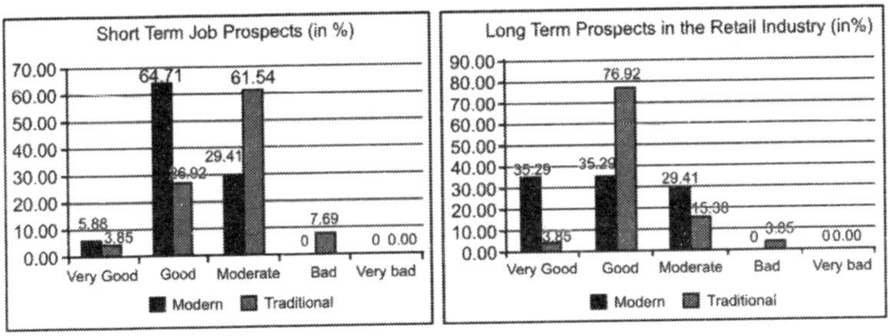

Overall, the survey results indicate that the remuneration, quality of work, and future job prospects are better in modern retail outlets when compared to traditional retail outlets. Moreover, it was found that a large number of traditional retail sector employees are seeking opportunities in the modern retail sector.

What Should Be the Right Employment Policy for Gujarat

The state of Gujarat is on a high-growth trajectory and hence per capita income is likely to rise. The retail sector is witnessing a double-digit growth – both modern and traditional retailers are growing. Unemployment is low in Gujarat; the government is actively initiating reforms (including investment in agriculture and supply chain) and the manufacturing sector is growing. The state is focused on attracting FDI, while many cities in Gujarat have attracted modern retailers. However, global retailers such as Wal-Mart Stores Inc., Metro AG, and TESCO plc have not selected Gujarat as the state for establishing their initial presence. The central government is now planning to open up FDI in multi-brand retail. All these have to be taken into account while designing an employment policy for Gujarat in the retail sector.

Since unemployment is low, Gujarat is well-placed to focus on the quality of employment. The survey analysis compiled in the section 'Retail Employment and Policy' shows that modern retail outlets provide better quality of employment. The ICRIER 2009 survey shows that prospects are considered good for both traditional and modern retail outlets. The modern retail sector is growing very fast and so are the job prospects. Hence, the state government should continue to promote modern retail.

However, existing studies have shown that modern retailers are facing a shortage of skilled workers in Gujarat. Thus, the problem of employability of personnel in modern retail outlets persists. The state government can help to mitigate this by focusing on skill development and training programmes for retail employees under public–private partnership. It can work with management and labour institutes to identify areas in which there is or could be skill shortage and respond appropriately to design suitable academic courses and training programmes to facilitate skill development. The training should focus on retail knowledge, product knowledge, customer dealing, customer orientation, and attitude.

As the retail sector modernizes, there can be some job displacements in the traditional sector. This may arise due to streamlining of the supply chain and direct sourcing that may displace the intermediaries. The pilot survey also shows that the requirements in modern and traditional retail is different and hence it may be difficult for an employee to just shift from traditional to modern retail. Modern retailers need not only higher skills in terms of qualifications but also product knowledge. Internationally, secondary and higher secondary school qualified employees are absorbed by the modern retail sector. However, in India modern retail seems to employ largely graduates. The government can focus on specific training programmes after higher secondary school (class 12) in collaboration with retailers to help these people to get into the modern retail sector. One of the key issues for the government is to identify the areas where unskilled and uneducated labour, displaced from the unorganized sector, can find alternate employment opportunities. These can be in construction, manufacturing activities such as agro-processing, warehousing, and cold chain development, among others.

In addition, the state government can help the traditional retailers to modernize and upgrade. The 2009 ICRIER survey found that the biggest problem of traditional retailers is poor infrastructure and finance. The government can improve the quality of supporting infrastructure like parking and power supply. Since this sector faces financial crunch, and small retailers are unable to offer collaterals for bank loans, government-owned banks, and micro-credit institutions can have innovative packages for meeting the specific requirements of this sector. Some banks, such as the Syndicate Bank, have already started microfinancing for small retailers. There could also be insurance schemes specially designed for small retailers. One of the biggest disadvantages of the 'mom-and-pop' stores in comparison with large retailers is the high purchasing/procurement costs. The state government can work with small retailers' associations to streamline procurement processes and encourage them to make bulk purchases through associations. The government could also work closely with them in the upgradation of technology, training of workforce, investment in infrastructure, and use of IT. All these aspects will enable the traditional retailers to grow, modernizes, and compete with the corporate sector.

At present, modern retail is growing at a fast pace in some cities which are mostly metro cities. There is a need for urban planning in these cities, which is largely the work of the local municipalities. The government could offer incentives so that modern retail spreads to other cities. This will lead to a more equal and holistic development. Besides, it will generate uniform employment opportunities across the state instead of creating pockets of employment. The local municipalities should also focus on streamlining the retail clearances process. For instance, in states such as West Bengal, there are easy clearance processes for certain types of retailers through green channelling. The single window clearance helps to save time and is cost-effective which is not there in seeking multiple clearances.

The state government should continue to push the central government for labour reforms and other reforms such as timely implementation of the single goods and service tax (GST) which will help retailers and logistic companies to set up supply chains through the hub and spoke model. This will increase sourcing from Gujarat to other states which would boost up manufacturing and create employment.

The state government should work with foreign retailers, especially food and grocery retailers, and encourage them to establish a presence in the state. This will help to develop the agriculture supply chain. In order to facilitate the growth of modern retail, the government should continue to undertake policies to strengthen the logistics and supply chain in Gujarat. This will lead to job creation in the rural areas and improve the earnings of farmers.

The government can also facilitate the cooperation between foreign retailers and SMEs in the state. There are examples of such collaborations in countries such as Vietnam with global retailers such as Metro AG.

The government should link developments in retail with other labour-intensive sectors such as tourism. For instance, countries such as Singapore and Malaysia have shopping festivals, which attracts tourists from across the world. These generate retail revenue and employment in both tourism and retail.

Notes

1. FDI up to 51 per cent in retail trade of 'Single Brand' products would be subject to the following conditions:
   (i) Products to be sold should be of a 'Single Brand' only.
   (ii) Products should be sold under the same brand internationally.
   (iii) 'Single Brand' product-retailing would cover only products which are branded during manufacturing.
2. All dollar figures are in US dollars. Conversion is done by using RBI annual average exchange rate in 2008–2009. ($1 = ₹ 45.99).
3. Source: DIPP Discussion Paper 2010.
4. Source: DIPP Discussion Paper 2010.

5. Share of employment in retail trade, according to the 2004–2005 NSSO Survey, was estimated at 7.3 per cent, marginally higher than its share as per 2007–2008 Survey.
6. For details see Mukherjee and Patel (2005), Kumar et al. (2008), and Joseph and Soundararajan (2009).
7. India Retail Report (2007).
8. Source: Own calculations from Central Statistical Organisation (CSO) database.
9. http://www.gujaratindia.com/.
10. Source: DIPP FDI Fact Sheet, March 2010
11. Conversion using RBI average annual exchange rate for 2007–2008. $1 = ₹ 40.24.
12. Source: Own calculations from CSO database.
13. Source: http://www.dnaindia.com/money/report_south-mumbai-to-get-a-pantaloon-central_1029625.
14. Reliance Retail Limited has purchased Adani Group's retail division in 2007.
15. Conversion using RBI average annual exchange rate for 2006–2007. $1 = ₹ 45.24.
16. By setting up a sourcing base in the state, foreign retailers aid employment creation in allied sectors such as manufacturing, and agro-processing.
17. Source: Mukherjee and Patel (2005).
18. http://www.ndtv.com/news/india/how-wal-marts-wooing-indian-farmers-19777.php.
19. See Sparks (1992) and Daniels (2007).
20. Others include Andhra Pradesh, Karnataka, Madhya Pradesh, and Maharashtra. For details see Report of the Working Group on Labour Laws and Other Regulations, Planning Commission, Government of India. http://www.planningcommission.nic.in/aboutus/committee/wrkgrp11/wg11_rplabr.pdf.
21. Labour is in the concurrent list as per the Indian Constitution. For any proposition, central approval is required.

References

Bagchi, A.K., Das, P., and Chattopadhyay, S.K. (2005). 'Growth and structural change in the economy of Gujarat, 1970–2000', *Economic and Political Weekly* 40(28), 3039–3047.

Daniels, R.C. (2007). *Skills Shortages in South Africa: A Literature Review*, Development Policy Research Unit (DPRU) Working Paper 07/121.

Hirway, I. (2000). 'Dynamics of development in Gujarat: Some issues', *Economic and Political Weekly* 35(35/36), 3106–3120.

Joseph, M., and Soundararajan, N. (2009). *Retail in India*. New Delhi: Academic Foundation.

Kumar, V., Patwari, Y., and Ayush, H.N. (2008). 'Organised food retailing: A blessing or a curse?', *Economic and Political Weekly* 43(20), 67–75.

Menon, S.V. (2008). *Drivers of economic growth in Gujarat*, Munich Personal RePEc Archive, January.

Mukherjee, A., and Patel, N. (2005). *FDI in Retail Sector in India*. New Delhi: Academic Foundation.

Sparks, L. (1992). 'Restructuring retail employment', *International Journal of Retail & Distribution Management* 20(3), pp. 12–19..

Reports

Kearney, A.T. (2010). *Expanding Opportunities for Global Retailers: A 2010 A.T. Kearney Global Retail Development Index*. http://www.atkearney.com/images/global/pdf/2010_Global_Retail_Development_Index.pdf.

DES (2008). *Socio-Economic Review – Gujarat State 2007–08*, Directorate of Economics and Statistics, Government of Gujarat, February. http://www.gujaratindia.com/pdf/ser0708.pdf.

DIPP (2010a). *Fact Sheet on Foreign Direct Investment (FDI): From August 1991 to March 2010*, Department of Industrial Policy & Promotion, Government of India, March. http://dipp.nic.in/fdi_statistics/india_FDI_March2010.pdf.

DIPP (2010b) *Discussion Paper on Foreign Direct Investment (FDI) in Multi-brand Retail Trading*, Department of Industrial Policy & Promotion, Government of India, July. http://dipp.nic.in/DiscussionPapers/DP_FDI_Multi-BrandRetailTrading_06July2010.pdf.

GAIC (2008). *Gujarat Agro Industrial Policy A.D. and Beyond*, Gujarat Agro Industries Corporation Ltd. http://www.gujagro.org/pdf/Agri.pdf.

GUDC (2008). *Gujarat Integrated Township Policy*, Gujarat Urban Development Company Limited, Urban Development and Urban Housing Department, Government of Gujarat, January.

IBEF (2008). *Gujarat*, Indian Brand Equity Foundation, February. http://www.ibef.org/download/Gujarat_171109.pdf.

KPMG (2007). *Accelerating Growth in Gujarat: A Discussion Note*. http://www.dtpt.com/pdfs/Gujarat_KPMGReport.pdf.

NSSO (2005). *Employment and Unemployment Situation in India Part-I and II*, NSS 61st Round, Report No. 515, July 2004–June 2005.

Planning Commission (2006). *Labour Laws and other Labour Regulations*, Report of Working Group, Planning Commission, August. http://www.planningcommission.nic.in/aboutus/committee/wrkgrp11/wg11_rplabr.pdf.

RAI (2010). *White Paper on Shops and Establishment Act* (Unpublished), Retailers Association of India.

World Bank (2008). *Doing Business in India, Sub-National Report 2009*, September. http://www.doingbusiness.org/Downloads/.

Websites

http://ic.gujarat.gov.in/industrial-policy/p2.htm

www.dipp.nic.in

www.gujaratindia.com/

www.mospi.gov.in

www.planningcommission.nic.in

13

Employment Potential in SEZs and SIRs in Gujarat

Lancy Lobo and Jayesh Shah

In contrast to the slogan – 'Land for Tillers' – in Gujarat during the 1970s, the present 21st century is poised to mark Gujarat as the 'Land for Industrialists'. The Government of Gujarat, which assisted the creation and promotion of Special Economic Zones (SEZs) and Special Investment Regions (SIRs), is also an additional vehicle for facilitating the distribution of land to industries. The promise of attracting foreign direct investment and creating employment and exports of goods in order to generate income in the state (by May 2010 about 60 SEZs (10–1,000 ha) and 13 SIRs (minimum 100 sq km)) has been under various stages of implementation in the state.

The increased utilization of land for industrial purposes has never been quite the same in the last 40 years and now the state of Gujarat in effect ranks third in the total industrial production in the country. However, the unemployment level ranges between 2 per cent and 5 per cent of the total workforce available (2010 estimates) monthly to daily variation. The Government of Gujarat estimates an investment of above ₹ 14–20 lakh crores in the industrial sector in coming 10 years (2020). The plan period targets growth rate from 10.5 per cent in the Tenth Plan to 11.5 per cent in the Eleventh Plan period.

Towards 21st Century Industrial Gujarat: A New Approach

Though Gujarat had been the forerunner so far as the industrial development in the country is concerned, its policy makers have never been satisfied with its share in the state domestic product (GSDP). According to the NSSO 64th round report (2007–08), the table on distribution of persons (per 1,000) by activity (principal + subsidiary) status for each state/UT shows the rate of unemployment at 5 per 1,000 persons in Gujarat against the national average of 9 per 1,000 persons. This figure is the lowest unemployment ratio among the states of India.[1]

The state has shifted its industrial policy from cluster and industrial estates (Gujarat Industrial Development Corporation – GIDC) based industries to SEZ during 2002–2004 and now have shifted towards industrial regions[2] and SIRs,[3] expanding the industrial influence areas to 200–400 sq km each. This shift in policy supports the states vision of becoming the largest business hub in Asia and the global investment destination (Industrial Policy, 2009). The state's five Vibrant Gujarat summits from 2004 to 2011 have successfully attracted industries to commit investments in various industrial sectors.

The creation of SEZs in the state is the result of an erstwhile industrial policy shift, post-2002 (SEZ-related policy) and later SEZ Act (2004). These provisions allowed investments by facilitating the industries to invest in the growth of industrial townships encompassing statutory powers. This also overrules the powers of the local bodies and the government to interfere in the day-to-day functioning inside these SEZs.

The concept of SIRs is fuelled by an ongoing Dedicated Freight Corridor (DFC) which encompasses 150 km and known as industrial corridor, namely, the Delhi-Mumbai Industrial Corridor (DMIC). The state government is also providing port connectivity and the necessary infrastructure to boost the demand of industrial investments in the state.

SEZs in Gujarat

Gujarat, like other states in the country, is now enabling the setting up of SEZs, which are to be created on demand; these are not based on central, state and regional (district) planning requirements but on the demands of private capital. About 60 SEZs under various stages of implementation have been formulated by the Gujarat SEZ Act, 2004 and its subsequent amendments in 2007. The lands for these SEZs are either acquired or purchased by public and private enterprises without any resettlement and rehabilitation package/policy. The GIDC is the medium through which land is being acquired from farmers and it is facilitating the setting up of SEZs for private capital.

The state has not only claimed lower amounts of agricultural lands for the SEZs, it has also successfully diverted the common or *gauchar* land (often referred to as wasteland) from listed properties in land banks to those industries promising high investment in the SEZs. At present, Gujarat has attracted investment to the tune of ₹ 2.63 lakh crores promising employment to 20 lakh people and has acquired nearly 32,000 ha of land.[4]

It is equally important to note that the state will be attracting a huge workforce over and above the 1.6 crores total workforce already available; 50 per cent of this workforce is engaged in gainful employment in the primary sector (cultivators and agricultural labourers), while 20 per cent is engaged as marginal workers in rural Gujarat. The human resources demanded in industries can only be met by a large influx of migrant population to existing urban centres as well as to proposed SEZ areas. In the absence of any impact assessment of the operational SEZs, it is difficult to assume the socio-economic impact of the SEZ.

According to the recent SEZ data available[5] from documents leading up to December 2010, it can be stated that Gujarat has three functional, 13 notified and operational, 29 notified, 45 formal, and 13 in principle approvals. The state would have 103 SEZs in the near future under various sectors, each acquiring land ranging from 10 ha to 6,000 ha in diverse districts.

Delhi-Mumbai Industrial Corridor

DMIC is along the proposed western DFC from Delhi to Mumbai under the joint venture of the Government of India and the Japanese Trade Organisation (JETRO). Thirty-eight per cent of the DMIC zone falls within Gujarat state which is targeted for further industrial development in the state.

Western DFC

The western DFC would connect Delhi to Mumbai (1,483 km) covering four states in Western India. The DFC covers 588 km, which is approximately 40 per cent of its total length. The DFC is expected to have an impact on roughly 60 per cent of the total area of Gujarat (affecting 18 out of 26 districts in the state). About 74 per cent of the population (37.3 million) would be affected by this massive industrialization along 150 km on either side of the western DFC zone. This zone comprises 15.7 million working population of the state. Some of the cities along the corridors are Ahmedabad, Vadodara, Surat, and Bhavnagar with 0.5–1.0 million population. The state has proposed to develop industrial regions, SIRs, and port connectivity to western DFC.

Special Investment Regions (SIRs) in Gujarat

The State Government promulgated a legal framework – The Gujarat Special Investment Region Act, 2009. It has plans to create large-sized investment regions and industrial areas in the state of Gujarat to specially enable their development as global hubs if economic activity supported by infrastructure, civic amenities, centres of excellence and pro-active policy framework, and to set up an organizational structure with that purpose.

The SIR Act has provision for the development of such economic hub(s) with global standards. An investment region will be developed in an area of more than 100 sq km (10,000 ha) and an industrial area will be developed in an area of more than 50 sq km (5,000 ha). The ordinance provides for the establishment of a four-tier administrative mechanism for the establishment, operation, regulation and management of the SIRs. The structure will compose of an apex authority, a Regional Development Authority (RDA) for each region, a Project Development Agency and project-specific Special

Purpose Vehicles (SPVs). The government has already approved the formation of such a project development company in the name of Gujarat Industrial Corridor Company (GICC).

The state has identified potential locations for the development of industrial regions or SIRs as in Dholera, Pipav, PCPIR (Dahej), etc. The work on such projects has already been started by the state government. The Industrial Extension Bureau (iNDEXTb) document[6] lists 13 prospective SIRs and its land use plan to attract industrial investment covering total area of 4,600 sq km (460,000 ha) in the state. These sites are estimated to acquire 3,731 sq km of land for SIRs governed by the RDA as per the provision of the SIR Act of 2009. This includes an island SIR in Bharuch district, Aliya Bet, covering 163 sq km area primarily for aquaculture, film industry and recreation support to nearby PCPIR Dahej Special Investment Region. The combined estimates of the employment opportunity through SIRs are estimated to be above 31 lakh persons in the state.

Table 1

Area and Employment Estimates in Some SIRs

SIR	*Area (sq km)*	*Proposed employment*
Dholera, Ahmedabad	879	342,000
PCPIR, Dahej	453	120,000
Anjar, Kachchh	630	629,444
Changodar, Ahmedabad	319	462,287
Okha, Jamnagar	196	NA
Hazira, Surat	195	110,903
Santalpur	186	300,000
Navlakhi	182	685,000

Source: iNDEXTb (2010).

Issues and Consequences

From the land utilization data for the SIRs and SEZs in Gujarat state, it is evident that roughly 4.5 lakh hectares of land is expected to be utilized for industrial activities and townships.

As per the available information, the proposals are going to affect about 400 villages in the state, on an average affecting one million persons in the state. These villages compose of 78,000 cultivators and 74,000 agricultural labourers who would be directly affected by the utilization of their lands. Hence, their rehabilitation is of prime concern as livelihood deprival would cause extreme hardship.

The agricultural labourers, casual labourers and marginal farmers belonging to poor, dalit and tribal communities would be the hardest hit in the absence of active state intervention for their rehabilitation. Since these areas are expected to invite new migrants to the industrial sites which might result in an upsurge in the population (from 1 million to 5 million during the next decade). Thus, this would bring demographic transition in the project-affected areas associated with social changes. With the advent of new economies and activities, the local resident population would be marginalized unless they are trained and adaptive to new situations. The socio-economic impact of the industrial development on resident population and areas is still not clear.

Impact on Local and Regional Planning

The aggressive industrial development approach and the resultant desire to achieve social development goals are on the agenda of the state government. The present development is against the backward areas development norms where 'Agriculture First' strategy was adopted during the earlier plan periods. Traditionally the industries were supposed to have a functional relationship consistent with the region which was neglected during the current centralized industrial development by the state and centre. The question is whether industrial development is according to the central or state planning documents. This course would strengthen selective patterns of development in the developed regions and would benefit relatively better off sections of the population. It will neglect the comparatively backward regions which are environmentally degraded and weak in infrastructural facilities, as these regions may not lead to high return on investments in the short run.

It is also clear from the present policy that the state continues to promote the developed regions; whereas the resources of the backward regions are exploited even as cheap land is being utilized. Agriculture unfortunately remains a non-priority sector for the state's development policy under the influence of large corporations and private capital. This selective development would put constraints on state growth in the long run by (a) leaving agriculture weak and fluctuating, (b) widening regional disparities in growth, and (c) shrinking of overall size of market in the state. Thus, the present industrial development strategy would make the removal of poverty-level difficult in rural Gujarat in the long run, leading to wide-scale migration of people to project regions.

Creation of SIRs and SEZs in the state would fuel the urbanization of the remaining districts without taking appropriate reforms and development strategies for the existing small and medium towns. The neglect of small and medium towns by the state and the promotion of new urban settlements would have a serious impact on the survival and livelihood of the city and its people.

Significant power was granted to the local bodies under the 73rd and 74th constitutional amendments, whereby the local bodies played an active role in the development of the regions. In the present SEZ and SIR Acts, the local bodies are not to be consulted by the state or the industries. It is the state which decides the location of industries without even consulting the State Pollution Control Board. Thus, mainland Gujarat from Mehsana to Vapi has already seen the concentration of industries since early 1960s. Further industrialization in these belts would cause serious damage to the environment as stated in the environments reports prepared by the Gujarat Ecology Commission.

Overemployment and Shortage of Labour in Gujarat

The state has the least unemployment ratios in the country, with only 5 per cent of the working population unemployed. It is believed that the state with its aggressive industrial policies would allow multiple, increased employment choices to its people. It can thus be estimated that the state is already short of labour force as concerns the agricultural, industrial, and services sector of its economy. With major industries such as the diamond and textile industries failing to meet labour supply from traditional sources employ mainly migrants from poorly developed states. The success of the rural employment guarantee schemes in many parts of India including Gujarat would provide an initial setback in the supply of labour. Moreover, the cost of the production and labour accumulation in the state is slated to increase as the demand between the sectors is going to increase. At present, 60.99 lakh persons are employed in 24.26 lakh establishments engaged in different economic activities other than crop production and plantation in the state. The proposed SIRs and SEZs are expected to generate employment to an additional 50 lakh persons in the next decade requiring high and semi-skilled workforce. This might result in the diversion of increased working population from the primary sector to the secondary and tertiary sectors. Despite the primary sector facing labour shortage required for commercial crops such as cotton and tobacco, industries would further prompt the exodus of people from this sector. Thus, though Gujarat would have good capital investments, but it could face severe shortage of labour and skilled persons in the near future.

Notes

1. NSSO (2009), NSS Report No. 531: Employment and Unemployment Situation in India: July 2007–June 2008.
2. Industrial regions: Industrial nodes identified for the large-scale industrial development by state or national organizations.
3. Special Investment Regions (SIRs) formulated under the Special Investment Region Act, 2009.
4. See MoCI, Data released on web, New Delhi, on 31 May 2010.
5. See www.sezindia.nic.in/asez-sez-granted-under2005.asp for PDF download and latest information.
6. See iNDEXTb (2010) *Special Investment Regions: Sector Profile*, Vibrant Gujarat 2011, Government of Gujarat.

Index